Also available at all good book stores

9781785316470

9781785313929

9781785315466

9781785315381

9781785317286

9781785316869

9781785316906

9781785317262

9781785317309

WHERE THE
COOL KIDS
HUNG OUT

WHERE THE
COOL KIDS
HUNG OUT
The Chic Years of the UEFA Cup

STEVEN SCRAGG

First published by Pitch Publishing, 2020

Pitch Publishing
A2 Yeoman Gate
Yeoman Way
Worthing
Sussex
BN13 3QZ
www.pitchpublishing.co.uk
info@pitchpublishing.co.uk

ISBN 978 1 78531 683 8

Typesetting and origination by Pitch Publishing

Printed and bound in India by Replika Press Pvt. Ltd.

Contents

Dedication

For my Uncle David, who we lost this year. You could go years without seeing him sometimes, but safe in the knowledge there was always a beer and a mad story or two to be offered by him when you did eventually catch up. I don't think I ever saw him when he wasn't laughing about something or other.

Acknowledgements

THIS IS my second book, both of which were conceived of a podcast. A couple of years ago, for *These Football Times*, we created a three-part podcast series about the glory days of the European Cup, the European Cup Winners' Cup and the UEFA Cup, from where a throw-away, yet semi-serious remark, from my fellow senior writer, Will Sharp, resulted in the birth of the book *A Tournament Frozen in Time*.

As an example of how rising to a tongue-in-cheek challenge can sometimes get completely out of hand, *A Tournament Frozen in Time* ended up being shortlisted for the Football Book of the Year, by the Football Writers' Association, while nods of agreement had already been made between myself and the wonderful Jane Camillin that we really should put together a sequel, all about the peak years of the UEFA (Yoofa) Cup – essentially, the two-legged final era, which was largely played out before football was partitioned off from all but those that could either afford the extortionate price of a ticket, or a costly sports channel subscription.

Before long, the marvellously talented Duncan Olner had conjured up the front cover and just as with my first book, he translated the image I had in my mind's eye perfectly. The two covers share a link. A goal has been scored in a final and it is being celebrated. The combined thrill and fear of seeing the cover to a book you've dreamt up is indescribable.

As was the case last time around, the encouragement of my *These Football Times* colleagues has been invaluable. Just like Will, with his initial suggestion that I needed to be writing a book, without the faith of Omar Saleem, the creator of *These Football Times*, this book would not exist. His long-standing belief in the words I write has been an inspiration that made the difference between me extending myself to write books, or not.

Furthermore, my fellow podcast partners, Stuart Horsfield, Gary Thacker and Aidan Williams have always been there with timely and rambling conversations about the subject matter, which have been crucial on those days when the words aren't flowing as easily as I'd have liked them to. Each have their own books in creation, and it has been a breath of fresh air to talk about those topics with them, too.

Chris Weir, Dan Williamson, Matt Evans, Andrew Flint and Jon Townsend have all cheered on from the sidelines too, often rounding people up on Twitter, to crowd round, when announcements about the book have been made, at times when some have their own books to worry about.

Hyder Jawád was once again a heroic figure, while Jeff Goulding, Karl Coppack and Trevor Downey have been the greatest unpaid social media publicists an author could wish for.

I have also drawn great strength from the continued support of my dad, my sister and brother, Alison and David, my unofficial soul sister, Hayley Coleman, plus the always enthusiastic backing of Andrew and Carrie Knott.

And then there has been my wife, Beverley. Counsellor, comforter, defuser of pandemic-related stresses and bringer of curry, she has always been everything, as have our children, Sam, Elsie and Florence, without whom this book would not have been.

Introduction

THE UEFA Cup, when compared to the European Cup and the European Cup Winners' Cup, always felt like a thoroughly modern tournament. Futuristic even. Born in 1971, its archive footage of games is predominantly to be found in colour, apart from the odd exception here and there due to the vagaries of the staggered phasing out of black and white television across Europe.

If I were to be asked for a mental image of the European Cup in its early years, I would offer you the 1960 final between Real Madrid and Eintracht Frankfurt at Hampden Park (despite me not being born until 1974), while for the Cup Winners' Cup I would give you the 1963 final, as contested by Tottenham Hotspur and Atlético Madrid.

Both these games flicker across the screen enigmatically, in a black and white monochrome manner. It is football, but not as a child of the 1970s and 80s would know it. While I embrace the black and white and pre-television era enthusiastically now, as a child it was an entirely different matter. I looked scornfully at archaic black and white footage of games, with its heavier ball, clumsy boots and cumbersome, billowing, cotton kits.

Sacrilege it might be, but Kenneth Wolstenholme's voice always sounded older than it was. When he commentated on the 1966 World Cup Final, he was only a few months older than I am now, but when his tone was attached to black and white images, he almost sounded 30 years older than he was.

Conversely, Wolstenholme's voice combined with colour footage jars, yet it shouldn't. David Coleman, the harder-edged BBC football voice of the 1970s, who had lived in Wolstenholme's shadow throughout the 1960s, was born less than six years beyond his former colleague, yet his voice suits colour footage better than it does black and white.

This is where the UEFA Cup was born, to an era of colour broadcasts and Airtex kits, of players not seeming like they could just as easily pass as RAF pilots, rather than the footballers they were. In this respect, Liverpool beating Borussia Mönchengladbach provides the images I most associate with the formative exchanges of the UEFA Cup, and they are images not delivered in a sepia-tinted black and white hue, but on a steamier and vibrant colour landscape.

Despite the dated hairstyles and the type of mutton chops Mungo Jerry would be proud to call his own, when I watch the goals of the 1973 UEFA Cup Final first leg, it feels like something I could reach out and touch, whereas the seven goals that Alfredo Di Stéfano and Ferenc Puskás put past Eintracht Frankfurt's Egon Loy in the 1960 European Cup Final seem as if they are broadcast from the surface of the moon, as opposed to the surface of Glasgow's Hampden Park.

Added to this, the UEFA Cup was blessed with a significantly more artisan and handle-free trophy, compared to the European Cup and the Cup Winners' Cup. It's a towering octagonal and mottled silver edifice, which is sat atop a marble base, where at the foot of the silver is clustered a collective of twisting and turning players, symbolically bearing the weight of the trophy, in a visage that loosely resembles the Eton Wall Game, or those crowded and generally lawless 12th-century street games of a football-related activity, which were eventually banned for a few centuries due to the carnage they left in their wake.

It was at the Bertoni workshops, in Milan, that the trophy was made. Amazingly, it took 20 years until one of Milan's iconic clubs finally got their hands on the UEFA Cup, Internazionale eventually breaking the hoodoo in 1991, winning it twice more and contesting a further lost final before the decade was over.

Other aspects contributed to the distinct and modern feel of the UEFA Cup. The extra winter round that the tournament boasted over its siblings was an alluring bonus, while the two-legged final gave with one hand and took away with the other. The two-legged final denied supporters the concept of travelling en masse to a pre-decided, neutral final venue in the way the finals of the European Cup and Cup Winners' Cup did, yet the two-legged final gave so many more supporters the chance to see their team play in a major European final, as half of the UEFA Cup Final was played out on their own doorstep. Meanwhile, the most intrepid supporters would head off to the return game in smaller numbers.

What the UEFA Cup also had, largely year-on-year, was a cluster of great teams from each nation. Three, sometimes four teams from the biggest-hitting leagues would find themselves drawn into the tournament, as opposed to the European Cup and Cup Winners' Cup criteria being one team per nation, except for the holders being given the right to defend their title.

For example, in 1976/77, when Juventus and Athletic Club went on to face one another in a closely contested final, the runners and riders had also included Ajax, Manchester United, Barcelona, AC Milan, Inter, Feyenoord, Celtic, Manchester City, Red Star Belgrade and a Magdeburg side that had won the Cup Winners' Cup as recently as 1974. Despite the strength of a line-up that also consisted of talented Derby County and Queens Park Rangers vintages, RWD Molenbeek and AEK Athens picked their way through to the semi-finals that very same year.

Basically, at least for the great and the good of European football, beyond qualification for the tournament, nothing came easy in the UEFA Cup. Every success was hard-earned. It was easier to pick up a place in the UEFA Cup, but once there, it was arguably tougher to win than the European Cup and the Cup Winners' Cup. Despite the stronger overall field of teams, the UEFA Cup was, however, classed as the lesser of the three major European tournaments. When push came to shove, you didn't need to win a domestic trophy to gain entry to the UEFA Cup in the same way that you did to qualify for a shot at the European Cup and Cup Winners' Cup.

While it might have been for teams that had finished 'there or there abouts' domestically the previous season, even the very name of the tournament felt modern. There was a wonderful propensity for British journalists to switch the U and E of UEFA around, to proclaim it to be the EUFA Cup, which led to a long-held pronunciation of 'Yoofa Cup' in certain circles. It all added to the growing mystique.

These glory days of the UEFA Cup were played out in parallel with the last three decades of the Cup Winners' Cup, all the way up until the moment that the Champions League began to admit multiple teams per nation. The game then changed, at first subtly, but irrevocably. I would suggest that those in charge of football benefited from these alterations far more than supporters did. Something special was auctioned away in the name of shepherding Europe's biggest names into one elite tournament.

Yet, what went before these changes combined to create a distinct personality for the youngest of the three major European tournaments, and just like the peak years of the European Cup and the wonderful randomness of the Cup Winners' Cup, this personality blossomed on a Wednesday evening beyond the alluring theme tunes of *Sportsnight* and *Midweek Sports Special*, where you were presented your football in a highlights format by the boxing commentator, Harry Carpenter and the former TV-am frontman Nick Owen, who would serve these wonderful European football tutorials in broadcasting compendiums that often included greyhound racing and ABA boxing events. It was truly magical.

Between 1971 and 1997, the UEFA (Yoofa) Cup really was where the cool kids hung out, and this is the story of the tournament's chic years.

Chapter One

The Inter-Cities Fairs Cup and the Dawning of the UEFA Cup

BEFORE THE UEFA Cup came into existence, there was the Inter-Cities Fairs Cup. A peculiarity of a tournament, with an elaborate set of terms and conditions when it came to participation; a tournament that ran from 1955 to 1971, and one which was won with a trophy that wouldn't have looked out of place had it been presented to the snooker player Doug Mountjoy at the Preston Guild Hall in 1988, when he unexpectedly beat Stephen Hendry in the final of the UK Championship.

This oddity of silverware carried the name of the Noël Beard Trophy – Beard seemingly having little to do with football other than being a Swiss entrepreneur whose son branched out at one stage into the manufacture of silver trophies.

Stretching for a lifespan of 16 seasons, the eccentricities of the Fairs Cup meant it was only won 13 times, while during the 1968/69 season it was won twice.

The first playing of the Fairs Cup was an unwieldly business. Scheduled to be contested over a two-season span, between 1955 and 1957, it took an extra year to complete, despite only ten teams taking part. Games were scheduled to coincide with international trade fairs, acting as a unique added attraction.

Groundbreaking, the inaugural Fairs Cup campaign consisted of a first round of group games, which was never again repeated in the tournament. This experiment was launched a full 36 years prior to group stages being implemented in the 1991/92 European Cup – an adjustment that was a dry run for the following season's rebrand to the Champions League.

With an original field which had consisted of 12 teams, only for the city representative collectives of Cologne and Vienna to hastily withdraw from the tournament before they were expected to kick a ball in anger, the first contesting of the Fairs Cup stretched from 4 June 1955 to 1 May 1958.

The tournament, which was the combined brainchild of Ernst Thommen, Sir Stanley Rous and Ottorino Barassi, was only initially open to teams from cities that hosted trade fairs. Thommen was vice-president of FIFA; Rous the secretary of the Football Association and FIFA president to be; and Barassi a founding father of FIFA, known for keeping the Jules Rimet trophy hidden under his bed during World War Two.

Under such criteria, league positioning held little in the way of sway when it came to qualification. Most participants were city representative collectives, drawing players from across multiple clubs and indeed 'London' played in the Fairs Cup's opening game and reached the very first final, where they were heavily defeated over two legs by a Barcelona XI that was inhabited almost exclusively by Barcelona players. Despite the token input of one Español player, Barcelona, as a club, claim the 1958 Fairs Cup to be their first European honour. It is a claim that is recognised by FIFA.

Indeed, as a testament to just how long the first Fairs Cup took to complete, the second leg of both the semi-final and the final took place at the newly built Camp Nou while the Barcelona XI home group game had taken place at the *Blaugrana*'s previous home, the Camp de Les Corts.

There were exceptions to the city representative rule from the off, however. When Aston Villa refused to allow their players to play for a combined city of Birmingham team, Birmingham City took up the tournament invite instead. It was a similar situation in Milan, with Internazionale competing – AC Milan understandably hoarding their own players to take part in the inaugural contesting of the 1955/56 European Cup instead.

Compact but rambling in nature, whereas the first Fairs Cup took three years to complete, the first European Cup was played out within one season. This meant that in technical terms the Fairs Cup was the footballing version of the Betamax, compared to the European Cup's VHS. Amid this, it goes largely unrecognised that the very first Fairs Cup game took place three months before the first European Cup game, yet by the time the first Fairs Cup was won, Real Madrid were a short few weeks away from winning their third European Cup.

Equipped with a more streamlined format for the 1958–60 playing of the Fairs Cup, when Barcelona defeated Birmingham City in the second final, they did so with the birth of the Cup Winners' Cup creeping ever closer. The Fairs Cup had to pull its socks up if it were to survive. From the 1960 final onward there would be a Fairs Cup Final every calendar year.

This came with a twist, however, as the 1960/61 and 1961/62 finals didn't take place until the following seasons had begun, with these decisive games being played out in September and October. The finals of 1966, 1967 and 1968 were also contested beyond the summer interlude. Leeds United prevailed in the 1968 final over the course of the August and September, while Newcastle United won the 1969 final in games played in May and June. Thus the 1968/69 season ended having contained two Fairs Cup finals.

Shapeshifting structurally, the Fairs Cup constantly struggled to find a comfortable pattern. City representative XIs eventually vanished from the tournament beyond the 1962/63 season, while even the one city, one team rule was temporarily jettisoned for a couple of seasons, before being reintroduced once again. The requirement to be based in a city at all was also dropped. On top of these alterations, the 1964 and 1965 finals were then played as one-off games, with the two-legged final being shelved, only to be revived once more in 1966.

It was only over the course of the last three seasons of the Fairs Cup that it fell into a closer sync with the pattern that the UEFA Cup would take on. While in England, their representatives were decided in a continually scattergun manner, across the continent the teams finishing in league placings directly below the domestic champions became the automatic qualifiers, apart from those instances when more than one team from any one city finished in the eligible positions.

Yet, as a mark of the outlandishness still at play in England, when Newcastle qualified for, and went on to win, the 1968/69 Fairs Cup, they did so from a tenth-placed First Division finish, some five positions behind Everton, who were barred from taking part due to third-placed Liverpool qualifying ahead of them. While league consistency went unrewarded in some circumstances, others prospered thanks to geographical good fortune.

For the first few seasons of the UEFA Cup, English football continued to adhere to the Fairs Cup's one city, one club rule, despite no such rule being transferred from the old tournament to the new. Arsenal twice missed out on UEFA Cup qualification in those early days – firstly, for the 1972/73 season, after Tottenham Hotspur usurped them as holders, and then in 1973/74, despite finishing First Division runners-up the previous season. Tottenham again took London's space, having won the 1973 League Cup Final.

This one city, one club issue continued in English football until things came to a head at the end of the 1974/75 season, when UEFA warned the Football Association and the Football League that they were running the risk of having their quotient of UEFA Cup berths lowered. Again, it was Everton who were set to miss out, until European football's governing body intervened.

Arguably viewed with initial suspicion, by the time the UEFA Cup was born, the more condescending football observers branded it the 'Runner-Up Cup'. English teams prospered throughout this period of handover, however. By the time of the Fairs Cup discontinuation, the end came when First Division clubs dominated, with the last four being won by English teams. This was, however, what could be classed as the third segment of a three-epoch tournament.

With the Fairs Cup arguably being the personal fiefdom of Barcelona in the formative years of the tournament, other LaLiga clubs sat up and took notice.

Valencia prevailed in 1962, against Barcelona, retaining it the following year, before losing out in another all-LaLiga final in 1964 to Real Zaragoza. Zaragoza in turn lost the 1966 final to Barcelona. The only thing to punctuate this Spanish monopoly was AS Roma with their win in 1961, a success which perplexingly still stands to this day as *I Giallorossi*'s only major European honour.

Between these periods of dominance from Spain and England that compellingly bookended the 16-year history of the Fairs Cup, there was a rise from the east. Dinamo Zagreb, beaten by Valencia in the 1963 final, went one better in 1967 against Don Revie's Leeds United. Two years beforehand, it was the evocative Ferencváros who were claiming Hungary's one and only major European trophy, when they defeated Juventus in Turin, in the second of the two one-off Fairs Cup finals.

Leeds' 1967 defeat to Zagreb, however, acted as a pivot, a turning point for English teams in the Fairs Cup. The latter years of the tournament were a far cry from the oddity and confusion of the London representative team which had contested the 1958 final.

In 1958, when London travelled to Barcelona for the second leg of the final after a 2-2 draw at Stamford Bridge, they did so with seven changes to their line-up and a different manager to the one who had led them in the first leg. Jimmy Greaves, for instance, had played and scored in the first game but was unavailable for the return encounter as he was required by Chelsea to play in the FA Youth Cup Final second leg instead. Greaves was effectively on the losing side in two cup finals on the same day.

Following in London's footsteps, Birmingham City subsequently lost the finals of 1960 and 1961, thus ending English interest in the Fairs Cup Final until Leeds lost out to Zagreb six years later.

1968 proved to be a watershed year for Revie and Leeds after a spate of near misses when it came to their attempts to chase major honours. They not only lifted the Fairs Cup that year, but the League Cup too. Yet, attendances remained uninspiring at Elland Road for Fairs Cup games, the stadium barely half full, for both the home legs of the semi-final against Dundee, and the final against Ferencváros. In comparison, when Leeds headed to Budapest for the second leg of the final, it was a game played in front of 76,000 spectators.

Just under nine months later, the tournament was embraced more enthusiastically 83 miles further north, at Newcastle United's St James' Park; 60,000 eager souls clicked through the turnstiles to witness the first leg of the 1969 final, the Magpies' first major cup final for 14 years.

While their entry into the tournament had been gained in peculiar mid-table circumstances, Newcastle more than made up for that with a sparkling run to glory, which took them past an array of dangerous and successful opponents.

European champions to be, Feyenoord, were dispatched in the first round, swept aside in the first leg, 4-0, on an evening when the Rotterdam club fielded eight members of the team that would beat Celtic, in Milan, in the 1970 European Cup Final. This was a game that was won just 24 hours after Leeds had departed the Hungarian capital with the trophy, having held Ferencváros to the goalless draw that was enough for them to win the 1968 final.

More significant victims would fall by the wayside to Newcastle. Sporting CP, winners of the 1964 Cup Winners' Cup, were beaten next, followed by previous Fairs Cup winner and once beaten finalist, Zaragoza. The Zaragoza games had the added peculiarity that the first leg, at La Romareda, took place on New Year's Day, 1969.

Newcastle came away from Aragon with a 3-2 defeat, a 2-1 second-leg victory seeing them through on the away-goals rule, in an oddity of a system where penalty shoot-outs were still a few years away, leaving games that were tied, where both legs ended with identical scorelines, at the mercy of being decided by the toss of a coin with no replays being implemented.

It made for a strange series of events for its English participants when it came to the 1968/69 Fairs Cup. While Newcastle benefited from the away-goals rule, Leeds progressed beyond Napoli in the second round thanks to the toss of a coin, while Liverpool and Chelsea exited the tournament on the call of heads or tails against Athletic Club and DWS of Amsterdam respectively.

Continuing the eccentric theme, Hamburger SV then withdrew from their projected quarter-final against the Turkish club Göztepe A.Ş, fearing a fixture backlog domestically and potential repercussions should they not have returned from İzmir in time to fulfil a Bundesliga fixture, against Bayern Munich – a lost opportunity of European glory for HSV, given that they had reached the final of the Cup Winners' Cup the previous season.

As for Newcastle, they bludgeoned their way past Vitória de Setúbal in the quarter-finals, running up a healthy first-leg lead, before hanging on grimly to it during the second leg in Portugal.

This set up a 'Battle of Britain' semi-final against a Rangers team that had been unfortunate to lose the 1967 Cup Winners' Cup Final. After a goalless draw at Ibrox Park, Newcastle came through strongly in the second half of the second leg, back at St James' Park. This was an underestimated masterpiece of a result for a Newcastle side that had never played competitive European football prior to this campaign.

By comparison, Rangers had two Cup Winners' Cup finals and a European Cup semi-final under their belt. The Scottish side were by far the more experienced team when it came to European competition, going on to gain their own European success three years later.

Awaiting Newcastle in the final were Újpesti Dózsa of Hungary – the team that had ended Leeds' defence of the trophy in the quarter-finals. Just as was the case for the outgoing holders, in winning the 1968 final Newcastle would have to emerge from Budapest jubilant if they were to win the 1969 Fairs Cup Final. A 6-2 aggregate scoreline serves to shield how hard they were made to work, for what is still to this day their last major honour.

Kept at bay in the first leg by a determined and skilful Újpesti side, a side that would go on to dominate Hungarian domestic club football throughout the 1970s, it took Newcastle over an hour to break the deadlock at St James' Park. What followed Bobby Moncur's opener was a 20-minute span where the home team's sheer force of will managed to breach the Újpesti goal line on two more occasions, firstly by Moncur again, and then by Jim Scott.

With Newcastle's manager, Joe Harvey, feeling that one hand was on the trophy, it was with a rude awakening that they went in at half-time in Budapest 2-0 down on the night. Ferenc Bene and János Göröcs had brought Újpesti to within a goal of Newcastle, on aggregate, during a blizzard of magical first-half football at the Megyeri úti Stadion.

As swiftly as Újpesti had drawn themselves back into contention, however, they let their chance of glory slip away at the start of the second half, when Moncur scored again. Moncur would score only three league goals throughout the entire 12 years of his time at Newcastle, yet here he was, scorer of three goals over the course of the two legs of the 1969 Fairs

Cup Final – as heroic a captain's contribution as there possibly could be.

Moncur's goal halted Újpesti's momentum with a near immediate effect. Four minutes later, Newcastle's era-defying Danish international midfielder, Preben Arentoft, had levelled the scores on the night, with a wonderfully volleyed effort. To rub salt into Újpesti's wounds, the 19-year-old Alan Foggon then snatched a third for Newcastle, within minutes of his introduction as a substitute, forcing his own rebound off the crossbar over the line.

In keeping with the eccentric path Newcastle had taken to Fairs Cup glory in 1969, the second leg of the final is notable for Újpesti's striped goalposts. It adds to the mesmeric nature of the footage of what is, after all, the last occasion Newcastle lifted a major trophy. Even the commentator on duty for the BBC was the retrospectively lesser-heard Alan Weeks, rather than the more familiar tones of Kenneth Wolstenholme or David Coleman.

Their qualification for the 1968/69 Fairs Cup might have been an oddity, but Newcastle's success is one of the finest by an English team in any European club competition. Yet, it remains largely obscured behind the strangely hypnotic name of Újpesti Dózsa and the eventual birth of the UEFA Cup.

Unwittingly, with only two seasons of the tournament remaining, the Fairs Cup continued its gradual metamorphosis. In the summer of 1969 there was an alteration of name, from the Inter-Cities Fairs Cup to the European Fairs Cup. This change was announced on the eve of the second leg of the 1969 final, and it was accompanied by the draw for the first round of the 1969/70 edition.

Despite this, that old ad hoc nature of the Fairs Cup persevered, even to the point that, with little over 24 hours to go until the second leg of the 1970 final, the Fairs Cup committee still hadn't decided if the away-goals rule would be in operation or not while, once again, the English had made heavy weather out of identifying the teams that would represent the First Division. For the 1969/70 playing of the tournament, Everton, Chelsea and Tottenham all missed out, despite finishing the previous season in third, fifth and sixth positions respectively. Southampton were instead invited, having finished seventh.

Beyond the lack of decisiveness of the Fairs Cup committee, the 1969/70 season was arguably its best yet. They even managed to factor in the early ending of the European domestic seasons, due to the late-May start of the 1970 World Cup.

Arsenal made it three successive winning English teams, ending a 17-year trophy drought in the process and soothing the pain of losing the previous year's League Cup Final to Third Division Swindon Town. Lifting the Fairs Cup would also act as the springboard to Bertie Mee's side going on to complete the league and cup double the following season.

Their domestic woes of 1969/70 were impressively brushed aside, to the extent that Arsenal even defeated the Ajax of Rinus Michels and Johan Cruyff in the semi-finals. It was an evening of surprise and wonderment at Highbury when they accumulated a 3-0 lead to take to Amsterdam.

This was of course an Ajax side that would return to London a year later, to win their first European Cup, at Wembley, the opening part in a hat-trick of successes, yet they had also contested the 1969 European Cup Final, which they had lost to AC Milan. In an ocean of general Highbury mediocrity, this convincing Arsenal victory over Ajax was both majestic and shocking.

It also acted as the precursor to a sobering series of nights that Cruyff experienced in England in the UEFA Cup. He would go on to draw at Anfield in Barcelona colours in the 1976 semi-final second leg, a result that saw Liverpool through to the final. Cruyff went on to suffer a 3-0 loss at Portman Road against Ipswich Town in the third round in 1977/78, although this was overturned in a second-leg penalty shoot-out. He then played through the pain barrier to put Barcelona into a 2-0 lead at Villa Park in the first leg of the very next round, only to see his team-mates throw it all away for a 2-2 draw after he was withdrawn late on.

Even in his one solitary season as a Feyenoord player at the end of his career, a season in which he helped Ajax's bitter rivals to a domestic league and cup double, Cruyff shared a team with an emerging Ruud Gullit which was defeated at White Hart Lane, as part of Tottenham's winning run.

One heavyweight overcome in the last four by Arsenal, Internazionale had been the team expected to emerge from the other tie, after they had departed Brussels with a 1-0 win against Anderlecht from the first leg of their semi-final.

At the San Siro, however, Anderlecht had stunned their hosts in the second leg, returning to Belgium with a 2-0 victory and a place in the final. From a heavily presumed Ajax vs Inter clash, the 1970 Fairs Cup Final was instead an encounter between Arsenal and Anderlecht.

Only a week split the second leg of the semi-finals and the first leg of the final. Arsenal found themselves faced with a wall of sound from the stands of the Émile Versé Stadium, the venue that would be renamed as the Constant Vanden Stock Stadium some 13 years later. On the pitch, they were faced with beautifully skilled and balanced opponents.

A footballing lesson was served to Arsenal and they were lucky to restrict Anderlecht to a 3-1 win. The home side had two compelling penalty appeals waved away, before the prolific Belgian international, Johannes Devrindt, scored the opening goal of the first leg, while the dangerous Jan Mulder netted the next two. Mulder would later go on to play for Ajax, before becoming a journalist, broadcaster and actor.

There was a ray of light for Arsenal, however, as they snatched a goal with eight minutes left to play. The 18-year-old Ray Kennedy powered in a header, having only been on the pitch for five minutes. It was just the second goal of his professional career.

Kennedy, having thrown Arsenal a lifeline, watched on from the sidelines six days later, as Anderlecht struggled with a Highbury pitch that resembled a mudflat. As the visitors stuck to the purity of their approach to football, they were undone by a combination of the inspired goalkeeping of Bob Wilson and a central defensive weakness to an aerial ball.

This isn't to say that Arsenal relied solely upon an agricultural path to glory. Their build-up play was compact and neat, they passed and moved as they probed for their openings. The first goal was a fine strike from outside the penalty area by Eddie Kelly, a goal that came midway through the first half and electrified the atmosphere at the famous old stadium.

Made to wait until 15 minutes from time to level the aggregate score, it was that aerial weakness which Arsenal capitalised upon to swipe the Fairs Cup from Anderlecht's loosening grip. At the back post, John Radford got his head on the end of a perfectly flighted cross from Bob McNab to make it 2-0 on the night.

It took just 90 further seconds for the outcome to be settled. Again, an aerial approach was to torment Anderlecht. This time a high cross-field ball from Charlie George caught the Belgians on the chin, which was collected by Jon Sammels, who charged into the Anderlecht penalty area to drill it beyond the reach of Jean-Marie Trappeniers and into his bottom right-hand corner.

As Arsenal made the most of their Fairs Cup springboard, going on to dominate English domestic football in 1970/71, it was Leeds who reclaimed the trophy, in turn becoming the last winners of the Fairs Cup. This time, it was a shot at European glory that was embraced in West Yorkshire much more enthusiastically than it had been three years earlier.

Maybe it was with a sense of regret over their partial indifference to winning the tournament in 1968, especially having then watched Newcastle and Arsenal lift the Fairs Cup within effusive circumstances for the following two years, that

Leeds' 1971 success drew more spectators to Elland Road for the home leg of the final than had been the case against Ferencváros.

There were several extenuating reasons for this upturn in interest, other than simply a greater regard for the tournament, however. What would have undoubtedly facilitated this was that the home leg came second this time around and that Leeds had set themselves up for the return game nicely, having gained a 2-2 draw in Turin during the replayed first leg, after it had initially been abandoned early in the second half, 48 hours beforehand. When question marks were raised over the potential for the rearranged game to be washed out too, Leeds' opponents made the bold gesture of agreeing that, if this were to happen, then they would allow both legs of the final to take place at Elland Road the following week.

Juventus being the opposition will have also piqued local interest in Leeds, as will the Football Association's refusal to allow the BBC to broadcast the game live, or even in the form of highlights, decreeing that, with them showing the European Cup Final the night before, there was more than enough televised football scheduled for that week.

Added to this, Leeds had narrowly overcome Liverpool in a high-profile, all-English semi-final, thus throwing a bright spotlight on the run of Revie's team before the final had come into view upon the horizon.

Leeds edging their way into the final, at Liverpool's expense, deprived football history of the sensory overload that would have been offered by Bill Shankly's team playing the home leg of the final at either Goodison Park or Old Trafford – both of which were mooted possibilities, due to Anfield being out of action, as construction of their new Main Stand gained pace to ensure it was operational for the beginning of the 1971/72 season.

Ultimately, it was to be Leeds that kept the late English charge on the Fairs Cup going. A 1-1 draw in the second leg meant that they took it on the away-goals rule. Leeds then went on to face Barcelona, at the Camp Nou, in a play-off for the right to the permanent possession of the Noël Beard Trophy. An out-of-form Barcelona beat an understrength Leeds, 2-1.

And so, the Fairs Cup ended, after a protracted two-year period of baton-passing from the Fairs Cup committee to UEFA. A tournament which, based on its initial conceptual idea, should have been shelved long before it was, yet a tournament that by the time it was discontinued had laid the groundwork and evolved into the pattern that the UEFA Cup would be born with.

As for the men behind the creation of the Fairs Cup, Thommen was outlived by his tournament and Barassi died a short few months after the Barcelona vs Leeds play-off game. Meanwhile, Rous would remain in his role as FIFA president for another three years, until he was overthrown by his former protégé, João Havelange. He eventually passed away in July 1986 at the age of 91, some 15 years after time had been called on the Fairs Cup.

Chapter Two

A Very English Handover

THERE WAS a step-by-step route to the UEFA (Yoo-wafer) Cup being mistakenly branded in the UK as the EUFA (Yoofa) Cup. Often referred to as the 'European Union Cup' or 'European Union Football Association Cup' in the build-up to its inception, there was a pronunciation schism from the very start, and it took a generation for it to be resolved.

Tottenham Hotspur were there from the word go. They were in Iceland on 14 September 1971, to face ÍBK Keflavik, where they plundered a 6-1 victory and Graeme Souness played the only 20 minutes of first-team football he ever would with a cockerel on his chest.

They had never appeared in the Fairs Cup, yet here they were as a fully paid-up member of the UEFA Cup club from the beginning. It was love at first sight for Tottenham.

While Leeds United went out at the first hurdle of the new competition, effectively as holders of a tournament that had only just been born, joined in a hasty exit by Southampton, Wolverhampton Wanderers followed Tottenham into the second round, when they brushed the attentions of Académica de Coimbra aside with ease.

For Leeds, it was a seismic shock to throw away a 2-0 first-leg lead, capitulating to a 4-0 defeat at home to Lierse. The two legs of this game also straddled the Fairs Cup play-off game in Barcelona, making for a regrettable, if unforgettable, European campaign for Don Revie's side, who would go on to win the FA Cup and marginally miss out on the league and cup double.

Beset by injuries, it had still been a stunning turn of events for Leeds against Lierse, as they were picked apart in a six-minute span during a first half where they conceded three times. So stunned was Revie that he had been compelled to substitute his goalkeeper at half-time, replacing the 17-year-old John Shaw with the experienced, yet mistake-prone Gary Sprake. While Shaw would never play for Leeds again, he did go on to make a solid career for himself as a First Division regular at Bristol City.

Despite their track record in the Fairs Cup, despite their runs to the 1973 European Cup Winners' Cup Final and the 1975 European Cup Final, Leeds never really got to grips with the UEFA Cup, failing to go beyond the third round during the two-legged final era in their four attempts. They did make the semi-finals, however, in 1999/2000 when, under better circumstances, they might well have made it to the one-off final in Copenhagen against Arsenal.

Intriguingly, for England's other Fairs Cup winners, Arsenal and Newcastle United, the two-legged final era of the UEFA Cup was also fallow ground. Both enjoyed their best runs in the tournament beyond the 1996/97 two-legged final cut-off.

For Tottenham and Wolves though, they embraced the new dawn with great enthusiasm. Wolves enjoyed an avalanche of goals against Den Haag, while Tottenham edged past Nantes in the second round. In the third round, it was easy pickings for both, as the north London club took apart Rapid Bucureşti, and the West Midlands outfit dismantled Carl Zeiss Jena in the second leg, at Molineux.

Tottenham's quarter-final reward was a tie against the unknown quantity, UTA Arad, who gave Bill Nicholson's side greater food for thought in the second leg at White Hart Lane than they had in the first leg in western Romania.

In comparison, the 1971/72 UEFA Cup campaign got very real for Wolves in the last eight, as they found themselves thrown together with the might of Juventus. Despite the size of the task in front of him, the Wolves manager, Bill McGarry, delayed his trip to Turin for the first leg in order to attempt to sign the Ipswich Town winger, Jimmy Robertson, while his squad went on ahead of him.

Rebuffed in his overtures for Robertson, McGarry found solace in a 1-1 draw at the Stadio Comunale, against an outrageously talented Juventus side that became as frustrated with themselves as they were with the visitors.

It wasn't an entirely problem-free evening, as McGarry's touchline exuberance saw him sent to the stands during the second half. A combination of attacking determination and inspired, if unconventional, goalkeeping from Phil Parkes helped procure Wolves an all-too under-heralded away European result of substance. It was Jim McCalliog who made a hero of himself, driving home Wolves' second-half equaliser to cancel out Pietro Anastasi's first-half opener for Juventus.

Wolves were perfectly positioned to take advantage of Juventus, at a time when Italian football was licking its numerous wounds. The early 1970s hadn't been kind to Serie A clubs in European club competitions, while the national team had suffered defeat at the hands of Greece just a few days prior to the first leg, and would go on to lose their two-legged European Championship quarter-final to Belgium, thus missing out on the chance to defend the title they had won in 1968.

It was with a valid sense of foreboding that Juventus headed to the Black Country. With one eye on their weekend clash with Torino, and the other on the wider scope of a Serie A title race that would rumble onward to the very last day of the campaign, the Juventus coach, Čestmír Vycpálek, rested six of his most valuable assets, while the burgeoning Roberto Bettega was also out injured.

A problem in disguise was posed to McGarry and Wolves by Vycpálek's insistence to downgrade in priority the inaugural UEFA Cup. Now, all the pressure to progress to the semi-finals belonged to the home side while, for those who represented *La Vecchia Signora*, there was an easing of the shoulders and nothing more than a chance to impress their coach or potential watching suitors.

Juventus's complex view on the task before them made for a tense evening at Molineux, one in which they came far closer to a place in the last four than should have been the case. When a Helmut Haller penalty dragged them to within one goal of the semi-finals, with only a few minutes left to play, Vycpálek seemingly remained unmoved, as he opted not to throw any late substitutes on to assist in the attempt to snatch the semi-final spot from Wolves' clutches.

For the remainder of the game it was a duel between the determined Haller for Juventus and a Wolves side who opted to counterpunch in the hope of a third goal, rather than err toward a safety-first approach of possession, or to gravitate to the corner flags.

This was all a far cry from how Wolves had chiselled themselves a deserved 2-0 lead, navigating their way past Juventus's physical and cynical approach to containment. Daniel Hegan had struck from distance shortly before half-time, while the legendary Derek Dougan glanced a header past Massimo Piloni not long after the restart.

Sigh of relief emitted, Wolves were through to a semi-final meeting with the enigmatic and handsomely dangerous Ferencváros.

Continuing the Anglo-Italian theme in the other semi-final, Tottenham were thrown together with Nereo Rocco's AC Milan. Bill Nicholson's response was to recall the discarded Alan Mullery from a loan spell with Second Division strugglers, Fulham.

Mullery had struggled for form and fitness for much of the 1971/72 season, eventually seeing his way back into the Tottenham first team blocked not only by his long-term contemporaries, but also by a new generation of midfielder at White Hart Lane.

An escalating injury crisis brought Mullery back into Nicholson's thinking, however, after player had convinced manager of the merits in letting him head to Craven Cottage, where Tottenham's club captain felt he could sharpen his match fitness better than he would while rattling around the reserves.

Bridging the end of March and the beginning of April, Tottenham faced a torturous four games in six days, of which the visit of Milan for the first leg of the semi-final was the last game of a punishing cluster of fixtures.

When John Pratt sustained a broken nose, it opened the door for Mullery to return, and Rocco was left to seethe over the ambiguities of UEFA's eligibility rules, when Italian regulations would not have allowed Rocco the same perk as the Football Association allowed Nicholson, had the master of *catenaccio* asked for such.

After a five-month absence from the Tottenham first-team picture, Mullery was seamless and imperious upon his high-profile return. While Steve Perryman, just a short few months beyond his teenage years, was the goalscoring hero of the evening, it was Mullery who orchestrated his team-mates, cajoling them, coaxing them into another superhuman feat.

As a testament to how much football Tottenham had had to play throughout the previous month, this was their tenth game in four weeks, whereas Milan had played half that amount over the same period. Tottenham's build-up to the arrival of Milan had involved not much more than a 48-hour rest, having played three games in four days, inclusive of back-to-back First Division fixtures on Good Friday and the Saturday of the Easter weekend.

Rocco fielded as strong a Milan line-up as was available to him, albeit a line-up minus the services of the talented goalscorer Pierino Prati and the influential midfielder Giorgio Biasiolo. While they had beaten Bologna a few days earlier, this was a Milan side that had become draw specialists domestically, with their weekend victory being only their third Serie A win since the turn of the year.

If Tottenham's players were feeling the weight of too much football during the lead-up to the visit of Milan, then they didn't outwardly project it. It was Nicholson's side that set the pace of the game and it was predominantly one-way traffic throughout the first half.

Opportunities came and went for Martin Chivers, Alan Gilzean and Martin Peters as the Milan defence was stretched to the outer limits of its capabilities. A blizzard of attacking football, it is uncertain which caused the greater shock: that Milan had managed to reach the 25th minute without their defence being breached or that they had ventured upfield to open the scoring when Romeo Benetti curled an effort into the top right-hand corner of Pat Jennings's net.

Undeterred, Tottenham stuck to their angle of approach and were rewarded within seven minutes, when Perryman capitalised on a loose ball just outside the Milan penalty area to score a spectacular goal of his own.

Rather than take a moment to compose themselves, having gained their equaliser, Tottenham ploughed forward again. Chivers and Gilzean shared and spurned a double-edged chance to give the home side the lead, while Mike England also came close. Amidst all of this, Gilzean was embroiled in a physical and private duel with Giulio Zignoli that often went past the blind eye of the Spanish referee.

As the second half started off where the first half had ended, Perryman again kept the Milan goalkeeper busy, with one dipping volley dropping just over Fabio Cudicini's crossbar. There is something utterly bewitching about watching the footage of these Tottenham chances, as Fabio's son, Carlo, a son who was still 17 months away from being brought into the world, would go on to become a Tottenham goalkeeper.

Perryman would not be denied for long, however, and it was with 25 minutes remaining that he struck the winning goal, a goal that was even more impressive than his first strike of the night. Cushioning the ball with one touch, before arrowing it beyond Cudicini's despairing dive to his right, Perryman had collected the ball when it was flicked into his possession by a Milanese head, in response to a corner which had been flung in from the right by Mullery.

It had been Mullery's second pivotal contribution in five minutes, as on the hour mark he played a starring role in Milan being reduced to ten men. There was even comedic value within the process of Riccardo Sogliano's sending off, in what amounted to a doubled cautioning for encroachment.

Sogliano had shown no intention of retreating the required ten yards when Tottenham won a free kick in a dangerous position on the right-hand side, some 25 yards or so from the Milan goal. As Mullery swiftly considered his options, Sogliano placed himself right in front of the ball, cutting off the chance for any quick free kick, prompting Mullery to pick up the ball and shove the Italian midfielder in protest.

This won Sogliano a yellow card, with Mullery escaping sanction for his own reaction, which included a pantomime threat to throw the ball in Sogliano's face. Eventually the incredulous Milan player backed away three yards, yet showed no intention of going any further, a stubbornness that only incited the referee to brandish a red card that seemed to initially go unnoticed by Sogliano, and momentarily stunned Mullery.

As Mullery pointed to the tunnel and beckoned to Sogliano that an early bath was being run for him, the Tottenham defender, Terry Naylor, stepped in to usher his captain away from the fray, to ensure that Mullery didn't fall under the attention of the suddenly erratic referee.

After Perryman had edged Tottenham ahead, the game petered out into a more sedate affair. Milan players were happy to take a 2-1 defeat, whereas Tottenham's began to fade as an understandable fatigue set in. Despite this, Nicholson's side had a vociferous claim for a penalty waved aside when it appeared that England fell into the penalty area after a robust challenge close to the 18-yard line. Perhaps to save himself from any further controversy, the referee didn't even award a free kick.

And so, the first leg of the semi-final ended with Tottenham harbouring a slender lead, Milan making for the airport with their precious away goal. A dominant display from the home team had gained a win, yet not reaped as big a reward as it deserved.

Wolves, meanwhile, were departing Budapest with a valuable 2-2 draw after the first leg of their semi-final against Ferencváros – a game where Wolves had drawn first blood in under 20 minutes, through John Richards, when he was left with an easy task to roll the ball into a largely unguarded net, thanks to a Dougan backheel, which dragged half of the home defence out of position. Yet, it was a moment of Dougan impudence that only served to antagonise Ferencváros into action. Within 15 minutes of taking their early advantage, Wolves were 2-1 down and nursing two second-leg suspensions as Bernard Shaw and Dave Wagstaffe found their names taken by the referee.

In the case of Shaw, he was penalised for handling the ball in the penalty area, the repercussion being István Szőke's expertly taken penalty sending Parkes the wrong way. Just three more minutes had elapsed when the legendary Flórián Albert gave his side the lead. Szőke again played a part; it was his run and cross that Albert calmly converted.

From here, it would have been easy for Wolves to hit the self-destruct button, but instead they came back with a considered approach to the second half that was both patient and mature. Even when Shaw gave another penalty away, Parkes managed to block Szőke's effort with his feet. It was a turn of events that took the wind out of Ferencváros's sails.

With ten minutes to go, Frank Munro plundered Wolves their equaliser, bundling the ball over the line when getting on the end of a Wagstaffe corner. It was to be the last goal of the game, a game that had pitted the skilled short passing, interplay and hypnotic movement of Ferencváros against the 'pic 'n' mix' approach of Wolves, which kept the Hungarians off balance.

McGarry had sent his players out to stretch Ferencváros across the width and down the length of the pitch, in a bid to drag their opponents out of their clusters and packs. Wolves' own attacking intent was in turn an eclectic one, mixing and matching traditional English wing play and an aerial bombardment with an understated deft opposite, as shown by Dougan's artistry to set up the opening goal. It made for a fascinating encounter.

Molineux was in raptures within 20 seconds of the start of the return game. Steve Daley, just four days beyond his 19th birthday and later to be the most expensive player in English football, gave Wolves the perfect start when he guided the ball into the Ferencváros net from a tight angle, after the visitors' goalkeeper, Bela Vörös, misjudged a deep cross from the future Arsenal FA Cup-winning hero, Alan Sunderland. Only 18 himself, Sunderland was an aspiring midfielder at the time, who was asked by McGarry to operate in place of the suspended Shaw at right-back.

Totally in keeping with the first leg of the game, Ferencváros took the tie straight back to Wolves, when Albert was unlucky to drift offside as he prodded the ball past Parkes for a disallowed equaliser. This was followed by a fine effort, which the dangerous László Branikovits hit from distance, and the Wolves goalkeeper somehow kept out, via an unorthodox low stop that he deflected up on to his crossbar. Even then, Lajos Kű failed to take advantage of the rebound when very well positioned to do so.

On the brink of half-time, Wolves made Ferencváros pay a costly price for their near misses, as another high ball to the back post reaped a second goal. This time it was Jim McCalliog finding the head of Munro, whose goal-bound effort could only be pushed into his net by the despairing Vörös.

Any ideas Wolves harboured that it would be a dispirited Ferencváros reappearing for the second half were quickly dispelled, however, as Kű made amends for his earlier missed opportunity when taking advantage of an off-balance Sunderland, before finishing coolly past Parkes, within a couple of minutes of the restart.

It set the remainder of the game up nicely for a tense finish, with Ferencváros now in need of just one goal to level the semi-final on aggregate and push the evening into extra time. The golden chance came sooner than anybody could have expected when, just one minute after his stumble had let in Kű to score, Sunderland handled in the penalty area.

Just as in the first leg, Szőke faced Parkes and the goalkeeper won the duel. Dropping low and sticking out a foot, the ball ricocheted away to safety. It was a terribly taken spot kick and it killed Ferencváros's momentum. It would be Wolves' last serious scare of the night and it was only the home side that looked likely to add to their goals from there, inclusive of Dougan hitting the crossbar.

Relief and joy swept Molineux at the full-time whistle. A hard-earned place in the very first UEFA Cup Final belonged to Wolves, but could Tottenham make it an all-English showpiece event? With their lead being a narrow one, Milan in possession of an away goal and the visitors denied the services of the injured Gilzean, it made for a difficult mission.

Milan flew at Tottenham in a frenetic opening five minutes. Twice, *I Rossoneri* came close to scoring the one goal that would hand them the advantage. Rocco had played for a 2-1 defeat at White Hart Lane to set up this very opening ambush at the San Siro.

Rocco was in for an unpleasant surprise, however, as, in the sixth minute, Mullery was once again his bone of contention when he curled a stunning effort from 25 yards beyond the reach of Cudicini and into the top corner, after a shot from Chivers was blocked and some intelligent reactions from Perryman.

A short period of adjustment was undertaken by both teams, as an insulted Milan lashed out like an angry bear, while Tottenham resembled a gazelle caught in the San Siro floodlights. Within this spell, England managed to head the ball against Jennings's crossbar.

Script soon discarded by Mullery and Tottenham, Milan lost heart as he dominated and dictated the midfield battle with Peters and Perryman. Even the genius of Gianni Rivera couldn't make Milan inroads against Nicholson's determined side, or not at least until they were invited to do so.

With little over 20 minutes to go, Milan were gifted a way back into the game, as Cyril Knowles brought down Alberto Bigon for a clear-cut penalty. Rivera converted and it provoked a fraught finale to the proceedings, in what were very wet conditions.

From sauntering their way into the 1972 UEFA Cup Final, Tottenham were now forced into a desperate rearguard action, in which they remained resolute. Even the returning Prati was unable to save Milan on this occasion. The north London side were deservedly into the final, to face Wolves.

For 36 years, the 1972 UEFA Cup Final would stand as the only all-English major European final. An anomaly in the record books, it never sat entirely comfortably on an early 1970s landscape that was dominated by Johan Cruyff and Ajax. It was, however, totally in keeping with the run English clubs had enjoyed in the Fairs Cup during the autumn years of the predecessor to the UEFA Cup.

Wolves, the great pioneers of European expansion of the 1950s – the club that had taken a swipe back at English football's Hungarian tormentors when defeating the mighty Honvéd at Molineux in December 1954, a friendly that induced the long-pregnant idea of a European Cup tournament – up against Tottenham, the first British club to lift a European trophy, the first team of the 20th century to win the English league and cup double.

Belatedly making their competitive European mark, Wolves would have been fitting winners of the first UEFA Cup. The

1960s had been a tumultuous decade for the club, however, and the glories of the 1950s had come to an end when they won the 1960 FA Cup Final.

Shockingly, in September 1964, the Wolves board of directors took the decision to sack their iconic manager, Stan Cullis. It was a turn of the card in which the club was rewarded with relegation to the Second Division at the end of the 1964/65 season. When they came back, two years later, they returned in a steady and unspectacular manner, eventually turning the corner for their mild renaissance of the early 1970s, a renaissance that brought them to the 1972 UEFA Cup Final, before winning the League Cup in 1974, via greater league consistency and other intrepid domestic cup runs.

Tottenham, meanwhile, had been one of the true heavyweights of English football throughout the 1960s. To go along with their 1961 league and cup double and that first British European success in the 1963 Cup Winners' Cup Final, they had retained the FA Cup in 1962 and won it once again, in 1967. They had arrived in the 1971/72 UEFA Cup on the back of winning the League Cup the previous season, Nicholson having evolved his team beyond the 1970 departure of Jimmy Greaves.

It made for a fascinating collision of contenders for the inaugural UEFA Cup Final – two teams that not only shared a nation, but had also shared an incredible 52 goals on the way to the final. All eyes were locked on Molineux for the first leg and the referee on duty was no less than the 'Russian linesman' from the 1966 World Cup Final, Azerbaijan's Tofiq Bahramov.

With neither finalist having lost a game en route to the final, something was going to give at some point, and it was Wolves who blinked first. Tottenham headed back to White Hart Lane with a 2-1 victory, thanks to two goals from Martin Chivers, the first of which was a guided header when he got on the end of a beautifully floated free kick from England. Parkes had been gripped by the indecision over whether to come for the ball or not and, in the end, he was caught between the two options, upon which Chivers took full advantage.

If the first half had proved to be something of a standoff, Chivers breaking the deadlock sparked an entirely different game into life. Wolves were on level terms 15 minutes later and it stemmed from a harshly awarded free kick, obtained after a period of sustained pressure from the home team. To add insult to the injury for Tottenham, Hegan took the kick quickly, to set up McCalliog, who smuggled the ball under the scrambling Jennings.

Encouraged by finding their way back into the game, Wolves were the better team during the last 18 minutes, and it was they who seemed to be seeking a winning goal as the clock ticked down. Yet, it would be Tottenham that snatched the advantage, completely against the run of play, and with only three minutes left, when Chivers launched an unstoppable drive past Parkes from almost 30 yards. Even then, after composing themselves, Dougan came close to a second Wolves equaliser.

Given that Tottenham had comfortably beaten Wolves in their league encounter at White Hart Lane earlier in the season, going into the second leg with a lead, plus two away goals, now made Nicholson's side heavy favourites to lift the UEFA Cup.

In between the two legs of the 1972 UEFA Cup Final, both Tottenham and Wolves had other dramatic duties to occupy their time.

Five days beyond the first leg, Molineux played host to what was meant to be the coronation of Leeds as league champions, a game that took place just two days after Revie's side had beaten Arsenal in the FA Cup Final. The league and cup double were Leeds' to be claimed, yet a determined Wolves ensured it was to be Derby County's title instead, on an evening when Liverpool also failed to clinch the prize. Three nights later, Tottenham completed their own league programme, with a 2-0 victory at Highbury against Arsenal.

Four days before the second leg, Chivers and Peters were on international duty with England in Munich for the second leg of the European Championship quarter-final against West Germany, where Sir Alf Ramsey's team failed to overturn their 3-1 first-leg deficit.

It added an extra layer of end-of-season fatigue to the players who were walking out at a packed White Hart Lane to decide the winner of the very first UEFA Cup, on what was a beautiful summer evening, a stark contrast to the damp conditions that had been on offer at Molineux a fortnight earlier. While there were two unchanged line-ups on display, Wolves were bolstered by the return of their captain, Mike Bailey, who was on the bench being out injured since early January.

Just short of the half hour, Tottenham strengthened their position, when Mullery was yet again the hero, opening the scoring on the night and giving his side a comfortable-looking two-goal lead, when his flicked header found a way past the rashly advancing Parkes. The chance had been delivered to him by Peters from a quickly taken free kick, which was difficult not to be viewed as karma – taking from Wolves with one hand, having given to them with the other for McCalliog's equaliser in the first leg.

Up until Mullery's goal, it was almost as if there had been an uneasy and unspoken truce between the two teams to keep proceedings to nothing more than shadow boxing. The only other opportunity of substance had fallen to Gilzean, which he planted high over Parkes's crossbar from inside the six-yard box.

When Wolves' equaliser came, it was as spectacular as it was unexpected. Just four minutes before half-time, and after a period of pinball in and around the edge of the Tottenham penalty area, the ball fell to Wagstaffe, 25 yards from goal, from where he teed it up on his left foot before arrowing a beautiful and powerful effort past a helpless Jennings and in off his right-hand post.

Twisting on its axis, the whole complexion of the game altered in the second half. Wolves, just one goal from levelling the tie, began to apply pressure, increasing this when Bailey was introduced as a replacement for Kenny Hibbitt around the hour mark.

Jennings was at his defiant best, however, and, despite a hint of goal falling to not just Dougan, but also Richards and McCalliog, time ran out on Wolves' brave attempt to take the game into the period of extra time it probably warranted.

For Mullery, the comeback captain, lifting the UEFA Cup would be his final duty in a Tottenham shirt, returning to Fulham on a permanent basis in the summer of 1972, not long after the self-imposed ending of his international career and at a time when his stock as a top-level player of value had risen once again.

Perhaps it was dropping down a division that elongated his career, as Mullery's longevity was rewarded three years later when he played in the 1975 FA Cup Final alongside Bobby Moore for the Craven Cottage outfit, against West Ham United.

In the absence of Mullery, Tottenham's defence of their UEFA Cup in 1972/73 was still a strong one, but just not quite strong enough to hold on to the trophy. It also included another titanic, all-English, two-legged battle, this time in the semi-final, against Bill Shankly's Liverpool.

Confronting one another an incredible six times throughout the 1972/73 season, Liverpool had edged November's White Hart Lane, First Division encounter, 2-1, yet within not much more than a fortnight, Tottenham had knocked Shankly's side out of the League Cup, in a quarter-final replay in north London after a 1-1 draw at Anfield.

When the two sides then went head-to-head in the league once more, at Anfield at the end of March, it was a game that again resulted in a 1-1 draw. However, the remarkable thing about the fixture was that Jennings saved two Liverpool penalties, one from Kevin Keegan, the other from Tommy Smith, in a fixture that kicked off early so as not to clash with the Grand National.

This second league game of the season added extra spice to the first leg of the UEFA Cup semi-final, which came just ten days later and was again at Anfield. Once more, Jennings would prove to be pivotal, a man widely regarded to be the best goalkeeper in the First Division and quite possibly beyond.

Billed as a showdown between Liverpool's notoriously tight defence and Tottenham's stylish sense of attack-minded football, it was a case of roles reversed under the Anfield floodlights, as Nicholson's side spent most of the game repelling wave after wave of Liverpool attacks.

Defensive blocks and heroic saves batted away Liverpool chance after Liverpool chance. Miraculously, Jennings and Tottenham kept their hosts at bay until the 27th minute, when Alec Lindsay found himself in the right place at the right time, when a Smith free kick, swung into the penalty area, caused yet more chaos. The rebound fell sweetly to the Liverpool left-back, who made the most of his opportunity.

Perplexingly, Liverpool failed to add further goals despite their near-blanket domination over the visitors, who were restricted to the very occasional counter attack, in which a lack of support resulted in these rare forays forward, running into either the short shrift of Shankly's stubborn defence, or self-generated blind alleys. It came as both a surprise and a relief to Nicholson that his team managed to escape Anfield with only a one-goal deficit and everything still to play for in the second leg, a sensation accentuated by Jennings making outstanding saves from a thunderous and seemingly goal-bound Smith free kick, plus another effort from Steve Heighway that he tipped on to the crossbar.

A cause of frustration to Liverpool, this glut of spurned chances further irked Shankly's side when strong claims for a late penalty were waved away by the referee.

League title all but clinched, two days before heading to White Hart Lane, with a crucial victory over Leeds on Easter Monday at Anfield, Liverpool had not much more than 48 hours' recovery time before facing Tottenham in the second leg of the semi-final. Nicholson's side, meanwhile, hadn't played on Easter Monday and were afforded two extra days of rest before the resumption of UEFA Cup entanglements.

Also, in Tottenham's favour, Lindsay, Liverpool's match-winner from the first leg, wasn't fit to play, and neither was the influential Peter Cormack, who had picked up an ankle injury against Leeds. In their places were an 18-year-old Phil Thompson and the striker Phil Boersma, who got the nod from Shankly ahead of both John Toshack and the gravitational urge to bolster his defence.

With Thompson operating in midfield and Boersma offering a running option alongside Kevin Keegan, as opposed to the aerial presence that Toshack would have provided, Shankly decided that attack would be the most effective form of defence against a Tottenham side that would be a far more dangerous proposition than they had been at Anfield.

It made for a dramatic duel that twisted one way and then the other, battling for a UEFA Cup Final berth that could easily have fallen into the hands of Nicholson instead of Shankly – Liverpool, in search of their first European honour, against a Tottenham side that were desperately trying to hold on to the trophy they had earned a year ago, and to add further lustre to their growing reputation as seasoned collectors of European silverware.

At White Hart Lane, Liverpool edged the first half, successfully keeping Tottenham off balance as they hit on the break while offering their hosts little in the way of space and momentum when they ventured forward. No goals were scored, but Shankly's team were comfortably in control.

Within four minutes of the restart, all of this changed, however, when Liverpool were caught defensively flat-footed, as a long throw from Chivers, out on the right, was flicked on by Gilzean, from where the ball was met on the volley by the late run of Peters.

Undaunted, Liverpool continued to press Tottenham into reverse, and it was the work of Emlyn Hughes and Keegan that set up Heighway for Liverpool's crucial away goal, just over ten minutes after Peters had drawn his side level.

Hughes, operating at left-back in the absence of Lindsay, played a long ball down the left flank for Keegan to latch on to, the energetic striker forcing an error out of England before coaxing the advancing Jennings from his goalmouth leaving an unmarked Heighway with the simplest of tap-ins when squaring the ball to him for 1-1.

With Tottenham now needing two goals to reach the final, Liverpool were back in control, although the ice beneath them got progressively thinner. Peters, in startling form, put in a heroic captain's performance, rattling the Liverpool crossbar within minutes of Heighway's goal, John Pratt narrowly heading the rebound wide.

Peters wouldn't be denied for long though, edging Tottenham ahead on the night once again with a little under 20 minutes remaining when he capitalised as the ball fell to him after it had bounced off Thompson, following a spell of intense pressure from the home side.

With a grandstand finish set up, in a way the semi-final went full circle, with Liverpool's defence repelling the Tottenham attack in a similar manner at the end of the second leg to how Tottenham's defence had desperately fought to hold off Liverpool's rampant offensive during the first leg. Still willing to hit on the break, however, Chris Lawler came close to easing Liverpool's burden when he floated a header marginally wide of the post.

It was with a sharp sense of relief that Liverpool welcomed the full-time whistle, which brought with it a place in their second major European final. Beaten in the 1966 Cup Winners' Cup Final, Shankly's team would be aiming to go one better this time around.

Liverpool's defeat on the night against Tottenham in the second leg of the semi-final was their only reversal on their way to the 1973 UEFA Cup Final, in what had been a Germanic heavy set of hurdles to clear.

While Borussia Mönchengladbach were lying in wait in the final, Liverpool's run had also begun against West German opposition in the shape of future UEFA Cup winners, Eintracht Frankfurt. Advantage was taken by Shankly's side when Liverpool's greater fitness proved to be the decisive element during the first leg, at Anfield.

With the start of the new Bundesliga campaign having been delayed, due to the 1972 Munich Olympics, Erich Ribbeck's Frankfurt had stubbornly held Liverpool to 1-0 for over an hour, before they were finally breached with 15 minutes remaining, when Hughes headed in at the back post after some wonderful link-play between Keegan and Cormack.

A peculiar game, Liverpool's opening goal being allowed to stand seemed to take even the home side by surprise, when Keegan had appeared to be offside by a considerable margin. A glaring error by the officials, it would be the last time in the game that Keegan would be awarded the benefit of the doubt by the referee. Twice, he would be denied what seemed to be clear-cut penalty decisions.

Frankfurt absorbed this early blow and for all but the last 15 minutes they kept Liverpool contained and frustrated. Keegan was man-marked by the impressive Thomas Rohrbach throughout, while Uwe Kliemann was commanding at centre-back.

Yet, once Liverpool obtained their second goal, it acted as a catalyst for an avalanche of attempts upon the Frankfurt penalty area, with the visiting goalkeeper, Dr Peter Kunter, defying gravity, keeping the scoreline at 2-0 as he and his defence repelled wave after wave of attacks. Not only did both Keegan and Hughes spurn opportunities to add to their goals, but Lawler, Cormack, Heighway, Tommy Smith and Ian Callaghan also failed to convert openings that fell their way too.

At the Waldstadion, a fortnight later, Frankfurt tested Liverpool's defensive resolve to its limits, during a second leg in which Ray Clemence and his defenders were impenetrable. Even the loss of Smith, shortly before the hour, didn't weaken Shankly's stranglehold on a place in the second round, as in a rare Liverpool appearance, Trevor Storton covered the loss of Smith convincingly. A goalless draw saw Liverpool through.

Having navigated a comfortable passage beyond AEK Athens in the second round, Liverpool then faced back-to-back encounters with opponents from East Germany, firstly seeing off Dynamo Berlin in the third round, then Dynamo Dresden in the quarter-finals.

From Berlin, Liverpool returned home with a precious goalless draw, procured from a game where neither goalkeeper was seriously tested — a merciful turn of events for Clemence, who played while suffering from influenza.

In less than a minute of the return game kicking off, Liverpool's sense of security was further massaged as Boersma forced the ball over the Berlin line when following up the rebound to an effort from Heighway.

Missing both Keegan and Smith, Hughes dropped into defence to partner Larry Lloyd, while Thompson covered in midfield alongside Cormack. It was the Cormack–Thompson combination that propelled Liverpool into the last eight, after a seismic scare, when Wolf-Rüdiger Netz grabbed Berlin an entirely unexpected equaliser. It was a goal that provoked a wide-open spell of the game, as Liverpool strove to regain the advantage while Berlin were emboldened by the away goal they had claimed.

Wind was once again drawn from Berlin sails, however, when Heighway eased Liverpool's concerns midway through the first half with a deflected shot from distance, which wrongfooted Werner Lisha, for 2-1.

Spirit visibly draining from the East Germans, Liverpool's third goal killed the evening as a contest 11 minutes into the second half and eased any lingering fears of a second Berlin goal.

Toshack was the man who took advantage of a sleepy defence, as Cormack gained retribution for being cynically pulled back by Frank Terletzki when he executed a quick free kick, spotting the clever run of Toshack who collected the pass, turned and finished, for 3-1. From here, Liverpool began to turn on the party pieces, with an audacious act of skill and vision very nearly earning Lawler what would have been a spectacular goal.

Thrown together with Dresden next, this time Liverpool were at home for the first leg, in what was a mismatch in terms of physical stature. With over half of the Dresden line-up towering way above six feet tall, diminutive Liverpool players, such as Keegan, Callaghan and Brian Hall struck the appearance of ball boys that had wandered on to the Anfield turf. Ironically, it was Hall that opened the scoring with his head, instigating and finishing the move, via a Boersma cross.

Boersma, once again proving his value to Liverpool's UEFA Cup run, was the scorer of their second goal, just beyond the hour, accepting the second of two invitations to force the ball over the line, after a low and powerful effort from Heighway was blocked.

Under no illusions that they had been given their toughest European test of the season, Shankly and Liverpool knew that the job was only half done and that if they were to be underprepared for their second trip into East Germany, in less than four months, then their dreams of a first piece of European silverware could easily evaporate in Dresden.

At the Rudolf-Harbig-Stadion, however, Liverpool arguably produced their most grown-up away European performance to date, when becoming the first team to inflict a home loss upon Dresden in any competition for three years.

Liverpool's 1-0 victory was gained courtesy of a second-half goal from Keegan after he had had a first-half strike harshly disallowed, to go alongside another that was chalked off from Cormack. It was only the second defeat that Dresden had sustained all season, the first having been inflicted at Anfield.

With the steady supply of German opponents being disrupted by Tottenham and their spectacular all-English semi-final, Gladbach were Liverpool's fourth Germanic opposition of the season, when they went head-to-head in the final. Given that Liverpool had also faced Bayern Munich during their two previous European campaigns, Shankly and his team were now well accustomed to German adversaries.

Without that sense of acclimatisation to German teams for Liverpool, the 1973 UEFA Cup Final might well have ended very differently. Gladbach were a club on an inexorable rise, led by the shrewd tactician, Hennes Weisweiler.

When Weisweiler's team took to the waterlogged Anfield pitch for the first leg of the final on 9 May 1973, three of his line-up had been part of the West Germany side that had overwhelmed the Soviet Union in the 1972 European Championship Final less than 11 months earlier. A further three Gladbach players had been unused members of Helmut Schön's victorious squad.

Blessed by the presence of the enigmatic, stubborn, yet astoundingly talented Günter Netzer, Weisweiler's team could also boast the services of Rainer Bonhof, Berti Vogts, Herbert Wimmer, Jupp Heynckes and the future Ballon d'Or winner, Allan Simonsen. This meant that, for Liverpool, the danger was that Gladbach's inherent sophistication would simply be too much to cope with over the course of the two games.

Added to this, Gladbach were still within the stride of the run-in to the end of their domestic season. Not only was the final of the DFB-Pokal looming upon the horizon, a game that would prove to be Netzer's last for the club, but Weisweiler and his team still had four Bundesliga games to complete and their most recent competitive game had been a convincing 5-0 victory against a Wuppertaler SV side that were enjoying the greatest season of their existence.

A ray of hope lingered for Liverpool, however, as Gladbach had struggled to keep the ball out of their net for much of the season. Fifty-one league goals had been conceded up to this point, with over 70 shipped across all competitions. While Liverpool's determined defence would have their biggest test of the season ahead of them, Shankly was given cause for optimism that goals wouldn't be impossible to score.

Weisweiler, fully aware of the threat posed by Liverpool and the weaknesses of his own team, knew that an away goal would be crucial to Gladbach's chances of success. The first leg lasted for just 27 minutes, before it was abandoned due to the incessant nature of the rain.

For Shankly, the abandonment would be the pivotal moment of the final. Having watered the Anfield pitch during the days leading up to the game, under the impression that Gladbach would not react well to soft ground, the unexpected nature of the downpour that fell upon the city of Liverpool on the day of the final left the pitch resembling a swimming pool.

Yet, within those 27 minutes of football, Shankly had spotted what he felt was an aerial vulnerability in the Gladbach defence. When the second attempt to play the game was made 24 hours later, Hall was withdrawn from the starting line-up, to be replaced by the towering presence of Toshack.

Liverpool swept to a 3-0 win, Gladbach unable to cope with the high-tempo approach of the home team and the aerial advantage offered by Toshack. Twice, the Welsh international used his head to set up his strike partner, Keegan, to score, while Lloyd powered in a header for Liverpool's third goal of the night.

In an evening of drama, there was a blizzard of action during a 15-minute spell of the first half, where Keegan's goals were accompanied by him having a penalty saved by the West German international Wolfgang Kleff with the scoreline at 1-0, swiftly followed by Dietmar Danner striking Clemence's post. Liverpool might well have run up a 3-0 victory, but it was a comfortable margin of advantage that was attained via the finest of lines.

Even at 3-0 down, Gladbach still swept forward with a wonderful attacking verve and they would have been rewarded had Clemence not pushed a Heynckes penalty around his post with 25 minutes still to play.

Dictating the flow of play from there on, Gladbach were unable to obtain the away goal they so desperately wanted. In part, they were stunted by Weisweiler's decision to deploy Netzer in central defence, in the absence of Ulrich Surau.

With just under a fortnight between the two games, while Liverpool were largely left to their own devices without a competitive game to keep them sharp, Gladbach ran up 4-2 and 4-1 wins in the semi-final, second leg of the Pokal and a Bundesliga fixture, against Werder Bremen and Schalke respectively.

At the Bökelbergstadion, Liverpool walked into a Gladbach ambush. With Surau available once again, the midfield was handed to Netzer, who in turn kept the Liverpool midfield spinning on its axis, offering a consistent feed of passes for Bernd Rupp, a centre-forward by nature, but one who was asked by Weisweiler to drag the ball wide, allowing Heynckes to charge into the vacated space in and around Clemence's penalty area.

It was a ploy that worked perfectly. Despite a glaring early miss by Rupp and a diving header from Heynckes that narrowly missed the target, Liverpool failed to heed the warnings. Just before the half hour Gladbach had their breakthrough, as Rupp latched on to a loose ball to the right of goal – the pace of it taking a shot out of the equation, he squared it to the onrushing Heynckes, who side-footed home for 1-0.

Not much more than ten minutes later, Heynckes struck again. Rupp involved once more, he received the ball from Vogts on the edge of the penalty area, with his back to goal, before twisting and turning his way towards his target while evading the advances of Lloyd, Lawler and Smith, then laying it off for Heynckes to curl a stunning effort into Clemence's top left-hand corner.

Both goals converted by Heynckes and teed up by Rupp, as clinical and impressive as they were, Gladbach had partly benefited in both instances when Rupp had initially miscontrolled the ball.

With five first-half minutes remaining, Liverpool were on the ropes, Shankly having again opted for the height advantage of Toshack ahead of either the extra man in midfield or the pace and ball-carrying talents of Boersma. The problem with this, however, was that Pavel Kazakov, the Soviet referee, blew for an infringement virtually every time that Toshack challenged for an aerial ball.

Unwittingly, Gladbach had blown the wind out of their own sails during their first-half fightback. When the game resumed after the interval, Liverpool's defence had regained its composure and Weisweiler's players were swiftly closed down whenever they were in possession.

Despite this, Heynckes wasted the chance to complete his hat-trick, when he glanced a header wide of the post, getting on the end of a wonderful cross by Wimmer. Gradually, however, Liverpool's grip on the UEFA Cup continued to tighten, Gladbach's pressure being repelled. Boersma, replacing Heighway as an outlet during the final stretch, could have grabbed a vital away goal, as could Toshack or Hughes.

A late Gladbach shout for a penalty was turned down and Liverpool had their first major European trophy, a trophy they had flown to West Germany with, when handed it by Tottenham, to return to the possession of UEFA for Liverpool's projected presentation. Netzer, Heynckes, Wimmer and Vogts had so nearly ensured that Shankly and his team returned home without it.

With the league title won, it meant that Liverpool would not return as holders to the 1973/74 UEFA Cup, instead taking part in the European Cup, yet this incredible run of English teams reaching the final of either the Fairs Cup or the UEFA Cup would continue in their absence.

In a wonderful baton-passing manner, as the UEFA Cup was handed from Tottenham to Liverpool, Shankly very nearly sent it straight back to Nicholson, as White Hart Lane again embraced a UEFA Cup Final. It was a comfortable progression to the final, against an eclectic set of opponents, plus a near miss on an all-English semi-final for Tottenham.

After seeing off Grasshoppers, Aberdeen had been circum-navigated in the second round, with a resounding 4-1 scoreline in the second leg, after a 1-1 draw at Pittodrie. The result at White Hart Lane masked the nature of the game, however, as Aberdeen had largely been the more expansive team, Tottenham simply being more clinical when their chances arrived.

In the third round there was a similar theme as Nicholson found himself up against the dangerously evolving Dinamo Tbilisi. Within eight years, Tbilisi would win the Cup Winners' Cup, but in the winter months of 1973 they went unrewarded for their industry during the first leg in Georgia when they were forced to settle for a 1-1 draw against their respected visitors.

Coates, Tottenham's most impressive performer in the first leg, gave his side the lead against the run of play and it was somewhat gravity-defying that Tbilisi were denied their equaliser until late into the second half, although a degree of luck was required to claim it, with the ball bouncing off Naylor to the grateful Kakhi Asatiani.

Asatiani, the Tbilisi hero, would follow the tragic pattern of several other players to represent the club, by dying in gruesome circumstances. In Asatiani's case, in November 2002, he was shot in the centre of Tbilisi, in what appears to have been a planned attack. A man of great footballing notoriety, he was the first player to be awarded a yellow card in World Cup finals history, in Mexico in 1970.

Back at White Hart Lane, on a night that was expected to be a much more taxing one for Nicholson's side, Tottenham brushed Tbilisi aside, with an aerial approach that largely went against the usual ethos of the club.

Chivers and Peters scored two each during a 5-1 victory that pitted a surprising show of Tottenham brawn against the artistic brain of Tbilisi. In the first leg, Chivers and Peters had been forced to drop deep and defend, more often than they had been able to spring forward in attack.

During a season of domestic inconsistency, Tottenham fell at the first hurdle in both the League Cup and the FA Cup, while their mid-table finish eventually came with a sigh of relief after spending the first half of the campaign a little too close to comfort to a relegation battle that would go on to claim Manchester United as one of its victims.

When Tottenham headed to West Germany to take on 1. FC Köln in the quarter-finals, they were a team low on impetus, fresh off the back of a convincing 3-1 defeat to Queens Park Rangers in the First Division that was flattering in its scoreline.

Struggling to settle on his favoured defensive combination and with his attack suffering through a crisis of confidence, Nicholson would have been forgiven for feeling a sense of foreboding about facing a Köln side that hadn't lost at home all season until a short few days prior to Tottenham's visit to the Müngersdorfer Stadion. Added to this, Köln had only lost once at home in their entire endeavours in European club competition.

Holed up in the picturesque Rheinhotel Dreesen, the hotel where Neville Chamberlain attempted to defuse the looming Second World War in summit meetings with Adolf Hitler, Nicholson successfully plotted an unexpected victory at the Müngersdorfer.

Shorn of the services of Coates, Nicholson ignored the more obvious options of Gilzean or Jimmy Neighbour as a replacement by bringing in an extra defender in the shape of Mike Dillon, an alteration that gave the teenage winger, Chris McGrath, a greater prominence.

With Peters and Chivers rising to the occasion too, McGrath was a constant threat to Köln and it was he who opened the scoring, after a powerful run and what seemed to be a mishit from Chivers, which fell to McGrath at the back post to side-foot in.

Incessant in their own sense of attack-minded football, Köln were blessed by the skilled presence of Wolfgang Overath, with the West German international just a few months away from being one of the pivotal components in his nation winning the World Cup on home soil.

Tottenham holding their lead at the interval, Dieter Müller clinically rolled in Köln's equaliser within ten minutes of the restart. For the next 20 minutes, Tottenham had to withstand a near constant wave of pressure from the home side. Striking out occasionally on the counter-attack, it was Peters who snatched the winning goal, with 15 minutes left to play, heading the ball past Gerhard Welz after some fine link-play with Naylor.

Despite their domestic struggles, it had been a classic Nicholson European masterclass and a result totally in keeping with Tottenham's UEFA Cup progression. The 1973/74 season was proving to be a clear double-sided coin at White Hart Lane.

Armed with their two away goals, Tottenham played with a wonderfully expressive freedom in the second leg, ending the tie as a contest within the first 14 minutes, when goals from Chivers and Coates curtailed any aspirations that Köln had about a potential comeback.

Peters added a third goal shortly after the restart, which still didn't stop the visitors from ploughing forward in search of a route back into the game. With their red shirts and white sleeves, however, Köln might as well have painted a target on the back of each player, and one challenge from England, on Heinz Flohe, was so well timed, yet uncompromising, that it wouldn't have looked out of place in a north London derby.

So emphatic in their defeating of Köln, Tottenham's split personality was perfectly encapsulated by their continued domestic inconsistencies. In the four league games they played, between the second leg of the UEFA Cup quarter-finals and the first leg of the semi-finals, Nicholson's European adventures won one, drew one and lost two.

It was probably a blessing to Tottenham that the potential of an all-English semi-final was ended, when Ipswich Town lost out in their quarter-final encounter on penalties to Lokomotive Leipzig. Almost mirroring Tottenham's season, Leipzig had offset their own domestic shortcomings with an inspiring UEFA Cup run. Before eliminating Ipswich, they had accounted for the exits of Torino, Wolves and Fortuna Düsseldorf.

Lacking in access opportunities to scout the form and shape of Leipzig in person, Nicholson leant on the advice and experiences of his old Wolves UEFA Cup sparring partner, McGarry, and those of Bobby Robson.

At the cavernous Zentralstadion, Tottenham defied the will of a partisan home support of 74,000 to return home with a 2-1 victory. It was a prize that could have been even more impressive, as Chivers somehow contrived to hit the post with a header shortly before half-time, the rebound hitting the Leipzig goalkeeper and rolling out of play, when it could easily have crept over the line.

Chivers's missed chance would have made it 3-0 to Tottenham, towards the end of an impressive first 45 minutes in which they had been utterly dominant, despite the absence of McGrath. Goals from Peters and Coates had swept Tottenham into a 2-0 lead, during a ruthless opening half hour.

Primed by Robson that Leipzig were a predominantly defensive team, Nicholson was wary enough of the sting the East Germans contained within their tail to insist his team didn't go for the kill during the second half.

Erring on caution, Tottenham went for a more traditional away European approach after the restart. It was a wise decision, as Leipzig attacked with greater fluency in the second half, locked within the realisation that their hopes of reaching the 1974 UEFA Cup Final lay in what they could salvage, before heading to London for the second leg.

Nicholson's tactics restricted Leipzig to pulling back only one of the goals they had conceded in the first half, when Wolfram Löwe powered in an impressive header, getting on the end of a Manfred Geisler free kick. Löwe would go on to play for East Germany at the World Cup just a couple of months later.

Flattering to deceive in the First Division once again during their games in the lead-up to the second leg, Tottenham were victorious at home to Southampton, before picking up a draw and a defeat at Chelsea and Stoke City respectively, the games against Southampton and Chelsea making up the Easter double header of fixtures.

When Leipzig arrived at White Hart Lane, Tottenham once more had the services of McGrath, but they also had a peculiar strand of pressure to contend with. Winning the first game of any two-legged European tie away from home brings with it a sense of expectation, almost trepidation, that the outcome is already assured, with only half the job done. The trailing team, with the freedom to throw caution to the wind, are left in a no-lose situation; for the team in arrears, the only thing that can be lost is a game they are expected to lose.

It was maybe with this in mind that Tottenham laboured their way through the first half of the second leg, while Leipzig probed and pressed for a route back into the reckoning. Impressive with their passing and movement, the East Germans met with an aggressive defensive front from Nicholson's side, with England strong in the tackle and John Pratt bending the rules to the very limits of their flexibility, to the point that even the White Hart Lane regulars were unenthusiastic about his interpretation of his defensive midfield duties.

Tottenham might have yielded much of the initiative in the first half, but in allowing Leipzig to get any notions of a comeback out of their system early, it left the second-half stage clear for the home team to cement their place in the final. McGrath was the man to break the deadlock, with a glancing and looping header shortly before the hour, thanks to a temptingly floated cross from Coates.

Still, Jennings was made to work hard by Leipzig, despite Tottenham taking a stranglehold of the game. Both the legendary goalkeeping of the Northern Ireland international and the crossbar barred Leipzig from making life uncomfortable for Nicholson and his players during the last half hour.

Chivers, with just three minutes remaining, gave the aggregate scoreline a much more generous tilt than it warranted, albeit with a wonderfully taken finish, after some swift and intelligent play from Perryman that drew three Leipzig defenders and opened up a clear angle of attack on goal for Chivers to roll the ball into the bottom right-hand corner.

Considering the last five years of the Fairs Cup and first three editions of the UEFA Cup, Tottenham reaching the 1974 final made it an eighth successive season in which there was at least one English representative contesting the prize, come the showpiece occasions.

Three years into the new tournament, Tottenham had been an omnipresent figure. Winners in the inaugural UEFA Cup Final, beaten semi-finalists in 1973 and now back in the final in 1974, as a club they had also never lost a major cup final of any description before. FA Cup winners in 1901, 1921, 1961, 1962 and 1967, with League Cup glory in 1971 and 1973, added to by European successes in 1963 and 1972, Tottenham had become English football's definitive 'cup team' and Nicholson was responsible for seven of those nine trophy-claiming days. Eight major honours, when you throw in his 1960/61 league title.

This would prove to be a bridge too far for Nicholson and Tottenham, however. Feyenoord ran out 2-0 winners at De Kuip, eight days beyond a 2-2 draw at White Hart Lane. Crowd disturbances marred the second leg, as Tottenham supporters clashed violently with both their Feyenoord counterparts and Rotterdam police, up and down the steep terracing behind one of the goals. The epicentre of the trouble unfolding at half-time, there had been flashpoints before the game and requests for calm were put out over the tannoy system prior to kick-off.

When Feyenoord took the lead shortly before the interval, it prompted the ripping out of wooden seats by Tottenham's followers, which were flung towards Feyenoord sections. It was an incendiary situation that has led to an uneasy relationship between the two clubs which exists to this very day, with renewing of hostilities in 1983/84 and 1991/92.

A heartbroken Nicholson relinquished his long-held role as Tottenham manager less than four months later, after a poor start to the 1974/75 season. Citing that he had suffered from burnout, it was a multi-faceted set of reasons that resulted in his departure.

Certainly, the hooliganism of Rotterdam had disappointed and perplexed Nicholson, but he was also struggling to reconcile himself with a new breed of footballer, who were more interested in the financial increments of prospective transfers to Tottenham than where they fitted into the club's on-pitch plans.

For Nicholson, it was still predominantly about the glory of the game as opposed to the personal rewards. Added to this, he was now also in possession of an ageing squad. Gilzean had retired, Peters, Knowles and England were over the age of 30, while Jennings, Beal, Chivers and Coates were all in their late 20s.

There was still a part of Nicholson's side that were yet to approach their peak years, Perryman the most influential of this collective, plus the emergence and impact of McGrath had been a massive bonus, but some substantial restructuring was looming, inclusive of the loss of significant figures.

Nicholson's appetite to rebuild will have been low when combined with his sense of disappointment over the events of Rotterdam and the rise of the money-hungry generation of player. All of this was then amplified when a disagreement over who should be his successor led to Nicholson departing the club entirely, after having initially agreed to stay on as an advisor. It was a spat that included the shelving of a planned testimonial game in his honour.

Tottenham's board of directors and Nicholson eventually made their peace, with him returning to White Hart Lane as an advisor to Keith Burkinshaw, having held a similar role at West Ham United for a short while, alongside Ron Greenwood, for John Lyall.

This return to Tottenham represented the wheel completing its full circle, as Nicholson was there to see Burkinshaw take the UEFA Cup back to White Hart Lane in 1984, ten years beyond the loss to Feyenoord.

English football's six-year run of Fairs Cup and UEFA Cup glory punctuated, 1974/75 proved to be something of a culture shock. Not only did the 1975 UEFA Cup Final take place without any English involvement, no First Division team made it beyond the third round.

With an era of English UEFA Cup influence nearing an end, 1975/76 offered one more spin of the wheel. Under new management, Liverpool would use the UEFA Cup as a springboard to launch themselves into a period of continental domination.

With Bob Paisley succeeding Shankly in the summer of 1974, the foundations laid by the former were used by the latter to build the empire that Liverpool became. Within the slipstream of winning the 1976 UEFA Cup, over the course of the next eight years they won the European Cup four times. The importance of their 1976 UEFA Cup success in acting as a springboard for what would follow tends to go unappreciated.

Just as in 1972/73, in 1975/76 Liverpool would make it a league title and UEFA Cup double. It was a season in which Liverpool made a defined switch from the Shankly version of themselves towards Paisley's image. Evolution was taking place.

On the way to lifting the UEFA Cup in 1976, Liverpool suffered only one loss and it came in the very first game of their run, in Edinburgh at Easter Road against Hibernian. Outplayed for the last hour of the first round, first leg, Paisley's team were fortunate to exit Scotland with only a one-goal deficit. Yet, they could also have punished their hosts late on, when Boersma, on as a substitute for the subdued Heighway, almost snatched an equaliser. Added to this, Phil Neal had a goal disallowed just before the hour mark.

For most of the opening act of this early season Battle of Britain, Liverpool were distinctly second best. Nervous in defence, dominated in midfield and starved of opportunities in attack, they were missing the defensive input of both Thompson and Smith, which meant that Lawler was deployed as an emergency centre-back, while in midfield Paisley sacrificed the misfiring Terry McDermott, bringing in Hall for his first start of the season. Up front, Keegan was joined by Ray Kennedy.

Despite what was a more than capable Liverpool line-up, it was Hibs that looked the team more likely to threaten the latter stages of the tournament and it only added insult to literal injury when it was left to the former Everton player, Joe Harper, to score the only goal of the evening.

Clemence was the man to sustain the injury, when he suffered a badly bruised thigh after a challenge from Harper. It proved a pivotal moment, as Clemence was in enough pain for it to be seriously considered by Paisley to replace him with Peter McDonnell, a back-up goalkeeper who would eventually depart Liverpool with UEFA Cup and European Cup winners' medals, yet never having made a first-team appearance for the club.

Playing on through the pain barrier instead, Clemence would be the hero of the evening for Liverpool, as with ten minutes remaining, he saved a John Brownlie penalty. It was a save that seemed to take the sting out of a Hibs offensive that would have been deserving of a wider lead to take to Anfield for the second leg. At the same time as Clemence was performing his heroics, McDonnell's chance of a Liverpool debut slipped through his fingers.

Disappointed or not by their failure to take greater advantage of Liverpool during the first leg, Hibs arrived at Anfield for the second leg in the mood to compete. Unfazed by the task that lay ahead of them, even when Toshack opened the scoring for the home side to level the aggregate score after 21 minutes, the visitors still swept forward in search of what would be a crucial away goal.

Hibs' boldness was rewarded in the 33rd minute, when Alexander Edwards coolly placed the ball past the outstretched reach of Clemence after some excellent interlinking with Des Bremner, a man who would go on to win the European Cup with Aston Villa.

Regaining their composure during the second half, Liverpool turned the game around within an 11-minute span from the 53rd minute onward, Toshack again with the goals, claiming himself a hat-trick of headers.

Paisley's side now harbouring a 3-2 aggregate lead, it was an advantage that left the game on a tantalising knife-edge, as a goal in retaliation from Hibs would hand them a place in the next round on an understated Anfield evening of European drama and tension that was criminally played out in front of what was not much more than a half-full stadium.

Liverpool rolled over the finish line and Toshack's hat-trick was a turning point for him personally after Paisley had failed in an attempt to sell him to Leicester City the previous season. The Welsh international would rekindle his partnership with Keegan, while Boersma would be moved on to Middlesbrough and Kennedy would soon undergo his conversion to a silken left-sided midfielder.

In addition, from the bench against Hibs had climbed Jimmy Case, who would soon make the right-hand side of midfield his own, while the likes of Lawler, Lindsay, Hall and Cormack would drift from contention, due to a combination of form, advancing age and injury. David Fairclough would balance out some of this when making his explosive contribution to Liverpool's run-in.

Paired with Real Sociedad in the second round, Liverpool swept through with a 9-1 aggregate victory, 3-1 winners in San Sebastián, followed by a 6-0 demolition at Anfield on an evening when Fairclough scored his first goal for the club and an impressionable John Aldridge watched on in awe from the Spion Kop.

Aldridge would later not only play for the team he grew up a supporter of, but he also became the first non-Basque footballer to sign for Sociedad.

Star of the second leg, however, was the 19-year-old Brian Kettle, who was drafted in at left-back, putting in a performance of high energy and pinpoint crossing, the first of which found the head of Toshack for the opening goal.

An attacking avalanche, Keegan was even able to see a penalty of his fly high over the Sociedad crossbar without repercussions. The eye of the Liverpool storm came in the second half, when they scored four goals in an eight-minute blizzard of forward momentum. The Sociedad goalkeeper recovered admirably from his Anfield experiences, however; Luis Arconada went on to win LaLiga titles with his club and to captain the Spanish national team.

Śląsk Wrocław were overcome in the third round, Liverpool claiming victories both away and at home – in Poland on an ice-encased pitch and at Anfield while shrouded in wisps of mist. Case scored a hat-trick in the second leg, denied more goals when striking the post and having what looked to be a perfectly good effort disallowed, on a night when he might have found himself amongst the substitutes instead, only being assured of his place in Paisley's team when Heighway was ruled out shortly before kick-off due to tonsillitis.

It was in the kinder weather and on the softer pitches of March that Liverpool renewed relations with Dynamo Dresden. A valuable goalless draw obtained from the quarter-final, first leg, behind the Iron Curtain, it was a game that had more to it than meets the scoreline.

Yet another fantastic UEFA Cup penalty save from Clemence, this time from Peter Kotte in response to a debateable awarding of the spot kick after Kennedy had sent Udo Schmuck to ground, was complemented with a textbook away European performance by Liverpool of containment and counter-attack.

Ten minutes from time, Thompson almost made it the perfect performance for Liverpool, when he got on the end of a Kennedy free kick with a wonderfully timed late run, only to see his well-directed header strike the angle of post and crossbar. It was a near miss that would be equalled by Dresden, when in the final seconds Hartmut Schade struck Clemence's left-hand post.

At Anfield, Liverpool had what seemed to be an unquenchable thirst for attack, as they created chance after chance. Neal and Kennedy went close from distance, Keegan had one tipped over the crossbar by Claus Boden, while Case hit the bar with a shot that was so powerful it had Thompson dropping to the turf to take cover.

Case, insatiable in his drive to break into the penalty area, was the man to open the scoring, when he got on the end of a Callaghan pass into the right-hand channel, from where he unnerved Gerd Weber and closed in on Boden before placing the ball just inside the bottom right-hand post. It was a goal of precision and the least Liverpool had deserved for their first-half efforts.

Just two minutes after the restart, Keegan made it 2-0, when he got on the end of a Smith cross that evaded its intended target, Toshack, plus the assortment of Dresden defenders that were surrounding him. Rather than slow the game down, Liverpool continued to plough forward, inclusive of Case hitting the crossbar yet again.

Dresden would not remain oppressed all evening, however. With 27 minutes left to play, they gained themselves an unlikely foothold in the game, when Gerd Heidler worked his way past both Hughes and Thompson, forcing the ball past Clemence to leave the outcome suddenly far more uncertain than had seemed possible.

From there to the final whistle, the game ebbed and flowed, as Dresden applied pressure for an equaliser that would be good enough to take them through on the away-goals rule, while Liverpool counter-punched in a bid to reassert their wider superiority. During this spell of the game, Toshack could have procured the goal that would have made Paisley's side much more comfortable, yet Dresden might have easily made their pressure tell.

Liverpool's prize for obtaining a place in the semi-finals was to be thrown together with Johan Cruyff and a Barcelona side that was now being led by the former Gladbach coach, Weisweiler, the man who was effectively the holder of the UEFA Cup, having won it with his previous team in 1975.

For Liverpool, it would prove to be an occasion marked with an historic victory and Joey Jones bouncing cushions off the heads of disgruntled spectators at the Camp Nou.

Toshack scored the only goal of the first leg in Catalonia to make Liverpool the first English team to beat Barcelona in their own stadium. No other English team would win at the Camp Nou until Liverpool did it once again in 2007.

As the game drew towards a close, irate locals began to throw the cushions they were sat on at the pitch in protest at their heroes' efforts. As some landed near the Liverpool bench, Jones, an unused substitute, took offence, thinking that they were aimed at the visitors, upon which he picked up a few of the cushions and began skimming them back into the crowd.

Finding his arm was true, Jones was getting the cushions to bounce off the heads of the Barcelona supporters, until Paisley pulled him back to the bench to inform him he was liable to provoke a riot and that the cushions were being aimed at the Barcelona players.

It was at a packed Anfield that the second leg unfolded. Cruyff in front of the Spion Kop for the one and only time, he played a huge part in the goal that Carles Rexach scored, seven minutes into the second half. On an evening when he was comfortably shackled by a resolute Liverpool defence, it was to be the one moment in which he was allowed the time and space for an act of genius.

Two minutes prior to Rexach's goal, Liverpool had taken the lead on the night extending their aggregate advantage when Thompson finished a move started by a Smith free kick, which was helped on by Keegan and Toshack, to the loitering Liverpool number four. Anfield erupted, before Rexach's swift reply stunned it into silence.

Deserved winners and the stronger team throughout the two games, however, it was Liverpool that progressed to the 1976 UEFA Cup Final, where they would face Ernst Happel's Club Brugge, who in turn had narrowly edged past Hamburger SV in the other semi-final, thus denying football history the tantalising image of Keegan facing his future employers in a major European final a year before signing for them.

Brugge travelled to Anfield in a more expansive frame of mind than Barcelona had, having dispatched not only the rising force of HSV, but also the increasingly considerable threats posed by Lyon, Ipswich Town, AS Roma and AC Milan. Against Bobby Robson's side, Brugge had even overturned a 3-0, first-leg deficit in their second-round clash.

Led by Happel, the visionary Austrian who had taken Feyenoord to European Cup glory six years earlier, it made for a fascinating meeting of footballing minds with Paisley.

Flying in the face of English footballing conventions of the era, Happel had his players out on the Anfield turf for their pre-match warm-up 20 minutes before kick-off. This meant that the Brugge players had been desensitised to the growing atmosphere and anticipation of the home support before the game began – while sufficiently loosened up, they also made a startlingly quick start to the first leg.

Already crowned as Belgian champions, while Liverpool still had a huge game ahead in their bid to win the First Division title, Brugge were blessed to have not only the home leg of the final second, but domestic matters all tied up.

Within 12 minutes, Brugge were in possession of a 2-0 lead, firstly taking advantage of an underweighted Neal header that was directed towards Clemence, where Raoul Lambert reached the ball first, putting his left foot to it as it dropped, looping it over the advancing Liverpool goalkeeper.

If that was an unpleasant surprise of a goal, seven minutes later came the shock to the Liverpool system, when an incisive combination of passes between Georges Leekens, Daniël de Cubber, Julien Cools and Lambert led to Cools hooking a left-footed shot into Clemence's top left-hand corner. The stunned silence of the home support was eventually punctured by the roar of the travelling Brugge followers.

Paisley's side were stung into retaliation and the only surprising thing was that it took until close on the hour for Liverpool to make their breakthrough, as a steady stream of chances were created and spurned, inclusive of opportunities that fell to Keegan, Smith, Kennedy, Case and Keegan once again.

Case had been brought on as a half-time substitute for the blunted Toshack, Happel having largely negated his aerial presence. It was on the ground that Liverpool were creating more traction, however, and with Fairclough staying on, it was with power, pace and swift movement of the ball that Liverpool drew themselves back into the game.

Kennedy struck first, with an explosive finish into the same top corner Cools had earlier found, this time from outside the Kop end penalty area, after being teed up by Heighway. It was a goal that lit the Anfield fuse and came just moments after Cools had dragged another Brugge opportunity wide.

Less than two minutes later, Liverpool were level, with Kennedy again pivotal when he profited from a wonderful turn and cutback by Keegan. This time his left-foot effort was low and inside the penalty area; this time Kennedy's shot hit the Brugge post, from where it rebounded, upwards, towards Case, who had the presence of mind to jump as the ball came to him, enabling him to side-foot it into the empty net, much to the delight of Liverpool's players and supporters alike.

Now incessant in their attacking intent, Liverpool had the lead four minutes later – Keegan taking responsibility for a penalty obtained by Heighway, when seemingly brought down just outside the penalty area. For Keegan, it was an assured spot kick, which it had to be, considering Paisley had given Neal the duties for the game.

With 25 minutes still to play, no further goals were added, despite Liverpool continuing the search for a wider lead to take to Belgium for the return game. Not for the want of effort, Keegan had what seemed set to be a certain goal cleared off the goal line from an unorthodox header, while Fairclough brought a stunning save out of the Danish international, Birger Jensen.

It was with mixed emotions that Liverpool departed the pitch with a 3-2 victory. Relief that they had turned a 2-0 half-time deficit around, yet frustration that having clawed their way into the lead, with a substantial amount of time remaining, they couldn't extend their advantage.

Six days later, Liverpool clinched the league title, with a dramatic 3-1 win at Molineux against Wolves. With a three-week gap between the first and second legs of the 1976 UEFA Cup Final, it was with no celebratory side effects that Liverpool walked out at Brugge's Olympiastadion in their bid to claim a second UEFA Cup success.

Just as in the first leg, it was Brugge that drew first blood. Rudi Glöckner, the referee who presided over the iconic 1970 World Cup Final, wasn't shy in pointing to the penalty spot with only 11 minutes played, much to the bemusement of the Liverpool players. No player having gone to ground, Smith was adjudged to have handled the ball just inside the Liverpool penalty area. From 12 yards, Lambert was utterly ruthless in his converting of his spot kick.

Four minutes later, however, Paisley's side were level on the night and ahead on aggregate once again when Hughes rolled an indirect free kick into the path of Keegan, who rifled it in hard and low, past the despairing Jensen. Only 15 minutes of the game had elapsed, yet no further goals were added, and the UEFA Cup belonged to Liverpool once more.

Despite the lack of further goals, there was to be no sedate finish to the game as both Liverpool and Brugge came close to adding to their tallies. Smith put the ball narrowly wide of Jensen's post when drifting in unnoticed as part of a clever Liverpool free kick, while in reply, Lambert agonisingly struck the inside of Clemence's left-hand post.

Unlike in the second leg of the 1973 final, when Gladbach ran out of steam in the latter stages, Brugge intensified their pressure on the Liverpool goalmouth as the minutes ticked down, during which a succession of chances and openings fell the home side's way.

After one last commanding piece of goalkeeping from Clemence and a subsequent downfield clearance, Glöckner blew the final whistle. It was a whistle that didn't just give Liverpool a second UEFA Cup, but it also marked the end of a period of intense English success and involvement in the end days of the Fairs Cup and the formative seasons of the UEFA Cup.

It was the culmination of a ten-year run, where there was only one final played out without the presence of an English team: a ten-season span when the trophy was claimed by a First Division side on seven occasions.

Due to the vagaries of football's wonderfully cyclical nature, five years would pass before an English team reached another UEFA Cup Final. In fact, due to the ban on English teams after the Heysel Disaster, followed by the near-blanket domination of the tournament by Serie A teams during the 1990s, beyond Liverpool's success in 1976, there would only be an English representative in two more two-legged UEFA Cup finals.

Dominant days unwittingly in the past for English football when it came to the UEFA Cup, the baton was now being passed on to mainland Europe to fight over, and it was the bewitching Gladbach who would place themselves front and centre.

Chapter Three

Gladbach All Over

THERE WAS a specific evening when Borussia Mönchengladbach hit the accelerator in the UEFA Cup, a defined launchpad from which they went on to reach the final four times in just eight seasons. Incredibly, during their 'down time' from the UEFA Cup, they also contested a European Cup Final and a further semi-final.

When Hennes Weisweiler oversaw a 5-0 victory against 1. FC Köln in their third round, second-leg encounter in December 1972, it acted as a facilitator in Gladbach's rise as a true European force and a conductor in the escalation of a modern rivalry that had been provoked by Weisweiler having been a former player and head coach of Köln, just 27 miles to the south-east of Gladbach's Bökelbergstadion.

Weisweiler would eventually return to the Müngersdorfer Stadion, via a season in charge of Barcelona. The relationship between Gladbach and Köln, on the back of this shared investment in a legend of a coach that created many of both clubs' greatest moments, has cultivated a rivalry that has elements that would be familiar to the supporters of Derby County and Nottingham Forest when they battle one another over possession of the legacy of Brian Clough.

Only their fourth European campaign, Gladbach's first foray into continental competition had been in the inaugural European Cup Winners' Cup campaign, during which they were thrashed by Glasgow Rangers 11-0 on aggregate, at a time when West German club football was still on an amateur footing.

Gladbach's second and third comings were much more purposeful, however. Fallers at the second round of the European Cup, in 1970/71 and 1971/72, to the substantial forces of Everton and Internazionale, they were only barred from a place in the 1972 quarter-finals by an ill-advisedly thrown can of Coca-Cola, which struck Roberto Boninsegna during a game that Weisweiler's team won 7-1, only for the result to be expunged as punishment. The Serie A team prevailed in the replayed fixture, going on to reach the final.

Excluded from the list of teams that contested the first playing of the newly formed Bundesliga, in 1963/64, Weisweiler took Gladbach into the new national West German top flight two years later, at the same time as Bayern Munich arrived, they too having been sidelined in the summer of 1963.

Consolidating, then maturing, Gladbach were champions for the first time in 1969/70, adding four further Bundesliga titles to their honours list throughout a decade in which they hypnotically went toe-to-toe with Bayern for the iconic *Meisterschale*, season in, season out. On only one occasion during the 1970s did West German football's champions' bowl not end up in the hands of either Gladbach or Bayern, that being in 1977/78, when Weisweiler took Köln to glory, edging his former team out on goal difference despite Gladbach running out 12-0 winners on the final day, at home to Borussia Dortmund.

Back in December 1972, however, Weisweiler's Gladbach took their 5-0 UEFA Cup demolition of Köln as their invitation to European greatness, despite going on to lose the 1973 final to Liverpool. Beyond dispatching Köln, Gladbach navigated another all-Bundesliga clash in the quarter-finals against Kaiserslautern, including a 7-1 victory in the second leg. They then acquainted themselves with Twente in the semi-finals, two years before the two went up against each other in the final itself.

Taking a sabbatical from the UEFA Cup in 1973/74, Gladbach were narrowly defeated by AC Milan in the last four of the Cup Winners' Cup. Prior to this, the culmination of the 1972/73 campaign had been a bittersweet one.

To offset their 1973 UEFA Cup Final loss, Gladbach won the DFB-Pokal, West Germany's domestic cup competition, beating Köln in a dramatic final that drifted into a tense period of extra time. The drama wasn't only confined to the pitch.

Günter Netzer, locked within the process of pushing through a transfer to Real Madrid and having spent much of the season struggling for form and fitness, was omitted from Weisweiler's starting line-up for the game. A row erupted, which almost resulted in Netzer refusing to take up his place on the Gladbach bench at Düsseldorf's Rheinstadion.

A game that was meant to be Netzer's glorious farewell to Gladbach was now a standoff. With the scoreline at 1-1, Netzer, the man for the big game, was called upon by Weisweiler to break the second-half stalemate. He refused to enter the fray, however, eventually going on, almost undetected by the Gladbach bench, at the beginning of extra time, from where, four minutes later, he had scored the winning goal, despite the initial poor reception he was greeted with from the Gladbach supporters.

Line in the sand drawn, by coach and player, it was with a surprising lack of ill-effect over the loss of Netzer that Weisweiler's Gladbach would go on to fulfil their fast-growing European potential, in 1974/75, something that came on the back of the disappointment of being pipped for the Bundesliga title in 1973/74.

After the rancour of Netzer's departure for the Spanish capital, the irony wouldn't have been lost on the former Gladbach playmaker when Weisweiler himself walked away from the Bökelbergstadion to take up the lucrative offer of employment in LaLiga, he was handed the chance to succeed Rinus Michels at Barcelona, where he would link up with another strong-minded footballing genius in the shape of Johan Cruyff. Before his move to Catalonia, however, Weisweiler had unfinished business at Gladbach. His last act as coach was a spectacular one, winning a Bundesliga and UEFA Cup double.

Beaten only once on their way to lifting the trophy in their first UEFA Cup outing of the season, away to Wacker Innsbruck, Gladbach were faultless from that initial defeat on their way to reaching a second major European final.

Winning nine games in succession, Gladbach overturned their first round, first-leg deficit against Innsbruck, before brushing aside the challenges of Lyon, Real Zaragoza, Banik Ostrava and, with much delight, Köln in the semi-final.

In the final, Twente were awaiting Weisweiler and Gladbach. An underappreciated Eredivisie force during the 1970s, the Twente of this era tends to be shielded by the rise of Feyenoord and Ajax as true European giants, while the escalating power of PSV Eindhoven also plays its part in this.

So close to glory at times, it was stunning that Twente ended the 1970s with only one KNVB Cup success to show for a decade of endeavour and style. Eredivisie runner-up in 1973/74, beaten by Gladbach in the 1973 UEFA Cup semi-final, they also lost the KNVB Cup Final of 1975 and 1979.

That 1975 KNVB Cup Final sat between the two legs of the UEFA Cup Final. When Twente left the pitch at the Rheinstadion, at the end of the first leg against Gladbach, with a very precious goalless draw, everything was stacked in their favour for a spectacular and silver-laden finish to the season.

An inspired goalkeeping performance from the controversial former West German international, Volkmar Groß, combined with Weisweiler being without the goalscoring services of the injured Jupp Heynckes, had ensured the advantage lay with Twente, with 90 minutes still to be played.

Blessed by the talents of the future Ipswich Town pair, Frans Thijssen and Arnold Mühren, Twente also had at their disposal the commanding centre-back, Kees van Ierssel, who had been a member of the Netherlands' 1974 World Cup squad, plus other past and future internationals, such as their captain and sweeper Epi Drost, his central defensive partner Niels Overweg and the free-scoring attacking triumvirate of Theo Pahlplatz, Jan Jeuring and Johan Zuidema.

With the skilled promptings of Thijssen at the centre of everything they did, it meant that Mühren found himself kept on the bench as a dangerous plan B. Beautifully balanced, clinical in attack, well marshalled in defence and aesthetically pleasing in the middle of the pitch, the goalless first leg had left Gladbach with a mountain to climb in the second game in Enschede.

Despite the dangers that lay within the Twente side, the first leg had remained goalless largely thanks to the heroics of Groß, who made a string of outstanding saves, inclusive of one majestic tip over the crossbar in the final seconds.

For Groß, it had been a personal as well as collective triumph at the Rheinstadion. At one point banned from football, when drawn into a 1971 Bundesliga bribery scandal, at a time when he had recently made his debut for the West German national team, the Twente goalkeeper had seen his hopes of involvement in the 1972 European Championship and 1974 World Cup evaporate.

It was perhaps with a sensation of shoulders easing that Twente were then surprisingly beaten by Den Haag, in the KNVB Cup Final eight days beyond the UEFA Cup Final, first leg, six days prior to the return game, at the now demolished Diekman Stadion.

One trophy having slipped from their grasp, Twente's over-enthusiasm was arguably their undoing when it came to their attempt to compensate for their KNVB Cup shortcomings with UEFA Cup success. With Heynckes available once more, Gladbach simply overwhelmed their hosts.

Setting up the excellent Allan Simonsen for the opening goal, with under 120 seconds on the clock, the landscape of the game had changed dramatically before it had had an opportunity to settle. All of Twente's hard work from the first leg had been picked apart ruthlessly by Heynckes and, before the ten-minute mark had been reached, the returning marksman had made it 2-0 when he capitalised upon defensive indecision to roll the ball under Groß.

Try as he might at half-time, Twente's coach, Antoine Kohn, the man who almost took his home nation Luxembourg to the 1964 European Championship finals, couldn't draw an early second-half response out of his stunned team. Within 15 minutes of the restart, Gladbach were 4-0 up, Heynckes again the tormentor, firstly with an intelligent lob into Groß's top corner, followed by being gifted a generous amount of space in the penalty area in which to head home his hat-trick-clinching goal.

Not a game that was entirely one-way traffic, Twente broke forward on a regular basis, only to see most of their attacks fail in the final third when they met with the determined Gladbach defence. The closest they came during that damaging first hour was when Pahlplatz struck the Gladbach post, with the score at 3-0, only to see the ball bounce cruelly, straight into the hands of the Gladbach goalkeeper, Wolfgang Kleff.

If the second leg hadn't been a free-for-all already, caution was completely thrown to the wind with the introduction of Mühren, at 3-0. Comfortingly, Twente did get the goal that their bravery and foolhardiness deserved when Drost struck a sumptuous dipping and swerving effort from 30 yards, which Kleff did well to get a touch to. The Twente captain's frustration clear to see, he simply stomped back into position for the restart, from where he promptly gave away a penalty ten minutes later after tripping Henning Jensen when the Danish international was bearing down on Groß.

Jensen's compatriot, Simonsen, converted the spot kick to finish the scoring at 5-1, two goals claimed by the future Ballon d'Or winner, the first step to him becoming the only man to score in the final of all three major European club competitions.

After celebrations that were generously joined by the Twente supporters, 15,000 of which had also made the trip to the Rheinstadion, Gladbach returned home to close out the

Bundesliga title and the last four games of Weisweiler's time at the club.

Surely torn over which way to turn when given the option of a new challenge with Barcelona or an attempt upon the European Cup with Gladbach, Weisweiler chose the Camp Nou, leaving a very attractive vacancy at the Bökelbergstadion.

Gladbach turned to Udo Lattek, the man who had been in the opposite corner at Bayern until being shockingly jettisoned in January 1975. Lattek had been to Bayern what Weisweiler had been to Gladbach and he transferred his Bayern successes to his new employer seamlessly. His first two seasons brought two Bundesliga titles and a European Cup Final defeat to Liverpool, before their amazing near miss on another Bundesliga title on that remarkable final day in 1977/78, when Weisweiler's Köln took the prize.

League runner-up in 1978, combined with a European Cup semi-final loss, again to Liverpool, it was back into the UEFA Cup that Gladbach went in 1978/79, a season in which they were shockingly inconsistent domestically, to the extreme that they could only labour to a tenth-place Bundesliga finish. It was their lowest placing since their debut Bundesliga campaign.

With Simonsen leaving for Barcelona at the end of the season and a clear job ahead to regenerate a Gladbach side that had been more than a match for an iconic Bayern era, it was to be Lattek's swansong too, leaving for Borussia Dortmund in the summer.

Domestic problems were forgotten on UEFA Cup nights, however, as Gladbach lifted the trophy for the second time, doing so without losing a single game. While Lattek's men were made to work hard in progressing through each round, they did so with at least two goals to spare on every occasion. Yet, this was offset by conceding away goals in all rounds, apart from the second round, where they were instead extended to extra time after 180 goalless minutes of football against Benfica.

Also navigating a way past Sturm Graz, Śląsk Wrocław, Manchester City and MSV Duisburg, in another all-West

German semi-final, Gladbach were thrown together with Red Star Belgrade in the 1979 UEFA Cup Final.

Red Star's path to the final had been one where they had skated upon the thinnest of ice. Berliner FC Dynamo had pushed them to a narrow away-goals victory in the first round, in which Red Star had needed to overturn a three-goal, first-leg deficit. Following this, Sporting Gijón, Arsenal and West Bromwich Albion had all been subjugated by slender one-goal aggregate scorelines. In the cases of the two English sides Red Star had faced, they were games which had been settled by late winning goals that stopped what had looked set to be periods of extra time at Highbury and the Hawthorns.

In their semi-final, Red Star had again relied upon the away-goals rule to see them past another Bundesliga team, this time Hertha BSC. All told, Red Star had ridden their luck tremendously, but they were dangerous opponents for Gladbach, led by the talented Vladimir Petrović, one of three players that they would supply for Yugoslavia's 1982 World Cup squad.

The first leg in Belgrade, at a packed Red Star Stadium was a game of attack and counter-attack as Gladbach attempted to absorb Red Star's pressure and strike for the crucial away goal to take back to West Germany.

Miloš Šestić was the man to draw first blood, for Red Star, when he stabbed the ball past Wolfgang Kneib midway through the first half, after Slavoljub Muslin unexpectedly found himself with a ridiculous amount of time and space in the Gladbach penalty area with which to pick out Šestić on the edge of the six-yard box.

Unable to build on their lead, however, a disciplined Gladbach were gifted an equaliser on the hour, when Ivan Jurišić inexplicably put the ball past his own goalkeeper, Aleksandar Stojanović, thanks to a wonderful diving header.

Undeniably in the driving seat, in the second leg, at a rain-soaked Rheinstadion a fortnight later, one goal settled the outcome. Simonsen procured a shockingly awarded penalty when he ran into Muslin after only 18 minutes, which he emphatically dispatched.

It was a glorious, but unsatisfactory way in which to end an indelible era for Gladbach. Red Star's Đorđe Milovanović was so incensed by the penalty being given that he spat on the ball before Simonsen took the kick.

Despite no further goals being added, the game remained on a knife-edge, Red Star only one goal away from forcing extra time, Gladbach looking for a second goal that would leave the visitors needing two to win.

Largely restricting Red Star to efforts from distance, Stojanović was kept busy by Gladbach, pulling off outstanding saves from both Rudi Gores and Wilfried Hannes before half-time, while in the second half, Hannes again came close, this time with a powerfully struck free kick, which stung Red Star into action, inclusive of Petrović and Dušan Savić combining to provide Nedeljko Milosavljević with a chance that should have hit the target.

As the game drifted towards the final 20 minutes the openings became more glaring, Simonsen having the time, skill and presence of mind to force another chance, while Muslin almost ended Red Star's frustrations when he struck the angle of Kneib's post and crossbar. Šestić then caught a corner on the volley at the back post with seven minutes remaining, which he just could not keep down.

A wonderful desperation enveloped the final minutes of the game – Red Star desperate in the hunt for an equaliser, Gladbach desperate in the defending of their narrow lead. Muslin again came agonisingly close when another effort drifted just the wrong side of Kneib's post.

Feeling ecstasy and relief in equal measure at the final whistle, Lattek and Gladbach had their last success together. For the ageing Berti Vogts, having missed most of the season through injury, 1978/79 was to be the end of the line for him too.

With a changing of the guard at the Bökelbergstadion in the summer of 1979, the new coach was a familiar face. Having retired as a player a year earlier, then acted as an assistant to Lattek while taking his coaching qualifications, Gladbach appointed Heynckes as their new coach.

Struggling to turn Gladbach into Bundesliga contenders again, Heynckes was able to draw upon his team's standing as UEFA Cup holders to cultivate another run to the final. Deprived of the iconic names he himself played alongside, Heynckes placed his faith in a prodigious teenager by the name of Lothar Matthäus.

Monopolised by Bundesliga teams, not only was the 1980 UEFA Cup Final an all-West German affair, but the semi-finals were populated entirely by their representatives too. With five Bundesliga teams taking part in 1979/80, Kaiserslautern, the odd one out of the five when it came to the last four, went as far as the quarter-finals.

Breezing past Viking in the first round, narrowly sneaking past Universitatea Craiova in the third round, there were iconic meetings to be had in the second round and the quarter-finals. Reunited with Inter in the second round, thrown together with AS Saint-Etienne in the last eight, these were duels of purpose.

It was with a sense of unfulfilled business that Gladbach overcame Inter, leftover frustrations from their expunged 7-1 demolition of eight years earlier hanging in the air at the Bökelbergstadion.

Heynckes's side managed to repel an early onslaught from opponents that were on their way to winning the Serie A title. Hannes opened the scoring five minutes before half-time, when turning and lashing the ball into the roof of Ivano Bordon's net after a penalty-box scramble, via a Gladbach corner. Inter then levelled the first leg ten minutes into the second half, when Alessandro Altobelli capitalised on an error from Kneib.

A wonderfully open game, both sides had their chances to claim a winning goal, Kneib redeeming his earlier mistake with important saves, Bordon proving his worth for Inter, both sides hitting the post.

Gladbach's UEFA Cup hopes were dealt a seemingly fatal blow a fortnight later at the San Siro; a new hero and an unlikely hero pulled off what had appeared an impossible task, after Altobelli opened the scoring midway through the first half when gifted a free header from point-blank range.

Kneib again made a crucial contribution, denying Inter what should have been a wider lead, with some outstanding reflexes, a long clearance of his paving the way for Harald Nickel to deliver a spectacular 35-yard sucker punch, catching the ball sweetly after bringing it down on his chest, crashing it in off the underside of Bordon's crossbar.

Nickel had been one of Heynckes's new summer recruits, purchased from Eintracht Braunschweig. He would end the season as joint top scorer in the UEFA Cup, impressing enough to break into the West German national side, being unlucky not to make Jupp Derwall's squad for the 1980 European Championship.

With no further goals added in regulation time, the game went into a fascinating period of extra time. Within four minutes, Altobelli had put the home team ahead again, with a brilliant glancing header that flashed across the helpless Kneib.

With the game no longer capable of going to a penalty shoot-out, Inter were left with the delicate decision of whether to go for more goals, or protect their slender lead. Stick, or twist?

Defending resolutely and springing forward with intent, Karl Del'Haye had a goal disallowed for Gladbach, while Kneib was called into action again. End-to-end football ensuing, shortly before half-time in extra time, the substitute, Norbert Ringels, became the unlikely saviour of Gladbach, driving the ball into Bordon's top corner when it fell perfectly to him on the angle of the six-yard box, after his team was awarded a free kick on the left-hand side.

Ahead on the away-goals rule, now it was Gladbach's decision whether they should attack or defend. Opting to absorb the pressure and strike on the break, Del'Haye won Gladbach a clear-cut penalty, with just over ten minutes remaining. Nickel converted it, with the confidence of a one-step run-up that Bordon was totally unprepared for.

Refusing to give up, Inter continued to plough forward, creating further opportunities and even having a goal of their own marginally ruled offside, before they began to lose both their spirit and composure late on. A stunning set of games, Gladbach had prevailed in a true UEFA Cup classic.

Spring brought Michel Platini and AS Saint-Étienne into view for Heynckes and Gladbach. Robert Herbin's footballing artisans hosted the first leg of the quarter-final at the Stade Geoffroy-Guichard. The home team was blessed by the presence of not only Platini, but also players of the calibre of Johnny Rep, Jean-François Larios, Dominique Rocheteau, Christian Lopez, Gérard Janvion and Jacques Santini.

A hipster's utopia, Gladbach and Saint-Étienne had been the best two teams of the 1970s not to win the European Cup. Gladbach were twice thwarted by Liverpool, once by European football's first-ever penalty shoot-out and by a stray Coca-Cola can, while Saint-Étienne had fallen at the hands of Liverpool too, as well as to Bayern Munich and Hampden Park's square goalposts, in the 1976 final.

This coming together of two iconic names of the 1970s represented an evocative marker in the eventual decline of the two clubs. Both would soon ebb away into the shadows, but in March 1980 they were still quite capable of greatness.

At half-time at the Stade Geoffroy-Guichard, Gladbach were 4-0 up after an incredible display of counter-attacking football. Twice Carsten Nielsen struck, either side of Nickel finding the net again, Ringels being the prime source of creation for the visitors. Shock and awe football, Gladbach scored those opening three goals within an eight-minute spell from the 14th minute. Sublime and ridiculous, it was football to warm the coolest of souls.

Stunningly fragile in defence, especially on their right-hand side, Saint-Étienne conceded the fourth in the 38th minute,

Gladbach breaking directly from defending a corner. Kneib released the ball quickly to Ewald Lienen, who set off on a wonderful run and finish.

Even Heynckes would have been shocked by those first-half events as his players walked into the dressing room for the interval. A performance of skill and speed, it was the evening that cemented the belief that Matthäus was set on a trajectory for superstardom.

No further Gladbach goals were added in the second half, Platini only managing to claw one back for Saint-Étienne, from the penalty spot, a goal that he was almost psyched out of, when the referee twice insisted the ball be spotted again. Kneib even managed to get a hand to it.

A fortnight later, it was an undeterred Saint-Étienne that tore into Gladbach at the Bökelbergstadion, Rocheteau coming close inside two minutes when he drove a low effort against the legs of Kneib. It was, however, only a fleeting flirtation with an impossible comeback, as within 15 minutes Gladbach were 2-0 up.

Firstly, Steen Thychosen chipped in with a wonderful, if rare goal in the colours of Gladbach, which was then added to four minutes later by Hannes, who took advantage of a loose ball and a kind deflection to score past Ivan Ćurković, to complete a 6-1 aggregate scoreline that was both deserved by Gladbach, yet insulting to a magnificent Saint-Étienne team.

One of a cluster of quarter-final results which set up an all-West German line-up in the 1979/80 UEFA Cup semi-finals, while Gladbach were drawn to face VfB Stuttgart, the other showdown was between Bayern and Eintracht Frankfurt, setting up the teasing possibility of a Gladbach vs Bayern final.

As so often occurs in such scenarios, however, the script wasn't followed, as, while Gladbach came from behind to overhaul their first-leg deficit against Stuttgart, Frankfurt pulled off a startling second-leg fightback of their own, against Bayern.

Leading 1-0 with less than five minutes remaining at the Neckarstadion, Gladbach succumbed to two late Stuttgart goals in the first leg of their semi-final, while over in Munich, at a sparsely populated Olympiastadion, Bayern were cruising to a sedate 2-0 victory.

Just under two weeks later, it was a Matthäus-inspired Gladbach that ran out 2-0 winners, at the Bökelbergstadion, to emerge with a narrow aggregate victory and a place in their fourth UEFA Cup Final.

To the south-east of Mönchengladbach, at Frankfurt's Waldstadion, Bayern came to within three minutes of joining their enduring 1970s rival in the final. Holding on to a 1-0 deficit on the night, clutching a 2-1 aggregate advantage, Bruno Pezzey became the home team's unlikely saviour. Having already scored the opening goal of the night, the Austrian international defender snatched the goal that took the game into extra time, making the most of an erratic evening of goalkeeping from Walter Junghans.

Powering on to a 5-1 victory, Frankfurt were still made to work for it, as a Wolfgang Dremmler goal, on the stroke of half-time in extra time, gave Bayern a temporary away-goal advantage, before the home team took control again during the last 15 minutes, thanks to a second goal for Harald Karger and the final strike of the night, via a Werner Lorant penalty.

This was a huge upset given that Frankfurt were heading towards a mid-table Bundesliga finish, compared to Bayern who would go on to hold off the challenge of Kevin Keegan's Hamburger SV to clinch the league title. As if the shock in the semi-final wasn't enough, the 1980 UEFA Cup Final would offer another unexpected twist to the tail.

Gladbach with all the European pedigree, Frankfurt with nothing to lose, it made for a fascinating final. Adding a further edge to proceedings, Frankfurt had beaten Gladbach 5-2 at the Waldstadion in the Bundesliga in mid-March, during a game in which Matthäus had injured the Frankfurt legend, Jürgen

Grabowski, when the two players came together in a challenge for the ball. Despite harbouring notions of being available for the second leg, it would unwittingly prove to be a career-ending injury for the World Cup-winning playmaker, the man who kept Netzer on the sidelines at the 1974 World Cup.

With the Bökelbergstadion only drawing a crowd of 25,000, those who chose to stay away missed a wildly open game that gave plenty of entertainment, without breaking into outright quality.

Frankfurt, drawing upon their cup instincts, forced the early pressure and it was Bernd Nickel that almost opened the scoring when picking the ball up from Karger and crashing it against Kneib's crossbar, after a hurried one-two off the head of his captain, Bernd Hölzenbein. Even the rebound offered opportunity for Frankfurt, and the wonderfully talented Cha Bum-kun was unfortunate to see his reactionary header fall straight into the arms of the Gladbach goalkeeper.

As Frankfurt had made the faster start, Gladbach were left to gradually feel their way into the game, Matthäus testing the nerve of the Frankfurt goalkeeper, Jürgen Pahl, with a series of probing crosses, not all of which were collected with ease. Conversely, however, he did make crucial saves from the Gladbach captain, Christian Kulik, and twice from the omnipresent Matthäus.

Having absorbed the mounting pressure admirably, Frankfurt then obtained the first goal, totally against the run of play, Karger beating Kneib to the ball in the Gladbach six-yard box, getting on the end of an arrowing corner from Nickel.

Losing all composure suddenly, Gladbach could easily have conceded again when Ringles headed against his own crossbar, soon followed by a rising shot from Lorant that had Kneib flinging himself across the face of his goalmouth.

The opening goal having been scored against the run of play by Frankfurt, the same could be said of Gladbach's equaliser, which came a minute before half-time and at a stage when the visitors were playing with a growing confidence. Even in conceding the goal, Frankfurt were lacking in fortune as Pahl had made yet another fine stop at the expense of Matthäus only to see the ball bounce straight to Kulik, who controlled, then caught it beautifully, sending it into the top corner and giving the Frankfurt goalkeeper little chance of stopping it.

Taking their end-of-first-half enthusiasm into the start of the second half, Gladbach were soon on the back foot again, as the game continued with its first-half pattern of the hard-earned initiative of one side being too easily handed back to the opposition. The veteran full-back Willi Neuberger became the latest Frankfurt player to extend Kneib. Further chances fell the way of Ronny Borchers for Frankfurt, then Lienen in response for Gladbach.

Borchers, having seen his opportunity saved by Kneib, was then pivotal in Frankfurt regaining the lead, with just under 20 minutes to play. Released into plentiful space in the right-hand channel, his cross was met by a spectacular stooping and diving header by Hölzenbein, which Kneib was slow to react to. While it will have taken the Gladbach goalkeeper by surprise, it wasn't an unstoppable effort.

Gladbach's reply was delivered five minutes later, when Matthäus drilled home their second equaliser of the game, after a determined but scrappy build-up that was generated primarily by the energy and desire of the indefatigable Lienen.

Perhaps content to settle for the draw, the last 15 minutes were gifted to Gladbach by Frankfurt. Held at bay until the 88th minute, it was with a beautiful sweeping move that Heynckes's men grabbed the lead, when Kulik put the ball away with a picture-perfect diving header to rival the one Hölzenbein had scored for the visitors.

Not over yet, there was still time for Neuberger to send in a swerving and dipping shot, which Kneib did brilliantly to tip over the crossbar, unnoticed by both referee and linesman. A game of immense action and end-to-end excitement, but littered with errors from both sides, it was with a mixture of delight, frustration and relief that the full-time whistle came.

In spite of the way the first leg ended, Frankfurt approached the second leg in a confident frame of mind. Owner of two away goals, they needed only a one-goal victory to lift their first major piece of European silverware. At a capacity Waldstadion, that is exactly what they managed to do.

A much more tentative encounter, there was a caginess at play that leant a sharp knife-edge to the occasion. Frankfurt were the braver of the two teams during the first half, however, almost taking advantage of the erratic goalkeeping of Kneib, but largely being kept to efforts from distance.

Frankfurt's best chance of the opening 45 minutes fell to Borchers, who ballooned the ball over the Gladbach crossbar, with Kneib absent from his goalmouth and only two statuesque defenders standing between the Frankfurt number nine and the deadlock being broken.

With the injured Grabowski watching on from the sidelines, Frankfurt began the second half where they ended the first, probing the Gladbach defensive lines and hunting for the one goal that would see them over the finish line. The best move of the game so far fell to Norbert Nachtweih, who shot straight at Kneib, after a fine passing movement.

Nachtweih, along with his team-mate Pahl, had defected from East Germany in 1976 while they were on duty for their national under-21 side. The DDR-Oberliga's Chemie Halle's loss proved to be Frankfurt's gain.

It was a near miss that awoke Gladbach from their self-imposed slumber. Matthäus soon tested the concentration of Pahl with a powerfully struck free kick, while Kulik spurned a golden opportunity in front of goal when he placed his shot too centrally at Pahl, the rebound falling perfectly to Lienen who also forced the Frankfurt goalkeeper into action. Gladbach's most dominant period of the second leg, this is where their chance of retaining the UEFA Cup came and went.

Just 13 minutes were remaining when Friedel Rausch, the Frankfurt head coach, replaced Nachtweih with the 19-year-old Fred Schaub. Four minutes later the substitute had procured the winning goal, when the Gladbach defence parted as it tried to second-guess the trajectory of a ricocheting ball.

Onwards Schaub plundered until faced with just Kneib, swinging his left foot at the ball, then watching on in hope until it nestled in the Gladbach goalkeeper's bottom left-hand corner, before wheeling away in unbridled joy.

Caution now thrown to the wind, Heynckes's side swept forward in search of the goal that would hand them back the UEFA Cup, an offensive desperation that gave Frankfurt the spaces to counter-attack at will. Schaub had a second goal rightly disallowed, while Cha Bum-kun forced a fine save from Kneib.

Time wasn't only running out on Gladbach's UEFA Cup Final hopes, as the last flickering motions of the clock were unwittingly counting down to the end of an incredible era for a team that had been one of European football's biggest stories of the 1970s.

Final whistle blown: it was an ecstatic Waldstadion that greeted Frankfurt's success. Grabowski, handed the UEFA Cup by Hölzenbein, was at the forefront of the celebrations, while Heynckes, his side and their supporters applauded their achievement.

Continuing to be a regular competitor in the UEFA Cup throughout the 1980s, the closest Gladbach came to return to the final came in 1987, when they were beaten by Dundee United in the semi-finals. Prior to this, there was also a remarkable capitulation at the hands of Real Madrid during the 1985/86 season.

Despite these brief instances of Gladbach rolling back the years, however, the prize remained elusive. Essentially a team frozen in time, for football hipsters of a certain age there is still a vigil being held, a dream that maybe one day Gladbach will once again return to the promised land of a major European final.

Chapter Four

Going Dutch

WHEN THE UEFA Cup came into existence, the Eredivisie's rise in the European Cup was its very epicentre. Feyenoord had beaten their great rivals, Ajax, to the punch by becoming the first club from the Netherlands to be crowned champions of Europe, when they defeated Celtic in Milan in 1970.

A year later, it was Amsterdam that was celebrating, as Rinus Michels and Johan Cruyff's vision of *totaalvoetbal* gained its immortal wings, upon Ajax winning the first of what would be a hat-trick of European Cup successes, the second and third parts of which were won when led by the underappreciated genius of Ștefan Kovács.

Amid this maelstrom, Twente were the first Eredivisie club to make an imprint on the UEFA Cup, with their run to the semi-finals in 1972/73, where they were convincingly beaten over two legs by Borussia Mönchengladbach.

It had been a voyage of European discovery for a team which falls under the radar when it comes to Dutch teams, for the wider breadth of football lovers. Cast into shadow, not only by the exploits of Ajax and Feyenoord, but also by the inexorable rise of PSV Eindhoven, who themselves would win the UEFA Cup in 1978, a decade later scooping the European Cup. Yet, as the fourth force of Dutch club football, it was nothing short of stunning that Twente exited the 1970s with only one piece of major silverware.

On that run to the 1972/73 semi-finals, Twente had overcome the gathering Georgian threat of Dinamo Tbilisi, hammered BK Frem of Denmark, away and at home, cruised past the volcanic island challenge of Las Palmas and then completed a stirring comeback against the Serbians of OFK Beograd, before Gladbach proved too strong in the last four.

Two years later they went one better, setting themselves up nicely for a shot at lifting the UEFA Cup, before capitulating so emphatically against the same opponents in the 1975 final. It was a blunt manner in which to end an impressive run that had begun with a first-round tie that would have reverberations echoing all the way to the 1981 final, via the October 1974 UK General Election.

Leader of the Conservative Party and former Prime Minister, Edward Heath, was sat in the Portman Road director's box, just hours after learning of the date for the second General Election of the year, but the interest in footballing terms was the presence in the Twente midfield of Frans Thijssen, the man who would play a starring role in Ipswich Town's glory seven years later.

Not the first time they had crossed paths, Twente and an injury-hit Ipswich had faced one another in the same competition the previous season. On that occasion, it was in the third round, with the English team progressing to the quarter-finals, although not without being tested, more so during a first leg which was played out across a snow-covered Portman Road pitch on an evening when the escalating fuel crisis meant that the Suffolk club had needed the generosity of a loaned generator from Bournemouth, so as to avoid the game having to take place during the Wednesday afternoon instead.

Two games that left a lasting impression on the Ipswich manager, Bobby Robson would capture the services of Thijssen in the summer of 1979, a year after the signing of his Twente team-mate, Arnold Mühren. A cluster of progressive football matches that appealed to the purists, their 1974/75 duels wouldn't have been out of place had they graced the final itself.

Ipswich had been the fastest team out of the blocks in the First Division, top of the table when they faced Twente and, widely praised for their style of play, Robson's side would eventually miss out on the title by just two points, while they were narrowly beaten by West Ham United in an FA Cup semi-final replay.

A majestically balanced 2-2 draw in East Anglia for the first leg, Twente struck first, in the 24th minute, when Johan Zuidema tucked the ball beyond Laurie Sivell, getting on the end of a nod down from Theo Pahlplatz at the culmination of some devastatingly intelligent interplay between midfielder and striker.

Ipswich's retaliation was just as spectacular, scoring twice within a five-minute stretch, shortly before half-time. Billy Hamilton got the first goal back, planting the ball past Hennie Ardesch (future father-in-law of Sander Westerveld) after a swift counter-attack, which was started by Kevin Beattie, when he broke up another Twente incursion, before powering downfield, crossing for Trevor Whymark, who then headed the ball on for Hamilton to finish.

An aesthetically pleasing equaliser, when Ipswich took the lead it was with something that little more Anglo-Saxon in approach, via a long ball from George Burley, which was then driven across the face of the Twente goalmouth by Whymark, for Brian Talbot to tap in.

Rather than capitulate, Twente took to the second half with a renewed enthusiasm, Zuidema coming very close with an opportunity he should have converted. The visitors, not content with the one away goal and a narrow defeat, thirsty for greater reward, instead took the game to their hosts when it would have been the easier option to retreat, in an attempt to protect what they already had.

Twente's endeavour would indeed be rewarded, when, with five minutes left to play, Pahlplatz charged through on Sivell for the leveller, with the Ipswich defence static and claiming offside.

Footballing soulmates, Twente and Ipswich could only be split by the away-goals rule a fortnight later. Just eight minutes had been played when Jaap Bos opened the scoring, blindsiding Colin Harper, cutting across him in collecting a wonderful cross-field pass from René Notten, before scoring past Sivell. As physically damaging as it was stylish, Bos injured himself during the scoring of his goal, lasting only five more minutes until he was replaced by Jan Jeuring.

Pain was followed by displeasure for Twente, as their hard-earned lead only lasted for seven minutes. Harper exacted his revenge with a deep diagonal cross-field pass, similar to the one he was caught out by for Twente's goal, which was collected effortlessly by Whymark, who then sent in a low cross from the right, which Hamilton dispatched beautifully on the volley.

Bohemian football, it was a match that had at one point been under threat of not taking place at all, as Robson had publicly pondered the idea of withdrawing from the competition in his bid to pour his team's entire focus on a burgeoning challenge for the league title.

Both teams having periods where they punched in attack, they would then fall back to defend furiously. It made for a fascinating clash and the chances came thick and fast; Zuidema, Pahlplatz, Notten and the marvellously named Kick van der Vall all came close for Twente, while in riposte for Ipswich, Hamilton, Talbot, Beattie, Allan Hunter and Colin Viljoen threatened.

And so, the game continued to ebb and flow to its conclusion, Twente edging through to the second round, but not before breathing a huge sigh of relief when Ardesch pulled off a spectacular save in the final minutes from the tireless Talbot.

Talbot made perfect contact with the ball from no more than eight yards, from which Ardesch twisted and arched acrobatically, punching the effort away with a save that was as valuable as a last-minute winning goal.

Made to fight for their continued participation in the 1974/75 UEFA Cup, Twente then went through a series of differing challenges against an array of eclectic opponents in reaching the semi-finals. While RWD Molenbeek were navigated comfortably in a Low Countries derby, it took a resounding second-leg victory to overcome Half Man Half Biscuit's team of choice, Dukla Prague, in the third round, after a 3-1 reversal in the Czechoslovak capital. It then required another Twente comeback to sneak past Velež Mostar in the quarter-finals.

Twente's prize for their exhaustive efforts was a last-four mission impossible against the mighty Juventus, four years on from the two having played one another in the quarter-finals of the last edition of what was, by then, the European Fairs Cup.

At home for the first leg, Antoine Kohn opted for a nothing ventured, nothing gained approach. They swept to a 3-1 victory, in which Zuidema was yet again the hero, scorer of two goals.

Serie A champions to be, whether Juventus simply underappreciated the threat posed by Twente or not, Carlo Perola's side were marvellously outplayed. Even the value of their away goal was wiped out within ten minutes of the return game at the Stadio Comunale, when Zuidema set off on an astounding solo run, weaving a way through a stunned Juventus defence before guiding the ball past the advancing Dino Zoff.

A startling 4-1 aggregate victory, in a way it was a turn of events that doomed the 1975 UEFA Cup Final to the margins of anonymity. Whereas a Juventus vs Borussia Mönchengladbach showpiece would have echoed through footballing eternity, so it could have with Twente being there, if it had not been for all their hard work throughout the campaign being so spectacularly undone during the early exchanges of the first half of the second leg.

Arguably, Twente became the invisible UEFA Cup runner-up. It was a tournament they never again threatened to win, despite periodically qualifying for it. A run to the quarter-finals during 2010/11, under the flag of the Europa League, after being knocked out of the Champions League at the group stages, was their best showing.

They did enjoy one last big 1970s European adventure, however, when Twente reached the semi-finals of the European Cup Winners' Cup in 1977/78, where they were comfortably dealt with by the enigmatic Rob Rensenbrink and his talented Anderlecht team-mates.

When Twente made their bewitching run to the 1975 UEFA Cup Final, they were bidding to keep the trophy in Eredivisie possession for a second successive season, aiming to procure the Netherlands a piece of major European silverware for a fifth season in a row.

While Ajax had abdicated as champions of Europe in 1973/74, Feyenoord had risen once again, to claim their second major European honour.

Given that Feyenoord took the Eredivisie title, pushed to the limit by Twente, doubling the glory with dominant performances in the UEFA Cup Final against an experienced but weary Tottenham Hotspur, it is jarring that their path to the final was littered with potential pitfalls, where their run could have very easily come to an abrupt end.

Östers IF represented Feyenoord's first and easiest hurdle, as the Rotterdam giants won both legs of their first-round encounter. Beyond this light introduction, Gwardia Warszawa came to within a goal of an away-goal victory in the second round. It was a near miss on elimination that would become symptomatic of the rest of Feyenoord's campaign. Before the Christmas, they scraped past Standard Liège on away goals, turning round a 3-1, first-leg deficit.

Ruch Chorzów were navigated next, in the quarter-finals, by the relatively sedate aggregate scoreline of 4-2. Yet, closer for comfort than the result suggests, the Polish side took the second leg into extra time.

Feyenoord had stumbled into the semi-finals, where they were drawn to play VfB Stuttgart. Continuing with their theme of misadventure and peril, Wiel Coerver's side shot themselves in the foot at De Kuip during the first leg. A win was garnered, yet with only a narrow one-goal lead and a costly away goal conceded.

A fascinating character, Coerver gave his name to a method of football teaching that saw his students learn via the classroom as much as they did on the training pitch in a near-academic system that took Boudewijn Zenden all the way to the Netherlands national football team and the World Cup finals, via a club career which took in spells at PSV Eindhoven, Barcelona and Liverpool, amongst others.

His dedication to this cause saw him walk away from frontline professional coaching in 1977, just three years after he led Feyenoord to their 1973/74 Eredivisie and UEFA Cup double, at a time when Coerver would have been one of the Netherlands' most employable coaches.

A footballing professor, Coerver earned Feyenoord their place in the 1974 UEFA Cup Final after surviving a nerve-shredding 2-2 draw at the Neckarstadion. A precious place in a major European final, obtained through a succession of stressful occasions.

It was against a domestically stalling Tottenham that Feyenoord battled for the UEFA Cup spoils. In one corner was the newly crowned free-scoring Eredivisie champions, while in the other was English football's great European explorers.

White Hart Lane played host to the first leg. Feyenoord, with only three survivors from the team that had won the 1970 European Cup Final, had still supplied nine players to Rinus Michels' 40-man provisional squad for the upcoming World Cup finals, seven of which would make the trip to West Germany.

Magnificently fluid in attack, Feyenoord were blessed by the goals of Lex Schoenmaker, who was supported and coerced in his thirst for the back of the net by the freedom and expression of the Danish international winger, Jørgen Kristensen and on the other side of the forward three, by Peter Ressel.

Balanced throughout, this talented attacking triumvirate was supplemented by the midfield drive of Theo de Jong, the guile of Willem van Hanegem and the discipline of Wim Jansen. All of this was built upon the foundation of a sound defensive unit, of which the goalkeeper and three of his defenders travelled to the World Cup.

With the opening 37 minutes played at a respectful distance of one another, the first leg burst into life during the last eight minutes of the first half. Tottenham finally made the breakthrough, when Mike England headed the home team ahead, arriving at the back post to get himself on the end of a beautifully floated free kick from Ray Evans.

The free kick had been given by an irritable Willem van Hanegem. The yellow card that accompanied it from Swiss referee Rudolf Scheurer also meant that he would miss the return game.

Channelling his anger in the most positive way he could, five minutes later, just as Tottenham were within touching distance of reaching the half-time break without conceding, Van Hanegem arrowed in the most perfect, but harshly awarded, free kick, from just outside Pat Jennings's penalty area, off the underside of the crossbar. A goal from the type of distance that would be classed as too close to score from directly, in contemporary translation, it was a sweetly struck goal, with no discernible run-up, the scorer leaning back to exactly the type of degree that meant the ball should have ended up in row Z instead.

It was with Van Hanegem's free kick that the 1974 UEFA Cup Final began to get away from Tottenham, despite the north London side reclaiming the lead midway through the second half courtesy of yet another set piece.

This time, Joop van Daele was the last man to touch the ball, putting through his own net, after being unsighted of another precision free kick, from Evans, distracted by the late run of England once more.

Electing not to defend what they already had, at 2-1 down Feyenoord continued to seek a second equaliser. Tottenham were meanwhile sporadically pressing for a third goal, a goal that would have given them greater hope for the trip to Rotterdam for the second leg.

A sweeping Feyenoord move, from one end of the pitch to the other, with only five minutes remaining, was the fatal blow to Tottenham. Kristensen and De Jong linking brilliantly, it was the latter who received the final unerringly weighted pass from the former, a pass that was almost, agonisingly, cut out by Steve Perryman, only for De Jong to score the last goal of the evening for a 2-2 draw.

In the case of Tottenham, while they had shown their UEFA Cup form during the first half, it was more like an unwelcome appearance of their inconsistent domestic personality during the second half. For Feyenoord, it had proved to be the perfect evening.

At De Kuip one week later, Feyenoord were faced with the task to simply avoid overconfidence. Holding all the cards, Coerver didn't only have his away-goals advantage in his favour, but his opposition number, Bill Nicholson, was dealing with injuries to Evans and Phil Beal, with Beal thought unlikely to play.

Beal did make Nicholson's starting line-up, however, as did Evans. A no-win situation for Tottenham, it was either field them, despite the doubts over their fitness, or opt for alternatives that might not be match sharp themselves.

Van Hanegem's absence aside, Feyenoord were at full strength and, having won their Eredivisie title with an average of three goals per game, the sense of foreboding for Tottenham must have been palpable, defending their proud record as a club that had never lost a big cup final.

A dark day for Tottenham, crowd disturbances before and during the game marred what should have been a fascinating 1974 UEFA Cup Final, second leg. Around 100 Tottenham supporters were arrested on an evening when Nicholson and his chairman, Sidney Wade, were asked to make pleas for calm.

Feyenoord's opening goal escalated the situation and the half-time interval offered only uncomfortable images from the stands of De Kuip, as seats were ripped out and thrown at opposing supporters, Rotterdam's police handed a warzone to patrol, rather than a football match.

Up until Wim Rijsbergen grabbed that first goal of the game, enabled by an uncharacteristically poor clearing punch from Jennings, Tottenham were in with a genuine chance. Chris McGrath had the ball in the Feyenoord net, only to see the goal disallowed, with Martin Chivers trailing back from an offside position.

A goal that would comfortably stand in eras to come, the whole complexion of the game hinged not only on the raising of the linesman's flag, to rule out McGrath's effort, but on two further Tottenham opportunities that would likely have been taken on another day. The first from a Martin Peters header, the other near miss came from Perryman, for whom Chivers conjured a fleeting glimpse of a free shot at goal, when looping a free kick over a Feyenoord defensive wall that was expecting a shot on goal.

It could be suggested that when Feyenoord took the lead they did so against the run of play. It was also a goal that came shortly before half-time, an interval in which a sizeable amount of Tottenham's focus was distracted by events in the stands.

After the restart, the home side were largely in the ascendancy, while the visitors struggled with the knowledge that only two goals would now suffice – a demoralising situation for a Tottenham team that had already had a goal ruled out and two very good chances go untaken.

Schoenmaker hit the foot of the post early in the second half, as a warning of how insurmountable the task was likely to be for Tottenham, swiftly followed by De Jong seeing a strong header tipped over by Jennings. The same player would again be denied by the Northern Irishman, this time from distance.

Tottenham's play became more ragged, while their players started to lose some of their legendary composure. Still, chances presented themselves and Ralph Coates was unfortunate not to score, frustration being further provoked when an indirect free kick inside the Feyenoord penalty area, which was twice taken, came to nothing.

Then came the killer blow of Feyenoord's second goal, Ressel shooting low and diagonally across Jennings, leaving the Tottenham goalkeeper with no chance of stopping it. It was a goal that came with little more than five minutes left to play and it was at the end of a passing move of great patience and intelligence.

For Tottenham, it was a bitter pill to swallow. A first taste of cup-final defeat, in a set of games that fine lines dictated were to go against them. Even the venue itself made the loss that little bit rawer, as De Kuip had been the backdrop of Nicholson's Cup Winners' Cup glory of 1963.

Shifting UEFA Cup sands, the Netherlands had its first success in the tournament and Feyenoord would lift the trophy again, once more at De Kuip, 28 years later, but on that occasion in the one-off final era, when Rotterdam had been given the hosting duties on merit.

A brooding relationship consummated, Feyenoord and Tottenham would cross paths in the UEFA Cup again almost a decade later.

After Twente's rise to the 1975 final, Eredivisie's clubs laboured in the UEFA Cup over the course of the next two seasons, but an evolving Dutch European force was ready to stake their claim, to the south-east of Rotterdam, over in Eindhoven.

Despite the prominent successes of Feyenoord and Ajax, PSV Eindhoven had been the first Dutch team to compete in the European Cup, in the tournament's inaugural campaign of 1955/56, when they were comprehensively defeated by Rapid Wien in the first round.

Eight years before they got the chance to try again, PSV made the quarter-finals of the same competition in 1963/64 in what was a statement of greater intent for their future European showings of the 1970s.

Narrowly denied a place in the 1971 Cup Winners' Cup Final by Real Madrid, PSV made the last four again in 1975, this time beaten by the ruthlessly stylish Dynamo Kyiv. Building a fast-growing reputation for themselves, a first European Cup semi-final was reached in 1976, where only one goal was the difference between PSV facing Bayern Munich at Hampden Park rather than AS Saint-Étienne. The two faced off once more in the second round the following season when the exact same result was generated.

By 1977/78, PSV were primed for continental success. Eredivisie champions for the third time in four seasons, with two recent KNVB Cup successes to their name and the owners of an escalating presence in European club competitions, the 1978 UEFA Cup Final represented an unwitting high-water mark for this generation of PSV. Regression was on the way, but not before collecting a first major European honour.

Benefiting from an Eredivisie power vacuum, created by the struggles of Ajax, post Cruyff, plus Feyenoord suffering their own dip after winning the 1974 UEFA Cup, PSV were in the right place at the right time to dominate the second half of the decade, until a new Ajax rise materialised in 1978/79.

PSV's 1974–78 rise was so pronounced that they supplied six members of the Netherlands squad for the 1978 World Cup finals, double that of Ajax and three times the contribution made by Feyenoord.

It really could have been eight considering that their legendary goalkeeper Jan van Beveren and captain Willy van der Kuijlen had largely been the casualties of the 1970s powerplays for positions of favour within an outrageously talented international set-up that was vulnerable to internal rancour, civil war and politicking.

With the Van de Kerkhof twins, René and Willy, at the core of everything PSV achieved during this era, Kees Rijvers's side had the perfect mix of skill, strength and balance.

A run that began in Lurgan, County Armagh, at Glenarvon's Mourneview Park, a run that had an influence that came via Merthyr Tydfil, PSV brushed the Northern Irish outfit aside, 11-2 on aggregate, going on to navigate a way into the quarter-finals beyond loosely defended, but comfortably won encounters with Widzew Łódź and Eintracht Braunschweig in the second and third round respectively.

In the last eight, 1. FC Magdeburg stood between PSV and a fourth major European semi-final of the decade. Having risen to Cup Winners' Cup glory just four years earlier, the East German side won the first leg with the only goal of the game.

At the Philips Stadion, a fortnight later, a dramatic evening unfolded in which Magdeburg came to within 90 seconds of going through to the semi-finals. Instead, PSV enjoyed the type of good fortune that had previously eluded them at the most pivotal of European moments.

It was a spectacular 90 minutes of football, which erupted during the last ten minutes of the first half. Martin Hoffmann opened the scoring, guiding the ball in after a wonderful surging run and eventual cutback from Jürgen Pommerenke. PSV were now left with the need of three goals to progress.

Four minutes later, however, PSV gave themselves hope when Ernie Brandts headed home from a corner. It was a sense of hope that was soon replaced by optimism, when on the brink of half-time Wolfgang Seguin glanced another header in for the home side. Given Seguin was a Magdeburg player, this was an unfortunate turn of events.

Still needing one more goal to go through, the second half started with a high degree of energy from PSV, yet the next goal went to Magdeburg once again. Pommerenke from distance, with an effort that Van Beveren really should have kept out, seemed set to be the goal that would kill off PSV's chances of reaching the semi-finals. Carelessly on Magdeburg's part though, PSV struck back within a minute, Brandts levelling the tie, on aggregate, to set up a nervous finish.

The final seconds of the game were ticking away, when Harry Lubse scored PSV's winner. It was a goal that combined the general untidiness of the desperate situation the home team found themselves in, with a fine passing movement to create the opportunity that put PSV into the semi-finals, all topped off by the scruffy nature of the need for plundering in the rebound when Lubse was the first to the ball after his initial effort bounced back off the Magdeburg goalkeeper, Dirk Heyne.

A classic European evening in Eindhoven, there was still time for PSV to very nearly throw away their hard-fought place in the last four. Delight and relief in equal measure, the prize for prevailing against Magdeburg was a semi-final meeting with the Barcelona of Rinus Michels and Johan Cruyff.

First leg at the Philips Stadion, it was a stunning performance of misadventure from a Barcelona side that not only boasted the influence of Cruyff, but also the reassuring presence of Johan Neeskens.

Antonio Olmo scored the first goal of the game after only ten minutes, PSV again benefiting from an outrageously beautiful own goal, another header, this time a spectacular diving one, which flashed past the Barcelona goalkeeper, Pedro Artola, into his top right-hand corner.

Another two goals were to be gifted by the high-profile visitors, the second of the evening falling to Lubse, just seven minutes after the opener, when he ran through on Artola thanks to some poor defending, finishing smartly.

Paul Postuma, a second-half substitute, made it 3-0 to PSV when taking advantage of a wild back pass and a badly attempted clearance, having only been on the pitch for two minutes. When Van Beveren then made a spectacular late save, Barcelona's misery was complete.

At the Camp Nou a fortnight later, PSV held their nerve to reach a first major European final. Pushed to the limits of their durability, however, they had had to hold on desperately for the last 25 minutes at 3-1 down on the night, 4-3 ahead on aggregate, blessed by an away goal that was procured by a man who had begun his career at Merthyr Tydfil.

Nick Deacy's Football League experience had been collated at Hereford United and during a loan spell at Workington, before he was recruited by PSV in 1975. There are meteoric rises and then there is Nick Deacy.

From performing at Merthyr Tydfil's Penydarren Park to scoring a crucial UEFA Cup semi-final goal at the Camp Nou in four short years was a journey of wonderful unlikeliness.

Carles Rexach opened the scoring from the penalty spot with only ten minutes played and, when Paco Fortes curled a second Barcelona goal beyond the reach of Van Beveren with less than 20 minutes having elapsed, the writing had swiftly been daubed on the walls of the second leg for PSV.

Composing themselves, PSV managed to get to the interval without conceding another goal, but they returned for the second half minus the services of Postuma. This is where Deacy entered the fray and within three minutes of the restart, he had grabbed his goal, as he drifted in from the right to cut across one of his own team-mates and roll the ball into the far corner.

Breathing space obtained, it was midway through the second half before Rexach struck from the penalty spot again, this time after Cruyff had made the most of an innocuous challenge. PSV rode the wave, however, and no further goals were scored.

In the final, the aesthetically pleasing SEC Bastia were waiting for PSV. Boasting the right-footed sorcery of Johnny Rep and the supreme talent of Abdelkarim Merry, who played under the nickname of Krimau, it was a partnership that benefited from the laconic playmaking of Claude Papi and the midfield intelligence of Jean-François Larios.

Papi, a tragic figure, was Bastia's favourite son. A one-club star, a Corsican born and bred, his form was so compelling throughout their run to the 1978 UEFA Cup Final that he won himself a place in the France squad for the World Cup finals that summer.

Sadly, Papi died of a ruptured aneurysm in January 1983, just a short few months after he had retired from football. He was only 33.

Perpetual midfield motion, alongside Larios and Félix Lacuesta, Papi was the dynamo of the Bastia side that had finished the 1976/77 French First Division campaign in third place, a team that collectively scored 82 goals, yet also conceded a generous 53, during a season of lax defending across the breadth of the French top tier, where only Saint Étienne had conceded fewer goals than the number of games they had played.

It was within this spirit of open and attacking endeavour, offset by a loosely bolted defence, that Bastia found themselves involved in a succession of magnificent games. In the first three rounds, narrow home, first-leg victories, in which potentially costly away goals were conceded, were followed up by heroic and at times dramatic wins on their travels.

Twice in arrears in Corsica in the first round against Sporting CP, despite a François Félix hat-trick, Bastia headed to Lisbon for the second leg in a vulnerable position. At the Estádio José Alvalade the visitors came to within four minutes of an away-goals exit, until Rep was the beneficiary of some hopeful, rather than decisive, build-up play by his team-mates. With Sporting's resolve broken, Félix added a second Bastia goal in the final seconds.

Next came Newcastle United, who opened the scoring early at the Stade Armand-Cesari when Paul Cannell bundled the ball over the Bastia line from one yard in the eighth minute of the first leg. Entirely unrepresentative of how the rest of the game panned out, it was in defiance of footballing gravity that Bastia were held at bay until the second half, when Papi capitalised twice on the type of defending that would lead Newcastle into the Second Division by the end of the season. The most stunning aspect of the evening was that it took Bastia until the 89th minute to obtain their narrow lead.

In the north-east of England, any thoughts Newcastle had of making hay of their away goal were obliterated within the first eight minutes of the start of the return game. A performance at St James' Park that was entirely fitting for a team that was sat at the bottom of the First Division, the Magpies were 2-0 down swiftly, sliced apart ruthlessly by Lacuesta's skill, as he slalomed his way into the Newcastle penalty area, the ball eventually falling to Jean-Marie di Zerbi, who drove it beneath Steve Hardwick. Only three minutes had elapsed.

Five minutes later, Rep and Papi combined beautifully to open the Newcastle defence yet again, with the Netherlands international lashing in Bastia's second goal. Lacking in confidence, Newcastle's fragility was all too clear. Picking and choosing when to expend more energy, Bastia added only one more goal, midway through the second half, another for Rep, this time from even greater distance, powering the ball into Hardwick's top right-hand corner.

Alan Gowling's headed goal, which brought the score back to 2-1 before the interval, proved no more than a disputed consolation. A push in the build-up, obvious yet undetected, was animatedly protested by Rep, earning only a yellow card from the referee.

Three weeks later, Torino arrived at the Stade Armand-Cesari for the third round, first leg. When Paolo Pulici flicked the ball up and hooked in the opening goal in the 24th minute, it already seemed as if Bastia had been given a mountain to climb if they were to reach the quarter-finals.

This was a Torino side that had been Serie A champions in 1975/76, narrowly missing out on retaining their title 12 months later. Blessed by the presence of the future World Cup winner, Francesco Graziani, they would again end their domestic league campaign in a healthy position. Upon this occasion, third.

Bastia absorbed the blow of the away goal and were on level terms before half-time. Papi was both the generator and the scorer, as he cut a swathe through the Torino defence, eight minutes prior to the break.

Upping the pressure, Bastia pressed Torino back during a relentless second half, in which the visitors could only occasionally strike forward in counter-attack. Larios and Papi both came close, before Rep converted with a coolly slotted finish, after a deft lay-off from Lacuesta. Yet, try as Bastia might to increase the lead that they would be taking to Turin, Papi again coming agonisingly close, Torino managed to hold on for the remaining 27 minutes, beyond Rep's goal.

So, a fortnight later, in freezing temperatures, at the snow-surrounded Stadio Comunale, Bastia pulled off what was arguably their finest-ever result on the European stage, emerging triumphantly with a 3-2 victory and a place in the last eight.

It was Larios who opened the scoring, with a spectacular effort from outside the Torino penalty area, set up by the intelligence of Rep and the vision of Lacuesta. Graziani, however, would strike twice, either side of the interval, to level the aggregate scoreline, all away goals having been cancelled out.

Rather than panic, Bastia took a deep breath and restored their advantage within three minutes of Graziani's second goal. Krimau, in the right place to benefit from a slumbering Torino defence for his first of the evening, would also strike on the break with 25 minutes still to play, keeping his composure to roll the ball home, after running half the length of the pitch toward the unguarded Luciano Castellini.

In the quarter-finals, Bastia were part of an avalanche of 15 goals with Carl Zeiss Jena – an incredible 9-6 aggregate victory, in which seven different players scored for the Corsican team. Bastia won the first leg, 7-2, before holding on to a 4-2 reversal in the second leg at the Ernst Abbe Sportfeld.

One hundred and eighty minutes of football during which all defensive tactics were rendered redundant, these were two games that swayed from the sublime to the ridiculous. While there was great beauty in some of the goals, others were hypnotically scrappy and relied upon a Bastia weakness at set pieces. Larios and Papi were largely at the centre of everything that was aesthetically pleasing about the first leg.

In East Germany, in the return game, Papi's first-half away goal blew any vague doubts of potential capitulations away. It was another well-worked effort and, along with the increasingly familiar sight of Krimau hitting decisively on the break, it all meant that Jena's four goals were rendered relatively meaningless, although within them were a spectacular volley from Lutz Lindemann plus the unfortunate sight of the Italian referee, Alberto Michelotti, being credited with an assist during the build-up to Eberhard Vogel's goal for 3-1, which temporarily gave the hosts a glimmer of hope in pulling off an impossible comeback.

With just one last challenge standing between Bastia and a place in the 1978 UEFA Cup Final, avoiding the more obvious dangers of PSV and Barcelona in the semi-final draw, they were paired up with Grasshopper Club Zürich.

Another marvellously open game then unfolded at the Hardturm, a stadium that, like Bastia's, offered an atmospheric, yet unique experience, where, with the backing of an impressive travelling support, the visitors struck first, through Krimau who worked his opening skilfully after being supplied by an outstanding and fluid break from their own half, via Larios, Papi and Lacuesta.

A lead that lasted only four minutes, Heinz Hermann levelled the scores, after a counter-attack that was just as incisive as the one that Bastia had struck from. The game was then turned on its head by the 31st minute, when a lapse in Bastia's concentration led to a Grasshopper penalty, which was confidently converted by Raimondo Ponte.

With neither team able to take a defensive stranglehold on proceedings, just six minutes later, Rep won Bastia a penalty of their own, which Papi calmly placed in the top right-hand corner to level the scores at 2-2.

Undone at yet another corner in a more sedate second half when Francis Montandon headed past Pierrick Hiard to make it 3-2 to Grasshopper, the only surprise was that, with well over half an hour still to play, no further goals were added to the scoreline. Although, it wasn't for the lack of endeavour.

Back at the Stade Armand-Cesari a fortnight later on a wet, yet electric night, Papi was the fitting hero, breaking the stubborn deadlock with 23 minutes remaining, after Bastia had seen chance upon chance repelled by a combination of the waterlogged pitch, desperate Grasshopper defending and the inspired goalkeeping of the Swiss international, Roger Berbig.

Lacuesta twice, Larios and Jean-Louis Cazes had all come close, before Papi dug out a majestic half-volley that arced out of the desperate reach of Berbig to nestle into his bottom right-hand corner. The resultant pitch invasion of celebrating Bastia supporters was as memorable for the interloper's struggles to keep their feet upon a sea of water and mud as it was for their unbridled joy. What elation had remained confined when Papi scored was unleashed upon the final whistle.

Bastia became France's first UEFA Cup finalist, the first of only two occasions that a French club ever reached a two-legged UEFA Cup Final. In a seemingly cursed situation, still to this day, France awaits its first UEFA Cup/Europa League winner.

Marseille, three times a beaten finalist during the one-off final era, might have outstripped the achievements of Bastia in terms of the tournament's greatest French exponents, but these were finals which came beyond the UEFA Cup's finest days, whereas Bastia and Bordeaux reached such heights as the tournament was enjoying its peak years.

It was at a vibrant but still saturated Stade Armand-Cesari that the first leg laboured to a goalless draw. It was a great disappointment that Bastia were unable to play to their ball-playing strengths when given home advantage. It proved to be a game where the outcome was dictated by the goalkeepers, as much as it was the conditions.

What could well have been a beautifully balanced set of games effectively became a one-off final on home soil for PSV, and they made the most of the situation. Circulating the ball with ease and almost teasing Bastia at times, the home side opened the scoring in the 24th minute via a beautifully fluid movement in which Willy van de Kerkhof ran the ball towards the Bastia penalty area exchanging passes with Gerrie Deijkers and taking possession once again as he ran towards goal, from where he seemed to prod the ball past Hiard.

An uneasy truce then set in, where neither team ran the risk of overstretching themselves, PSV wary of conceding the away goal, Bastia afraid of falling further behind. It was a stasis that remained in operation until midway through the second half when Deijkers hooked home PSV's second goal of the evening, Bastia making hard and ultimately damaging work of attempting to clear their lines.

Handbrake now released, PSV turned on the party pieces in a wonderful last quarter of the game. It was a freedom of expression that was never better represented than the sublime few seconds in which René van de Kerkhof played a private game of keepie-uppies, inclusive of flicking the ball up and over the head of his twin brother. It was a slice of footballing audacity that rivals that of Ajax's Gerrie Mühren, when he hypnotised Real Madrid and the Santiago Bernabéu five years earlier.

One last goal was procured by PSV, when Van der Kuijlen hammered home his own rebound, after a beautiful initial effort bounced back off the post, returning immediately to his possession. It was a goal that spoke not only of the inspiration of PSV's football, but also of the forlorn nature of how Bastia's own magical run was ending. Deijkers and Van der Kuijlen's goals were separated by just two minutes and they could easily have been added to.

A success that would eventually be overshadowed by their European Cup glory a decade later, PSV's success in the 1977/78 UEFA Cup is one that goes criminally unheralded. In this respect, it sits perfectly with the lack of wider recognition of Bastia's own indelible run to the final.

Two majestically talented teams shielded by the 1988 European Cup Final and a waterlogged Stade Armand-Cesari, PSV and Bastia deserve more than a place in the unconsidered margins of UEFA Cup history.

Chapter Five

The Start of Something Beautiful?

OF ALL the *Sliding Doors* moments in football, there are few more pronounced than the one that unfolded in the city of Milan in the summer of 1976. With a more than willing Giovanni Trapattoni in the palm of their hand, AC Milan looked elsewhere for a new head coach to lead them into the 1976/77 season.

A player of huge importance to them for over a decade, throughout the 1960s and into the early 70s, Trapattoni had twice been asked to temporarily guide Milan, during the turbulence of 1973/74 and 1975/76, a period of time when he was mentored by the legendary Nereo Rocco, who took on the role of technical director.

Trapattoni took Milan into the 1974 European Cup Winners' Cup Final and then guided them to a respectable third-placed Serie A finish in 1975/76, only to be overlooked in the summer for the role on a permanent basis, losing out to Paolo Barison, a former Milan team-mate of Trapattoni's, who had an unerring facial resemblance to his rival for the job.

Barison would last just five games, before being replaced by Giuseppe Marchioro, Milan contriving to limp home to a tenth-placed Serie A finish in 1976/77 – a far cry from Trapattoni's soothing guidance of the previous season.

With an increased appetite for frontline coaching, falling back into the junior coaching ranks at the San Siro wasn't an option for Trapattoni, a man who had played the vast majority of his football in the red and black stripes of Milan, winning two Serie A titles, the European Cup twice and a Cup Winners' Cup.

Expected to reappear at one of Italian football's mid-ranking Serie A clubs in order to gain more experience before striking once again for one of the top jobs, it came as a huge surprise that when Juventus were left to consider a successor to the departing Carlo Parola they swooped for the newly available Trapattoni.

When Milan ended the 1976/77 season a little too close for comfort to the relegation zone, the sight of Trapattoni leading Juventus to *lo Scudetto* will have been a painful one. The man they had passed on, one of their own, leading Juventus to glory in Turin, was a sensation Milan would become all too familiar with over the course of the next decade.

With Milan seemingly cursed during his time at Juventus, by the time Trapattoni returned to the city in 1986 to take over at Internazionale, *I Rossoneri* had suffered one demotion, due to the *Totonero* scandal, plus a further relegation to Serie B on the pitch, while they had won just one Serie A title and one Coppa Italia, both of those successes before *Totonero* broke.

Conversely, for Trapattoni and Juventus it was a glory-laden ten-year union in which they collected 14 major honours. It was a run of success that began at the 1977 UEFA Cup Final.

Up until this point, Italian teams had underachieved massively in the UEFA Cup. While Juventus had fallen at the semi-final stage two years earlier, only Milan, in the very first season of the tournament, had travelled as far. Whether this was down to the shifting sands of 1970s European football or due to a lack of respect for the UEFA Cup from a Serie A perspective is open to interpretation, but during the first three seasons of the UEFA Cup's existence, Milan reached the Cup Winners' Cup Final twice, while Inter and Juventus contested one European Cup Final each, which suggests it might have been the latter scenario.

This possible UEFA Cup ambivalence, or simple difficulties of dealing with a dense field of talented teams, certainly seemed to have been carried across from the Inter-Cities Fairs Cup. With AS Roma the only Serie A club to win the predecessor to the UEFA Cup, a success that had come 16 years prior to Juventus's 1977 run to glory, the only other Italian team to reach a Fairs Cup Final had been Juventus themselves, twice, defeated by Ferencváros in 1965 and then by Leeds United in 1971.

Italian teams weren't alone in their early high-profile UEFA Cup underachievement, however. Spain's LaLiga representatives were just as slow off the mark. Athletic Club, Juventus's opponents in the 1977 UEFA Cup Final, were the first to reach the showpiece event from the Iberian nation.

Whereas Serie A's clubs had largely laboured through the Fairs Cup, LaLiga's had excelled in, and dominated, the early years of the tournament, winning six of the first eight played, before relinquishing their grip, with no Spanish team reaching another final beyond 1966.

Into the formative years of the UEFA Cup, no LaLiga team had reached even as far as the semi-finals, until Rinus Michels and Johan Cruyff took Barcelona there in 1976. So, it seemed entirely apt that Serie A and LaLiga would simultaneously get their acts together in 1976/77.

Juventus began their UEFA Cup campaign on Moss Side, beaten 1-0 at Maine Road by Tony Book's Manchester City, undone by as stereotypically an English goal as imaginable. Brian Kidd the scorer, with a header, in the six-yard-box, after Joe Royle flicked on a Dennis Tueart corner.

A fortnight later, with Manchester City opting for an attempted wall of defence, goals from Gaetano Scirea and Roberto Boninsegna handed Juventus the prize of another trip to Manchester, this time to face the team from Old Trafford.

With the first leg played out in Salford, it was a wonderfully open 90 minutes of football that ended with a 1-0 victory for the home side – a scoreline that was wholly unrepresentative of the fluidity of play and creation of opportunities. Franco Causio struck the post and Boninsegna forced Alex Stepney into a fine save, before Gordon Hill scored the only goal of the game, in the 32nd minute, with an excellent left-footed volley.

Juventus then shut up shop, only breaking away sporadically for an attempted sucker punch, as they contented themselves to absorb the pressure being applied by Tommy Docherty's side, Trapattoni happy for his players to complete their work back in Turin.

A heady combination of the finest of Italian goalkeeping from Dino Zoff, desperate defending from the international team-mates he reassuringly had in front of him, plus an increasingly frustrated set of Manchester United attackers being denied further goals, chances came and went, for Steve Coppell, Stewart Houston and Sammy McIlroy.

Manchester United, given no easy assignments in the opening rounds, had navigated their way past Ajax in the first round but their trip to Turin would be a bridge too far. Docherty's team were completely outclassed by Juventus, undone by intelligent movement, intense pressure, a passionate atmosphere; it all combined to facilitate a 3-0 win for Trapattoni's side on a night when it could have been so many more. Boninsegna struck twice, while it was a surprise that Juventus had to wait until five minutes from the end until Romeo Benetti scored the third.

As part of their travelling party, Manchester United had carried the England manager, Don Revie, so he could assess most of the Italian national team, who he would be facing two weeks later in Rome in a crucial World Cup qualifier. It seems that very few lessons were taken on board, as England were comfortably dealt with. Their 2-0 loss was a blow that England never recovered from in their hopes of reaching the 1978 World Cup finals.

Before 1976 had drawn to an end, Juventus had eased past Shakhtar Donetsk and into the quarter-final, progression powered by another 3-0 victory at the Stadio Comunale, this time in the first leg. All the goals came in the first half, the opener being a guided, deft finish from Roberto Bettega, the second, one in which the Donetsk goalkeeper, Yuriy Degtyarev, pulled off both an outstanding save, then a horrendous fumble, to help Marco Tardelli's effort over the line, then finally Boninsegna, who powered the ball into the roof of Degtyarev's net. A 1-0 defeat in Donetsk in the return game made for a hat-trick of inconsequential away UEFA Cup losses.

Athletic's progress, meanwhile, had worked on a similar, although not identical, pattern – convincing home victories offset by failing to pick off a win on their travels. Újpest FC, FC Basel and Trapattoni's former employers, Milan, had been put out of the tournament by Athletic.

It had been over two decades since Athletic, one of the biggest names in Spanish football, fiercely Basque, had claimed the last of their six domestic league titles. Since then, intermittent cup successes had sustained them, yet in their previous nine European campaigns they had never made it beyond a quarter-final.

Led by Koldo Aguirre as their head coach, a man who had been a midfielder of distinction for the club, like Trapattoni at Juventus it was his first season in the job too, having previously been assistant coach and, prior to that, in charge of Athletic's reserve team.

A team full of internationals to call their own, all of which were, of course, sourced from the Basque region, Aguirre could rely upon the likes of captain, goalkeeper and Athletic legend, José Ángel Iribar; Andoni Goikoetxea, who was the man that would eventually earn the nickname of the Butcher of Bilbao; the future Deportivo La Coruna LaLiga-winning coach, Javier Irureta; Ángel María Villar, a man who would rise and then fall within the very corridors of power, at both UEFA and FIFA; plus the future Athletic coach, Txetxu Rojo; the Barcelona legend to be, José Ramón Alexanko; and the enigmatic and prolific Dani.

A narrow defeat in Budapest against Újpest, remedied with a Dani-inspired 5-0 victory in the second leg back at the San Mamés, was followed by the ease of a 4-1 aggregate win against Basel in the second round, the second leg of which was refereed by the authoritarian English First Division official, Pat Partridge.

This then threw Athletic together with Milan. A tie that could so easily have signalled the end of their run, Athletic shrugged off the blow of conceding the first goal, plundered by Fabio Capello, by levelling the scores through a Dani penalty on the stroke of half-time.

Milan, seemingly still disorientated from conceding just before the interval, were 2-1 down within three minutes of the restart, with Carlos striking swiftly and decisively. Enthused by this quick turnaround in fortunes, Athletic went hunting for more goals with which to travel to the San Siro for the return game.

Whereas a Trapattoni-led Milan would likely have strangled the remainder of the game into submission, Marchioro's Milan fell apart in the last ten minutes, as both Dani and Carlos claimed another goal apiece to complete an impressive 4-1 victory.

Despite the solid foundation that Athletic had built for themselves at the San Mamés, there was still drama ahead at the San Siro, where Aguirre's side came to within two minutes of exiting the tournament.

Goalless until the 53rd minute, Athletic appeared to be gliding through to the quarter-finals. Egidio Calloni broke the deadlock with a towering header; however, seven minutes later Giorgio Biasiolo added to the escalating Athletic anxieties, when he volleyed home from six yards.

With half an hour still to play, Milan laid siege to the Athletic goalmouth, a goalmouth that seemed charmed, until Gianni Rivera unconvincingly went to ground with only six minutes remaining. The West German referee, Walter Eschweiler, pointed to the spot, however, and Calloni converted for a 3-0 lead. As things stood, Athletic were now heading out on the away-goals rule.

Yet, another twist was to come. With two minutes left to play, Rojo won the visitors a penalty of their own, which José Ignacio Madariaga confidently planted to Enrico Albertosi's left, with the former Italian international diving instead to his right. This was an incredibly nerveless act from Madariaga, as despite being right-footed, he struck the penalty with his left.

Relieved to have overcome Milan, no mercy was shown in the draw for the quarter-finals, as Athletic were paired up with the Rinus Michels-led Barcelona, a side that could not only still boast the services of Johan Cruyff, but those of Johan Neeskens too.

At the San Mamés, at the beginning of March, Athletic chiselled out a 2-1 victory, clawing their way back from a 1-0 deficit inflicted by Asensi. José Ignacio Churruca snatched the equaliser shortly before half-time, while Dani was once again the man for the big moment, when he scored from the penalty spot in the 63rd minute.

In possession of a fragile lead as they made for the Camp Nou for the second leg, a marvellously volatile game erupted in the Catalan capital. Wild challenges were answered by uncompromising retaliation, in an encounter where it was a stunning achievement by the referee that he managed to guide the game to its conclusion with a full complement of 22 players being on the pitch when the final whistle was blown.

On the offensive from the word go, Irureta twice gave Athletic the lead, with Cruyff twice being the man to level the scores. With 25 minutes still to play when the second of those Barcelona equalisers found the back of the net, Aguirre's side were left with a mountain to defend rather than climb. With a steely determination, Athletic did just that to book their place in the semi-finals, against RWD Molenbeek.

Perceived underdogs when facing both Milan and Barcelona, being the favourites against Molenbeek brought a different kind of pressure to Athletic. Within such proximity to the 1977 UEFA Cup Final, it was a test of resolve not to fumble this golden opportunity now.

Athletic returned from Brussels with a 1-1 draw after the first leg of the semi-final, a game in which José Ignacio Churruca's 25th-minute goal came to within two minutes of being the only one of the game.

Molenbeek's late equaliser was snatched by Jacques Teugels, a goal that provoked a safety-first response from Athletic in the goalless return game. A nervous occasion at the San Mamés was navigated, however, with the Basque giants reaching their first major European final.

For Juventus, having lost on their travels in all three of the rounds they'd played before Christmas, it was a smooth progression to the final into the new year. Neither Magdeburg, nor AEK, of Athens, posed a significant threat to Trapattoni's side. Bettega and Cuccureddu were the chief contributors for *I Bianconeri*, as Juventus scored nine goals over the course of their quarter-final and semi-final games, as aided by Benetti, Boninsegna and Causio.

Two finalists that drew massive attention, when all eyes locked on the first leg at the Stadio Comunale it was Juventus that made all the early running and it wasn't long before they carved Athletic open, creating the first serious opportunity of the game.

Like a prototype version of the chance Paul Gascoigne narrowly missed in the 1996 European Championship semi-final against Germany, on this occasion it was Boninsegna who desperately stuck his foot out when flinging himself towards the back post in an attempt to make contact with the ball, at the end of a beautiful move that was born out of an initially careless passage of play, instigated by a Causio free kick.

Before half-time, Juventus would suffer the blow of losing the services of Boninsegna, who was withdrawn in the 39th minute. The veteran striker, by now 33, scorer of Italy's only goal of their 1970 World Cup Final defeat to Brazil, had been so synonymous with Inter that the sight of him in the black and white stripes of Juventus had seemed to be an illusion.

A masterstroke of a signing, however, arriving the very same summer as Trapattoni, Boninsegna's Indian summer in Turin would yield not only this UEFA Cup success, but two Serie A titles too. Potential sensory overload for seasoned Serie A observers, while he was an Inter player, Boninsegna had been part of a magnificent rivalry with the Juventus defender, Francesco Morini, in which there was a huge sense of occasion whenever they went into battle against one another. Yet now, here they were, team-mates under Trapattoni, a man who had been Milan through and through.

Despite his advancing years, it is perhaps no coincidence that Juventus didn't add to the one goal they had attained at the time of Boninsegna's departure from the first leg, when he was replaced by Sergio Gori, another former Inter striker and fellow member of Italy's 1970 World Cup squad.

Linked to one another, without having shared a club simultaneously until 1976/77, in the summer of 1969 Boninsegna and Gori had swapped employers, when the former signed for Inter and the latter headed in the opposite direction, to Cagliari. Stunningly, it was Cagliari and Gori that ended the 1969/70 season as Serie A champions, rather than Boninsegna and Inter, who would be made to wait another 12 months for that prize.

Valuable, yet left-field a signing as he was, that one Juventus goal of the first leg didn't fall to Boninsegna – it instead belonged to Tardelli, whose celebration, while not as iconic as the one he burst forth with five years later at the Santiago Bernabéu when scoring in the World Cup Final, was still one which made Claudio Gentile stand back, until he felt Tardelli was safe to approach.

Peculiar in nature, Tardelli's goal probably wouldn't have gone in had he made a clean contact with his attempted header. It instead was a half-botched effort, which he headed against his own left shoulder, only to see it loop up and over the despairing Iribar.

Despite Juventus working themselves other openings, the resolute defending of Goikoetxea kept Trapattoni's side at bay. Chances for Causio, Morini and Bettega were repelled during the first half, while Athletic had been restricted to only the most speculative of efforts at Zoff.

The second half predominantly being played out with Athletic on the back foot, Goikoetxea's enthusiasm for the tackle soon got the better of him, as he picked up the booking that ruled him out of the second leg.

Never losing focus or composure, however, Goikoetxea marshalled the Athletic defence majestically, with Gori joining the lengthening list of Juventus players to be denied in front of goal. Even with Causio in inspired form, Iribar would not be breached a second time and it must have been with a sense of great frustration that Trapattoni and his players met the final whistle. Juventus had effectively been played at their own game, by Aguirre and Athletic.

Carrying his injury into the return game, while he would play in Bilbao, Boninsegna lasted only an hour. This time, he was replaced by the former Italian international defender, Luciano Spinosi, as Trapattoni opted for containment.

Athletic's hard work from the first leg was undone within seven minutes, at the San Mamés, when an away goal procured by Bettega left Aguirre and his players needing to score three times over the course of the remaining 83 minutes.

Juventus had conceded three goals in one game, only once all season, so despite conceding a swift equaliser just four minutes after Causio's opener, a goal that Irureta had little say in scoring, when Churruca's misdirected volley hit the legs of his team-mate and ricocheted past Zoff, Trapattoni still wasn't tempted into a more open performance.

Irureta's goal brought on Athletic's best period of the game. Churruca was at the heart of most moves, while Dani was regularly the man who came close to capitalising upon the chances being created. A compelling shout for a penalty was ignored when Dani went to ground under the attention of Gentile, which was eventually followed by a disallowed goal, when use of an arm was adjudged during the build-up.

Shoring up his defence with half an hour still to play, Trapattoni had read between the lines of the first 15 minutes of the second half, with Athletic having picked up where they left off at the end of the first half. Tempers had frayed within a short few minute of the restart, when Benetti tried to keep hold of the ball a little too long after it rolled out of play.

As desperation and untidiness crept into Athletic's play, Juventus began to relax as the game reached the final 15 minutes. Spinosi's introduction had brought a soothing effect to Trapattoni's team, while his presence had been disruptive to the flow and rhythm of the hosts.

With 12 minutes remaining, the Athletic substitute, Carlos Ruiz, levelled the aggregate score, with a header that was as untidy as the general state of the game had become. Within the scramble to be the first to the ball, although the goal was credited to Ruiz, it could possibly have hit his arm on the way in, or even touched a Juventus player on the way through from the in-swinging corner that provoked the goal.

In possession of the away-goal advantage, Juventus eased their way to the finish line to collect not only their first UEFA Cup, but the club's very first major European honour.

Momentum had been everything in the end. Apart from losing on the evening at the San Mamés, Juventus had been without fault during a run-in that also saw them collect the Serie A title four days beyond lifting the UEFA Cup, narrowly pipping their cross-city rivals and the defending champions, Torino. It was an incredible four days which set the tone for the rest of Trapattoni's first spell in charge of *I Bianconeri*.

Between the two legs of the 1977 UEFA Cup Final, Trapattoni had guided Juventus to crucial Serie A victories at the San Siro, against Inter and at the Stadio Comunale, against Roma. In comparison, Athletic had perhaps focussed too much on their looming dates of destiny with Juventus.

While they had always been a step or two behind the arc of a title chase that proved to be a Madrid shoot-out between Atlético and Real, in which the Vicente Calderón would be the location of the celebrating champions, Athletic had been afforded the time and space to rest players, to be that little more circumspect in their approach and preparation.

Within that, however, comes extra thinking and worrying time. Having given themselves a strong position from which to strike at Juventus in the second leg, Athletic quite possibly froze during the early exchanges at the San Mamés. This is where Trapattoni and his ruthlessly in-form team dealt the decisive blow.

From this success, Trapattoni and Juventus struck out for much more, adding to their domestic haul the Cup Winners' Cup in 1984, then the European Cup on that horrendous night at the Heysel Stadium, a year later.

Through their disappointment, glorious days were soon on the horizon for Athletic too, as they won back-to-back LaLiga titles in 1982/83 and 1983/84, the second of those successes as part of a domestic double.

Together, Juventus and Athletic had finally broken the long-standing stranglehold that northern European nations had enjoyed in the UEFA Cup and the latter years of the Fairs Cup. Yet, the 1976/77 campaign acted as a mirage, rather than the start of a defined power shift, as the next seven UEFA Cups went north once again.

Not until the resurgence of Real Madrid in the mid-1980s did LaLiga have another representative in a UEFA Cup Final, while for Serie A it was an even longer wait, until Napoli's run to glory in 1988/89 signalled the beginning of a bewitching Italian monopoly on the tournament.

Chapter Six

Tractor Beam

THERE IS a strange and bewitching voodoo at play when it comes to Ipswich Town and the 1980/81 UEFA Cup; there is a strange and bewitching voodoo at play when it comes to Portman Road and European nights.

It's over 18 years since Ipswich last kicked a ball in anger in European club competition and, given their current and sad predicament in the third tier of English football, it could be a lot longer than that before they threaten to do so again.

On 31 occasions, Ipswich have purposefully stridden out beneath the Portman Road floodlights against continental opponents, and on 31 occasions they have returned to the dressing room undefeated. While their flirtations with Europe have been sporadic, that last campaign drifting into an ever-distancing past, they have always taken to European competition like a duck to water.

Of Ipswich's 12 European campaigns, ten of them took place in the UEFA Cup, eight of those ten coming during the two-legged final era. The one that hit the jackpot, in 1980/81, was their sixth attempt, having previously suffered from varying shades of misfortune and self-inflicted exits.

Healthy first-leg leads blown here, penalty shoot-outs lost there, until 1980/81 it was all too often a case of what might have been for Ipswich and the UEFA Cup. The biggest blows sustained came in 1973/74 when they were edged out in the quarter-finals on penalties by Lokomotive Leipzig, alongside 1977/78 when they headed to the Camp Nou to face the Barcelona of Rinus Michels and Johan Cruyff holding a 3-0 first-leg lead, only to see it swiftly evaporate before again going out on penalties. It all made for a painful learning curve.

Through it all, confidence was also banked. Yes, the 1977/78 Barcelona game might have blown up in Ipswich's face in the second leg, but you don't outclass Michels and Cruyff in the first leg without being left with an inkling of what might be possible. It would have been a familiar sensation to Bobby Robson's side, having also experienced eye-catching and mind-opening victories at Portman Road against the Günter Netzer-powered Real Madrid and the Giorgio Chinaglia-inspired Lazio.

Then came Arnold and Frans: Mühren and Thijssen, via Ipswich, having won the FA Cup before their respective arrivals. First came Mühren, in the summer of 1978, then on the back of his successful start, Thijssen was purchased in the new year to replace the Arsenal-bound Brian Talbot.

It all amounted to the reinvention of what was already a team of great potential, a team that had not only won the FA Cup but had previously threatened a league and cup double in 1974/75, only to see both prizes slip the net.

Under the guidance of Robson, Ipswich qualified for Europe in nine of his last ten seasons in charge. A wonderful run of consistency, during an era in which clubs such as Leeds United and Derby County swung from the high of league titles to the nothingness of relegation. It was a volatile era, one in which Manchester United and Tottenham Hotspur also befell the drop into the Second Division.

Within this, there is a propensity of some to question just how successful Robson's time at Ipswich should be considered. Yes, you can point to two major honours in 13 and a half seasons as being a sign of underachievement, yet that would be disingenuous.

At Portman Road, Robson built and rebuilt a team of skill, fluidity and consistency. They genuinely challenged for the First Division title on four occasions, there were two FA Cup semi-final defeats to go alongside the one they won, as well as a League Cup semi-final, while the great and good of Europe feared a trip to Suffolk.

Robson was also courted by countless clubs, sometimes on multiple occasions, yet his loyalty to the Cobbold family was such that it was only the England job that could successfully tempt him away, a job he took through a sense of pride and duty, when other far more lucrative options were available.

While other clubs operated in boom and bust formats, Ipswich cut a steadily consistent swathe through the 1970s and into the early 1980s. Between 1972/73 and Robson's last season in charge, 1981/82, the club finished outside the First Division's top six on just one occasion. That one exception being the season that Ipswich won the FA Cup.

The season 1980/81 represented the peak of Portman Road's attractive powers. A tilt at a treble that would eventually be condensed down to UEFA Cup glory, after the title was plucked from the palm of their hand by Aston Villa, while their bid for a second FA Cup in four seasons came unstuck in extra time, in a Villa Park semi-final against Manchester City.

Cruelly denied on two fronts, it would have been the easier option for Ipswich to sustain another body blow, but this was a balanced team with a great work ethic and a sense of skill, which was matched by their strength of character.

In Paul Cooper, they had a fine goalkeeper who would have ascended to the England team had he played in an era that wasn't inhabited by Ray Clemence, Peter Shilton and Joe Corrigan. An agile and reactionary stopper, he was a penalty taker's nightmare.

By the time the 1981 UEFA Cup Final took place, Ipswich went into it without their regular right-back George Burley, but Robson's side rolled with the punch. The 19-year-old midfielder Steve McCall slotted in at left-back, with the adaptable Mick

Mills switching to cover for the missing Burley, while central defence was marshalled by the England internationals, Russell Osman and Terry Butcher.

An artisan midfield, not only did it contain the talents of Mühren and Thijssen, but also the power, drive and eye for goal of the rampant John Wark, who ended the campaign with a truly ridiculous 36 goals.

A formation that was nominally a 4-3-3, up front Ipswich had the presence of Paul Mariner, the skilled Alan Brazil and the subtle probing nature of Eric Gates, who would at times drop deeper, to alter the formation to a 4-3-1-2, essentially turning the midfield into a diamond, when the need arose.

It all made for a flexibility to Robson's side that flew in the face of how he was often perceived to be, as a devout exponent of the 4-4-2, during his England days. He also had the wildcard option of throwing on the teenage winger, Kevin O'Callaghan, to stretch his midfield against teams that set out with narrower formations that were designed to congest Ipswich's fluid midfield cogs.

With such an expansive midfield, despite the fact that Wark, Mühren and Thijssen could battle when battling was required, the lack of a dedicated and disciplined midfield imposer was quite possibly the reason why, of the three trophies Ipswich were chasing in 1980/81, that it was the domestic honours that eluded them.

Brutal at home, but tentative on their travels in the early rounds, Ipswich were merciless during Portman Road first legs in the first three rounds against Aris, Bohemians Praha and Widzew Łódź, clocking up 5-1, 3-0 and 5-0 victories respectively, only to be beaten in the return games to varying levels of peril.

An explosive encounter with Aris; while Wark plundered four goals, it was Gates that was at the centre of everything. A busy night, in which he earned Wark three penalties and played a crucial role in a goal that ended with a Mariner volley from

20 yards, Gates also provoked the red card of Giorgos Foiros, who lost his cool as early as the 35th minute, swinging a punch at the newly capped England international.

Yellow cards also collected by Butcher and Mariner, it made for an aggressive evening, an atmosphere possibly provoked by rumours that Aris had approached Wark over a potential transfer to the Greek club during the summer. In the return game, in Thessaloniki, Ipswich found themselves 3-0 down with 15 minutes remaining, when Gates broke through to score what was now a crucial away goal.

When Bohemians travelled to Portman Road towards the tail end of October, they did so in a stubborn frame of mind. Ipswich endured a first half of frustration, as not even Mühren and Thijssen could crack the defensive blanket they were confronted by.

Nerves were eased within three minutes of the restart, however, as Wark was on target with a coolly taken finish, when the ball was rolled across his path. Six minutes later the Scottish international had his second of the evening, his sixth UEFA Cup goal of the campaign already, when capitalising on a rebound after Brazil hit the post.

A third goal was procured with just five minutes remaining, a goal that would prove to be a vital one. It was also a goal that came from a player that had become something of a ghost on the Portman Road wall.

Kevin Beattie was a supremely talented individual, a player that Robson reputedly rated to be as good as the legendary Duncan Edwards, but one that was also prone to injury, misfortune and, when he was younger, a propensity for misadventure.

Brought on as a late substitute, without a hint to the amount of football he had missed in recent seasons, Beattie found the top corner with a beautifully struck free kick. It would prove to be the decisive goal in the tie, as in Prague, in the return game, Ipswich were made to sweat, as they fell 2-0 behind having conceded early goals in both halves of the game, the second to the legendary Antonín Panenka, before holding out to narrowly progress to the third round with the help of Beattie once again, this time defensively, at one point clearing the ball when Bohemians hit the Ipswich crossbar.

In the third round, Zbigniew Boniek's presence wasn't enough to disrupt Ipswich's run, when Robson's side navigated their way past Łódź, a team who had already ejected Manchester United and Juventus in the previous two rounds, a team that two years later would reach the semi-finals of the European Cup, defeating Liverpool along the way, and were considered by some observers to be the favourites to win the 1980/81 UEFA Cup.

It made Ipswich's 5-0, first-leg victory one that was almost as astonishing as their iconic 6-0 demolition of Manchester United the previous season. Łódź were left disorientated after their early composure soon fell apart in the face of Ipswich's frenetic approach to the game.

Another three goals for Wark and one each for Brazil and Mariner, Łódź had no answer to the avalanche of chances that were in equal measure skilfully created by the hosts and generously presented by the visitors.

A fortnight later, in Poland, Ipswich fell to a 1-0 defeat in sub-zero temperatures that were so piercing that both sets of players took to the pitch in tracksuit bottoms. Despite their exit, the Łódź players were applauded from the pitch by their supporters in recognition of the effort they had displayed, having performed well without three of their best players, inclusive of Boniek who had been sanctioned by their own football federation after they had been involved in a public row in an airport terminal with the coach of the Poland national team while on international duty.

When the quarter-finals came into view, Ipswich were riding the crest of their 1980/81 wave. With 13 goals scored in their three home UEFA Cup games, in which Wark had scored an incredible nine, anything less than riding the crest of their wave at this point might well have signalled the end of their run.

Top of the First Division, and with an FA Cup quarter-final against Nottingham Forest looming, Ipswich had reached the point of the season where every game was now a massive one. It was the perfect situation to be in to face the AS Saint-Étienne of Michel Platini, Johnny Rep and Jean-François Larios, opponents that had won 5-0 in Hamburg during the previous round.

When Rep powered in a towering header 16 minutes into the first leg at the Stade Geoffroy-Guichard, Ipswich could have been forgiven for fearing that a chastening night lay ahead of them. Yet, on an atrocious pitch, it was the illustrious hosts that chased the game from that moment onward and, within 12 minutes, Ipswich were level, Mariner with his own header, meeting the ball at the back post, converting a chance that was cleverly created by Mühren.

With no further goals in the first half, it didn't take long beyond the restart for Ipswich to steal the initiative, with Mühren scoring from distance in the 47th minute after an intelligent lay-off from Wark on the edge of the penalty area. It was a goal that sent shockwaves around the Stade Geoffroy-Guichard and out across the rest of Europe.

Ten minutes later, Mariner had his second and Ipswich's third, making sure a rebound found its way into the Saint-Étienne net after some wonderful build-up play, Robson's side resisting the urge for caution having edged in front so early in the second half. By the time Wark headed in Ipswich's fourth, with 14 minutes remaining, Platini's misery was complete.

This, combined with another comprehensive second-leg victory back at Portman Road and the springboard to UEFA Cup glory it created, went on to see Ipswich awarded the France Football European Team of the Year award, ahead of a Liverpool team that won the European Cup via some incredible performances of their own, plus the hypnotic force that was Dinamo Tbilisi, who lifted the Cup Winners' Cup in style.

Two hard-fought 1-0 victories against the Rinus Michels-led 1. FC Köln saw Ipswich into the 1981 UEFA Cup Final, games that were surrounded by the club's domestic capitulation, amid a fixture backlog that saw them take to the pitch four times in between the two legs of the semi-final.

First leg settled by a Wark header, Köln spurned a hatful of second-leg chances, the prime culprit being Stephan Engels, paving the way for Butcher to snatch the only goal of the game, with Köln's aerial weakness again taken advantage of.

An underappreciated achievement, getting past Köln was no simple task, being that they were a team that could call upon not only the coaching genius of Michels but the playing talents of Harald Schumacher, Harald Konopka, Gerhard Strack, Rainer Bonhof, Pierre Littbarski, Dieter Müller, Yasuhiko Okudera and the England international, Tony Woodcock.

While the 1981 UEFA Cup Final is widely respected as an act of football greatness, and Ipswich's convincing victories over Saint-Étienne are massively admired, their semi-final performances against Köln fall beneath the radar of many general football lovers, when they should be as celebrated in equal measure.

Awaiting Ipswich in the final were AZ '67 Alkmaar – an aesthetic like-for-like, who left Mühren and Thijssen feeling completely at home; a team that had just clinched their very first Eredivisie title, after a run of near misses which had come to an end with a 5-1 drubbing of Feyenoord at De Kuip.

Guided by Georg Keßler, the West German coach had put together a compellingly balanced team that domestically in the Netherlands had broken the traditional hegemony of Ajax, Feyenoord and PSV Eindhoven. Cast by a strong spine that had boasted the man who kept goal for Feyenoord in the 1974 UEFA Cup Final, Eddy Treijtel, a defence marshalled by Hugo Hovenkamp, a midfield powered by the future Real Madrid, Nottingham Forest and Tottenham Hotspur colossus, Johnny Metgod and stylised by the duo of Jan Peters and Kristen

Nygaard, with the goals scored by Kees Kist, it meant that Ipswich would have their work cut out to succeed.

A relatively sedate route taken to the final, AZ were unbeaten when they arrived at Portman Road, bearing gifts of giant cheeses, as handed over on the pitch prior to kick-off by women dressed in traditional lowland garb. Ipswich, meanwhile, carried injuries on to the pitch. Cooper, Thijssen, Gates and Mariner all dragged their bodies into action for a greater good that led them to a 3-0 victory.

Wark from the penalty spot, some marvellous opportunism from Thijssen and a glancing contribution from Mariner, to deny Brazil what would have been the goal of his career, sparked wild celebrations in Suffolk. It was as if Ipswich had suddenly been reunited with the kind of form that had carried them to the end of March, before the painful experiences of April.

A fortnight later, in Amsterdam at the Olympic Stadium, Ipswich got off to a dream start, when, within four minutes, Thijssen had volleyed in an away goal, taking the aggregate score to 4-0 and leaving AZ in need of five goals to prevail.

Whether it was a case of Ipswich becoming blasé about the situation or that the conceding of an away goal liberated AZ from the prospect of playing in hope of provoking one of Ipswich's second-leg self-destruction acts of previous European campaigns is all open to conjecture, but after Thijssen's goal, AZ most certainly came into the game, while Ipswich lost focus.

It was the Austrian international, Kurt Welzl, who scored what initially seemed to be no more than a consolation goal for AZ, heading the ball past Cooper after some determined work from Metgod. Before half-time, AZ would have two more, Metgod grabbing the second himself, Pier Tol volleying in the third.

With Wark having volleyed in a second for Ipswich, in between AZ's second and third goals, despite the escalating nature of the situation, Ipswich still harboured a 5-3 aggregate lead at the interval, which left Keßler's side needing three second-half goals with which to pull off the impossible.

That Ipswich restricted AZ to only one further goal is testament to the discipline Robson's side performed with, as AZ visibly wilted after Jos Jonker struck a fine goal from outside the penalty area, to make it 4-2 on the night.

The 1980/81 season was one of wonderful, expansive football, in which Robson's side had chased a treble, yet a season that was in danger of Ipswich ending without a trophy had they thrown the 1981 UEFA Cup Final away, then the immediate repercussions might have been seismic.

With Everton, Manchester United and Sunderland all courting his attention, armed with lucrative contracts, Robson was left with a difficult decision whether to stick, or twist, in the summer of 1981. Considering his team to be the best in the land and with the England job a year away from being available, he eventually opted to stick for one last push for a league title that again eluded them, in 1981/82, before taking up the opportunity to succeed Ron Greenwood as England manager.

A peculiarity, Robson never managed to transfer his sense of expansion at Portman Road on to the international scene with England, all too often selecting a rigid 4-4-2 formation and placing an over-reliance upon Bryan Robson.

For Ipswich, the 1981 UEFA Cup remains their last major piece of silverware. Upon Robson's departure in the summer of 1982, he was succeeded by his assistant, Bobby Ferguson, who, like so many great number twos, never quite hit the same heights when handed the top job.

Ferguson dismantled Robson's side with too much haste and Ipswich eventually limped to relegation in 1986, from where they have since spent only five seasons in the English top flight. A proud club that retain a special affection from football hipsters everywhere, without finding themselves an oil or gas rich oligarch, it is hard to see how they can ever scale those dizzying heights once again.

And within that, football is a poorer sport because of it.

Chapter Seven

The Hypnotic Rise of IFK Göteborg

IFK GÖTEBORG are easily lost in generational translation.

A club that hasn't made it to the main draw of a major European competition since the 1999/2000 season, yet, as late as the 1994/95 campaign, the shifting sands of football hadn't altered enough to stop them being a genuine European force of substance.

In what was just the third season of the Champions League era of UEFA's blue riband event, Göteborg were still potent enough to reach the quarter-finals, at the expense of knocking Alex Ferguson's Manchester United out in the group stages, topping a group that also contained Barcelona and a fast maturing Galatasaray, before being narrowly edged out in the last eight, on away goals, by Bayern Munich.

A team that could still boast the much-admired and sought-after Jesper Blomqvist, one of seven members of the Sweden squad for the 1994 World Cup finals to be supplied by Göteborg, a World Cup in which Sweden finished third, it was a run that acted as one last European hurrah for the team that arguably suffered more than any other in such a position of prominence due to the redrawing of the rules of European footballing engagement, from the 1997/98 season onward and the dawning of the Bosman Rule.

Winners of the UEFA Cup in 1982 and 1987, the first of those being under Sven-Göran Eriksson, Göteborg became a widely feared force throughout the 1980s, one which also came to within a penalty shoot-out of reaching the 1986 European Cup Final.

A club that had endured a series of peaks and troughs, inclusive of relegation from the Allsveskan in 1970 while defending champions, they had enjoyed a meteoric rebirth after regaining top-flight status in 1976.

Historically renowned for their embracing of aesthetically pleasing styles of football, the arrival as head coach of Eriksson in 1979, aged only 31, was something of a culture shock to Göteborg. An eager disciple of the teachings of Bobby Houghton and Roy Hodgson, Eriksson was an unabashed pragmatist, implementing a rigid 4-4-2 formation that relied upon supreme fitness and relentless pressing. While the results were very positive, the style was, at times, unappealing.

With only three previous European campaigns behind them, just one of them having ventured beyond the first round, Göteborg were cast very much in the role of the quaint Scandinavian part-timers on their route to the 1982 UEFA Cup Final. It was arguably through the powers of underestimation that they prevailed the first time around.

Emerging from the second leg of the final, against Hamburger SV, not only had Eriksson's side stunned Europe by claiming the trophy, but they had also ended the campaign unbeaten. This being a run to glory that hadn't only accounted for an HSV side that was 12 months away from winning the European Cup, in what was the Bundesliga side's fourth major European final in seven seasons, but had also swept aside a Dinamo Bucureşti outfit that went on to reach the semi-finals of the 1984 European Cup, plus a Valencia that had lifted the European Cup Winners' Cup in 1980, and a steadily rising Kaiserslautern.

Eriksson played the situation to perfection. Humble and modest in the wake of positive results, he disarmed an unsuspecting continent. Even when Göteborg procured a late winning goal in the first leg against HSV at a drenched Ullevi, coolly scored by Tord Holmgren in terrible conditions, Eriksson seemed happy enough to let the plucky underdog narrative run its course, on an evening when the match ball was brought in by helicopter.

That Göteborg managed to conjure up any lead to take to Hamburg for the second leg was indeed a bonus, yet not because of their perceived position as an enchanting oddity, but instead due to the fact that in the first leg they had lost their most potent goalscoring threat, after just 19 minutes had elapsed.

Torbjörn Nilsson had been part of Sweden's squad at the 1978 World Cup, and alongside the veteran Ove Kindvall, it was their goals that had returned Göteborg to the Allsvenskan in 1976. While Kindvall had called time on his career in 1977, Nilsson had learned quickly from a strike partner that had been 11 years his senior.

So, it was a huge blow for Eriksson to lose his prized possession in the early exchanges of the first leg. Göteborg then lost the influential services of Tommy Holmgren, the younger brother of the first-leg goalscorer, Tord.

It was a theme of misfortune that carried over into the early stages of the second leg, as Eriksson lost the blossoming, future Fiorentina and Liverpool defender, Glenn Hysén, within the first 20 minutes.

Problems turned into opportunities, it just meant that Nilsson was ready to be unleashed upon the return game, against an HSV side that had travelled to the Ullevi in a state of near paranoia setting themselves up in an overly defensive manner.

Unwilling to chance their arm for an away goal in the first leg, with Ernst Happel deploying a safety-first mantra, HSV were made to pay a heavy price at the Volksparkstadion, when Dan Corneliusson opened the scoring for Göteborg in the 26th minute, powering the ball into the roof of the HSV net, when it had initially appeared that he had allowed it to run past him that little bit too far.

Having resisted suggestions to recall the ageing Franz Beckenbauer, HSV were left wide open to further goals in the second half, with Nilsson scoring the second on the break, after another desperate HSV attack broke down in midfield, while the third was added from the penalty spot just three minutes later.

Left in a state of shock, HSV, who were sat upon the brink of claiming the Bundesliga title, were forced to resort to wild efforts at goal that all drifted high and wide, while a belligerent Göteborg continued to set off on counter-attacks that should have led to at least two more goals.

Comfortable victors, Göteborg became the first Swedish team to win a major European competition, Malmo having reached but lost the 1979 European Cup Final. Yet, what made this success even more stunning was that the Swedish national team were four years into a 12-year exile from major international tournaments. While Göteborg were a club very much in ascendancy, the broader span of Swedish football was ailing.

With the great and the good of European football having sat up and taken notice, Eriksson was soon within the employment of Benfica, setting off on an odyssey that would eventually lead him to the door of the Football Association and a five-year spell in charge of the England national team, via stop-offs at AS Roma, Fiorentina, Sampdoria and Lazio, the Lisbon giants having previously approached the Manchester City manager, John Bond.

For Göteborg, there was life beyond the loss of Eriksson. Gunder Bengtsson had been his assistant and when Eriksson departed for Benfica, in time to take them into the 1982/83 Primeira Divisão campaign, it left a void for a Göteborg side that was only midway through their domestic season.

In stepped Bengtsson, who saw Göteborg over the finish line for both the Allsvenskan and the newly created

Swedish championship play-offs. Yet, he was subsequently overlooked as a permanent option, the job instead going to Björn Westerberg.

Westerberg was gone two years later, having delivered domestically only to struggle to make an impact in European competition. Meanwhile, Bengtsson had departed Göteborg, not to join up with Eriksson at Benfica, but to take the post of head coach at the Norwegian side, Vålerenga.

During his time at Vålerenga, Bengtsson delivered back-to-back 1. Divisjon titles, so when Göteborg were in the market for a successor to Westerberg, it was to him that they turned.

Beset by early frustrations, in his first two seasons Bengtsson's Göteborg were kept off the top of the Allsvenskan, while they were also beaten in the finals of both the 1985 championship play-offs and the 1986 Svenska Cupen.

By 1987, however, they were primed for greatness once again and, when they reached the UEFA Cup Final for a second time, it was Jim McLean's Dundee United who were waiting for them. A team that was another underappreciated hipster's favourite of the 1980s.

McLean at Dundee United, along with Alex Ferguson at Aberdeen, had risen compellingly to challenge the fabled Old Firm monopoly, taking the first half of the 1980s by storm and winning themselves not just a cluster of domestic trophies, but also the nickname of the New Firm.

Expanding into Europe, while Aberdeen had won the Cup Winners' Cup in 1983, Dundee United had been cruelly denied a place in the 1984 European Cup Final, in volatile and rumoured controversial circumstances.

A magnificent team, McLean's Dundee United oozed class and in my mind's eye they always seemed to feature on *Football Focus*'s Scottish goals round-ups on a Saturday lunchtime, when what felt to be every week Eamonn Bannon and Paul Sturrock were scoring 25-yard screamers past a variety of forlorn, yet sartorially elegant Premier Division goalkeepers.

A vision in orange and black, they leap from the screen and speak of a brand of Scottish football that was a million miles away from the generation upon generation of preordained textbook successes to have unfolded in Glasgow.

Despite having sold Richard Gough in the early weeks of the season, this was a Dundee United side that was built upon a solid defensive foundation, which was supplied by John Holt, Maurice Malpas, John Clark and the man who antagonised Brazil so beautifully into indelible 1982 World Cup action, David Narey. They also still had the services of the veteran Paul Hegarty, plus cover from Dave Beaumont and Gary McGinnis. It was a defensive unit that was securely marshalled by the Scottish international goalkeeper Billy Thomson.

In midfield, there was energy and skill aplenty, as Bannon, Billy Kirkwood, Jim McInally, Ian Redford and Dave Bowman dictated the pace, ably supported by Iain Ferguson, who could operate centrally, but also up front. Added to this, there was the former Everton player, Alan Irvine and the emerging teenager, Billy McKinlay.

Hunting goals, McLean could rely upon the talents of Sturrock and Kevin Gallagher, while the squad had such a depth that both Ralph Milne and Tommy Coyne were sold part way through the season.

A wonderful era for Dundee United, the 1987 UEFA Cup Final could have been the deserving crescendo for a team that would slowly regress in the years to follow, as a new wave of domination began to bubble up for Rangers, at Ibrox Park, led by Graeme Souness.

Equally cursed and blessed, Dundee United became as synonymous with the numerous near misses they had when it came to major honours as they did with the trophies they won, and no campaign illuminated this quite as much as the 1986/87 one.

Third in the league, beaten in the semi-finals of the Scottish League Cup, between the two legs of the UEFA Cup Final

Dundee United had even found the time to lose the Scottish Cup Final, in a seismic shock, against St Mirren.

Having departed Göteborg with a 1-0 defeat, the second leg wasn't beyond Dundee United turning it around, but just five days after losing the Scottish Cup Final, there was something undeniably flat about McLean's side as they stumbled to a 1-1 draw. Opting for an approach that attempted to match Göteborg in terms of physicality, rather than drawing on their own undoubted strengths, they played into the hands of the visitors.

When Lennart Nilsson opened the scoring midway through the first half, the latest in a string of early chances they created, it left Dundee United needing to summon up the physical and mental energy to find three goals. Despite Clark grabbing one back on the hour, the challenge was too much.

Just as in 1981/82, Göteborg had completed their run to glory unbeaten; they now stood at 24 games without a loss in the competition. Only the second time they had qualified for the UEFA Cup, they had won it on both occasions.

Göteborg had become a truly frightening entity, one which had overcome Internazionale in the quarter-finals, on away goals, matched in impressiveness by a Dundee United team that had beaten Barcelona at the Camp Nou, at the same stage, before pulling off a magnificent semi-final, second-leg victory at the Bökelbergstadion, against a briefly resurgent Borussia Mönchengladbach.

Dundee United had built to this moment, only to arguably lose it through a broken heart. They had become a genuine European force, enjoying and, at times, prevailing on massive European nights against the likes of Anderlecht, Monaco, PSV Eindhoven, Werder Bremen, Manchester United and, of course, Roma, Barcelona and Mönchengladbach.

Like so many others, however, they came unstuck against Göteborg, when they were so close to conjuring up a Scottish version of Ipswich Town's success. In so many ways, Dundee United and Göteborg were the perfect match for one another.

Chapter Eight

Anderlecht's Controversial Second European Coming and a White Hart Lane Uprising

IN THE 1970s and 1980s, in terms of European club competitions, nothing struck fear quite like being drawn to face a team that came from a far-off land, in an all-white strip, the proud owners of a name that had a jumble of consonants as part of its construction, where it seemed like at least one vowel was missing. Dinamo Tbilisi, I'm looking at you.

These all-white strips were that little bit more evocative if the sleeves and the sides of the shorts were adorned by the three thin Adidas stripes, or the one thick Puma stripe of the era. Yet, this wasn't a visual and sensory weapon owned by Real Madrid, funnily enough. Until the dawning of *La Quinta del Buitre* era, at least, Madrid's version of all-white belonged to a sepia-tinged 1950s and 1960s. Pristine all-white on a black and white landscape. Madrid were the kings of football's old money.

In a vibrant era of colour images, all-white meant not only Tbilisi, but it also spoke of Borussia Mönchengladbach, Club Brugge, Dynamo Kyiv and Anderlecht, amongst many others. I'm not entirely certain that part of Tottenham Hotspur's European adventures of the 1960s, 1970s and 1980s weren't partly wind-assisted by their use of all-white. AC Milan have famously favoured using the very same colours, when on European trophy-hunting expeditions of their own.

So closely associated to the European Cup Winners' Cup, having contested three successive finals between 1976 and 1978, twice winners, Anderlecht enjoyed a swift second European coming in 1982/83.

Harbouring only a small number of survivors from the last of those Cup Winners' Cup finals, while Rob Rensenbrink and François Van der Elst were long gone, Anderlecht still retained the services of Hugo Broos, Franky Vercauteren and Ludo Coeck, while being increasingly enveloped by a Danish influence which was led by Morten Oslen, Henrik Andersen, Per Frimann and Kenneth Brylle. In the summer of 1983 Frank Arnesen would also arrive at the Constant Vanden Stock Stadium.

Coached by the former Anderlecht playing legend, Paul Van Himst, in a season where the club would narrowly miss out on the Belgian First Division title, the UEFA Cup offered solace, in a gliding run where Anderlecht were measured, yet devastating.

Scoring 27 goals en route to the 1983 UEFA Cup Final, in the first three rounds Anderlecht did the groundwork in the first leg on all three occasions, stacking up convincing home victories, before being drawn into carefree and closely contested away legs, overcoming KPT Kuopio, the fast maturing FC Porto and FK Sarajevo, before the winter closure.

A third of their goals scored by the prolific Erwin Vandenbergh up to this point, from the quarter-finals the challenges were just as impressively navigated, except in reverse. Narrow away victories picked off in the first leg, followed by expressive, expansive football in the second leg, took Anderlecht into the final, past Valencia in the last eight, then the more subtle dangers posed by Bohemians of Prague in the semi-finals.

In the final, Anderlecht found themselves up against Benfica and Sven-Göran Eriksson, the man who 12 months earlier had taken IFK Göteborg to their incredible UEFA Cup glory. Now he was overseeing a renaissance in Portuguese football, in an environment where the continental fortunes of the nation's biggest club had drifted a considerable way since they had last reached a major European final 15 years ago. It had been a decay which had gone hand in hand with the diminishing returns of a national team that had not qualified for a major international tournament since the 1966 World Cup.

While Eriksson and Benfica would fall just short of restoring their halcyon days of the 1960s, in turn failing to banish the curse that footballing fables dictate Béla Guttmann to have cast upon the club, a brighter collective horizon was unfolding, and the following year Portugal would roar into the semi-finals of the 1984 European Championship, eight of the squad coming from the Estádio da Luz. Added to this, Porto would reach the final of the Cup Winners' Cup, going on to win the European Cup in 1987.

Unbeaten on their run to the final, Benfica retreated to Lisbon with a 1-0 defeat, plus a red card and second-leg suspension for José Luís, who really should have been joined by Brylle, the former reacting to a poor challenge by the latter.

Eriksson's side had sufficiently frustrated Anderlecht, who were restricted to a Brylle header that had unerring similarities to one of the goals that had beaten Bohemians in the semi-final; Vercauteren, after a spectacular piece of skill, curled in a beautiful cross with the outside of his left foot, for Brylle to head past a furious Manuel Bento.

A promising result, it could have been so much better for Benfica, as Fernando Chalana uncharacteristically missed two golden opportunities, slicing one wide when clean through, while striking the Anderlecht crossbar with the goal unguarded, deceived by an unfortunate bobble of the ball.

A fortnight later, it was a mature performance that saw Anderlecht over the line. Refusing to panic when Shéu opened the scoring in the 32nd minute, it was a beautifully weighted

Vercauteren cross that the Spanish-born Juan Lozano met with a back-post header just seven minutes later to stun a capacity Estádio da Luz into silence.

Happy to let Benfica come at them in the second half, Anderlecht played to a safety-first ethos as Eriksson's side threw themselves into attack. Nené missed a golden opportunity, while the substitute Zoran Filipović had a perfectly good goal disallowed, which denied the game a resounding climax, an unfortunate case of refereeing myopia from the high-profile Charles Corver. Corver was best known as the man who saw nothing wrong the previous year when Harald Schumacher rendered Patrick Battiston unconscious during the West Germany vs France World Cup semi-final in Seville.

As holders, Anderlecht swept to the final once more, but not without leaving a legacy of controversy behind them.

Neither Bryne FK nor Baník Ostrava offered Anderlecht too many headaches in the opening rounds, with the Belgians building first-leg leads to take to Norway and Czechoslovakia respectively, before making harder work than necessary out of their third-round encounter with Lens, edging through 2-1 on aggregate, yet scoring all three goals.

The Anderlecht goalkeeper, Jacques Munaron, scored a catastrophic 89th-minute, first-leg own goal at the Stade Félix-Bollaert to cancel out Vandenburgh's excellent and precious away goal, which he'd procured only two minutes earlier.

Just what was going through Munaron's mind as he attempted to control Brylle's back pass with his right foot, during an era when it was perfectly within the laws of the game to pick the ball up, only he will know, a ball that was travelling at sedate enough a speed for Olsen to let it roll through his legs, on its journey to the goalkeeper behind him.

In mitigating circumstances, Munaron was likely aiming to waste a few seconds with the ball at his feet, before picking it up, while a sizeable projectile was thrown in his direction from the Lens supporters behind his goal. Although, whether Munaron grasped this as a convenient reason to explain his aberration is wide open to interpretation.

Either way, violent riots erupted upon the terraces and the second leg provided a tinderbox atmosphere, both on the pitch and in the stands. Walter De Greef scored the only goal, after Anderlecht had already had what appeared to be a perfectly good goal disallowed.

More drama and footballing electricity lay ahead for Anderlecht into the new year. Spartak Moscow, in the quarter-finals, gave them food for thought, by walking away from the first leg, in Brussels, with two away goals.

A spectacular game of goals and incidents, Spartak took the lead in true Iron Curtain fashion, with a blinding flash of a counter-attack, in which Sergei Rodionov scored from just inside the penalty area, guiding the ball in with the outside of his right foot in the 18th minute.

Ten minutes later, high comedy and unconcealed subterfuge then took place, as, when Brylle headed the ball over the committed Rinat Dasayev, Sergei Bazulev pulled off an admirable double-fisted save on the goal line, when it looked like he might have reached the looping effort with the head he was soon hanging in sheepish shame.

Equaliser procured, Brylle himself calmly slotted the ball to Dasayev's right, as the legendary Soviet international dived the other way. Shortly before the interval, he had struck again, with a wonderful diving header from an unforgiving Vercauteren cross.

No further goals added until the last nine minutes, three would then arrive in a remarkable climax to the game that included a Vercauteren free kick, which caught out Dasayev as it dipped towards the foot of his left-hand post, a swift Valeri Gladilin riposte for Spartak, which took advantage of a slumbering Anderlecht defence and, finally, a harsh penalty, awarded against Vladimir Sochnov, which Brylle converted to complete his hat-trick.

Frustrated in a return game that took place in Tbilisi, Spartak missed a golden opportunity early in the second half, when Munaron pulled off an excellent save from a Yuri Gavrilov penalty. While Spartak did eventually make a breakthrough, Rodionov again on target, it was a well-taken goal that came too late to make the ultimate difference. A fine Spartak side, they had stunned Aston Villa with a late winner at Villa Park in the second round and, had fate smiled differently in their direction against Anderlecht, then they might well have come close to taking the trophy to Moscow, 21 years prior to CSKA managing to do so in 2005.

Anderlecht advanced towards a semi-final date of infamy with Nottingham Forest – an encounter that would forever tarnish the talent and reputation of what was a magnificent team.

Forest had been quite imperious on their run to the semi-final and the spectre of a second all-English UEFA Cup Final was one to be taken very seriously. Still unbeaten as they prepared to face Anderlecht, Brian Clough's side had undergone a period of transformation since their meteoric rise, a rise overseen by what was a polarising but legendary manager, who lifted the club out of a five-year Second Division exile, from where they were crowned league champions at the first time of asking, before going on to win back-to-back European Cups, all the while finding the spare time to reach three successive League Cup finals.

Having dismantled his all-conquering squad with an ill-advised haste, by the time of the 1983/84 Forest vintage, Clough had lost his talented right-hand man, Peter Taylor, while of the squad that won the second of their European Cups in 1980, only Viv Anderson, Gary Mills, Ian Bowyer and Garry Birtles were on duty against Anderlecht in the last four of the UEFA Cup four years later.

Perhaps, in a subconscious concession that Clough had made too many changes, too quickly, Mills, Bowyer and Birtles had departed the club only to later return. Birtles rejoined Forest after a disastrous spell at Manchester United, while Anderson was just a couple of months away from his own transfer, to Arsenal.

Clough had offset his over-eagerness for wholesale change by placing his trust in the City Ground youth system, a system that had produced talents such as Chris Fairclough, Colin Walsh and Steve Hodge, who were in turn supplemented by an eagle-eyed scouting network that had unearthed Steve Wigley from Curzon Ashton and Peter Davenport from Cammell Laird respectively.

With the reliable goalkeeping of Hans van Breukelen to call upon, this was a Forest side that was threatening a return to trophy-winning ways. While early exits had been made from the domestic cups, Forest would end the season in third place in the First Division, a promising league campaign in which they were always a couple of steps behind the champions, Liverpool.

The UEFA Cup, however, offered the very real possibility of a first piece of silverware in four years. Vorwärts Frankfurt were cruised past in the first round, before Forest impressively saw off a PSV Eindhoven side that Van Breukelen would go on to join in the summer of 1984, after Clough took exception to his goalkeeper's enthusiasm for international football.

A 'Battle of Britain' tie against Celtic could easily have brought a third-round exit, after Celtic departed a frozen Nottinghamshire with a valuable, but frustrating, goalless draw from the first leg, after largely dominating a game in which the crowd was evenly split, in terms of support for the two teams. With a sold-out away allocation of 11,500, many other pockets of Celtic's support were dotted around the City Ground and the collapse of a barrier and resultant crush saw the game held up for 11 minutes, while emergency repairs were made.

Widely thought to have all the work to do, Forest prevailed at Celtic Park a fortnight later; a Clough masterclass and goals from Hodge and Walsh saw the visitors through. It was as if Celtic played in constant fear of the away goal, rather than to their own strengths, strengths that had previously taken them past Sporting CP in a stunning second-leg fightback in the previous round that had led the green and white half of Glasgow to be optimistic that they might be on the brink of reliving their great European adventures of the 1960s and the first half of the 1970s.

In the slipstream of Forest's excellent performances, it came as something of a surprise that they then laboured past Sturm Graz in the quarter-finals, only booking their place in the semi-final thanks to a penalty from Walsh in the 116th minute of the second leg in Austria.

Handed the holders in the semi-finals, Forest's 2-0 first-leg victory was earned through two late Hodge headers, at the end of what had been a tense and closely contested game, in which Clough had had to come up with a plan that didn't include Birtles and the former Ipswich Town playmaker, Frans Thijssen, both of whom were out injured.

Up until Hodge's double intervention, Forest had been restricted to a series of dangerous, but uncapitalised, set pieces and an early, glaring miss by Mills. In reply, Anderlecht had created an increasing number of opportunities of their own during the second half, which left Hodge's goals feeling as if they were scored against the run of play.

Heading to the Constant Vanden Stock Stadium with a compelling lead to protect and an unchanged starting line-up, Forest were walking into a pre-paid ambush.

In 1997, one of football's worst-kept secrets was finally admitted to by Anderlecht, when they confessed that they had bribed the Spanish referee, Emilio Guruceta Muro, to facilitate a result that would be good enough to take them into the 1984 UEFA Cup Final. The referee in question had died a decade earlier, in a car crash, in the historic Aragon town of Fraga, and Anderlecht were reputedly being blackmailed over the information being publicly outed.

Further subterfuge was layered on top, when it emerged that UEFA had known of Anderlecht's guilt for several years before its public airing. An eventual, retrospective one-season ban from European competition was imposed on the club, but none of this changed the landscape of 1984 and even that ban was evaded, due to an appeal that went beyond UEFA.

A 3-0 victory sent Anderlecht into the final; 90 minutes of football where very little made sense, inclusive of Guruceta disallowing what appeared to be a perfectly good Anderlecht goal when the scoreline stood at 1-0.

Just what Guruceta was thinking at that point is entirely debateable. Did he forget his arrangement? Had he cultivated cold feet about the situation? Scifo had opened the scoring with a fine strike and, as Anderlecht were within the process of creating the perfect attacking momentum, a second goal here for the home side would have been entirely in keeping with what had already unfolded.

Essentially, Anderlecht were offering to make Guruceta's evening an easy one, yet with the excellent goalkeeping of Van Breukelen threatening to keep the Belgians at bay, it took the most suspicious of penalty decisions to level the tie on aggregate.

Brylle, the man to win the penalty, then converted it too. It was a passage of play that represented the perfect microcosm of this vintage of Anderlecht, as Brylle's turn to evade Kenny Swain was a truly special piece of skill, which was then offset by his fall to the turf, when the only part of the Forest full-back to touch the Danish international was his shadow.

With half an hour to go, this is where the alarm bells rang. Had Anderlecht's perfectly good goal in the first half stood, then they likely sweep to a victory that arouses no suspicion at all, as, for most of the game, it was a duel between Anderlecht and Van Breukelen. Between the home side's first and second goal, their disallowed strike was kept company by a string of near misses and included fine goalkeeping, the post being hit and a goal-line clearance. Yet, obvious ambiguity was permitted to envelop the game.

Anderlecht's second goal sparked not only on-pitch uproar, but violence also broke out upon the terraces of the Constant Vanden Stock Stadium.

Swinging back in the opposite direction, Anderlecht's winning goal was a beautifully crafted one, where Vandenbergh took the ball on his chest, cut between two Forest defenders and looped it over the helpless Van Breukelen. It was a goal which stemmed from the visitors needlessly losing possession in their own half.

Drama unconfined, but not completed, there was still time for Forest to be denied a law-abiding away goal that should have taken them through to the final, Paul Hart heading in from a late desperate corner in a stunning last roll of the dice.

Explosive scenes at the final whistle saw more violence erupt upon the terraces, while a furious Van Breukelen volleyed the ball in anger towards Guruceta, only narrowly missing his fleeing target. Clough, meanwhile, made a point of seeking the official out, to shake his hand and deliver a long, knowing and withering stare.

While corruption and bribery were hardly unique in football, this game was unique in the way it became such a high-profile incident, despite being so one-sided an encounter. Anderlecht were a great team in their own right, with talent and skill in abundance, and put in a performance that didn't need external assistance. Vanden Stock will, of course, not have been able to have forecast that, which makes it bespoke in the way the scandal belatedly exploded in the club's face and how they avoided significant punishment either at the time or retrospectively, apart from the smudging of their reputation.

Instead of Forest breathing a sigh of relief at riding their luck in Brussels and moving onward to the second all-English UEFA Cup Final, it was left to Tottenham Hotspur to put one of European football's biggest wrongs, at least partially, right.

The 1984 UEFA Cup Final would provide a fitting crescendo to the Keith Burkinshaw era at White Hart Lane and, while it was a success that marked the end of one north London epoch, it was an honour that was clinched by unexpected Tottenham heroes.

Burkinshaw had been in the job for an eventful eight years, taking over from the Arsenal-bound Terry Neill in the summer of 1976, immediately leading Tottenham into the Second Division before returning them, not only to the First Division at the first time of asking, but onward to a position of great prominence once again.

In future eras, Burkinshaw wouldn't have been afforded the chance to regenerate a big football club, after guiding it to relegation in his first season at the helm, but White Hart Lane reaped the rewards of patience, and back-to-back FA Cup wins in 1981 and 1982 were the biggest prizes that Burkinshaw had landed, prior to what was to be his swansong season in charge.

As gratefully received a return to the type of glory days that the club had become accustomed to during the Bill Nicholson era, Tottenham had come very close to other success in addition to those FA Cups. They came to within three minutes of winning the 1982 League Cup Final, against Liverpool, while in the very same season they also narrowly lost out to Barcelona in the semi-finals of the Cup Winners' Cup. Burkinshaw had also led them to greater league consistency, without sacrificing a style of play that was dictated by the bewitching Glenn Hoddle, in conjunction with the aesthetically pleasing Osvaldo Ardiles, and until his 1983 departure, Ricardo Villa.

More than a simple homage to flair, Burkinshaw's Tottenham was built upon a solid defensive foundation and was blessed with a forward line that could be punishingly prolific. It was also a team that could still draw on the metronomic presence of Steve Perryman, the only survivor of the club's 1972 UEFA Cup Final-winning team.

In Ray Clemence, they had a goalkeeper who had won the competition in 1973 and 1976, casting a watchful eye over a balanced back line of the very talented Danny Thomas, the wonderfully consistent Chris Hughton and the underrated central defensive partnership of Graham Roberts and Paul Miller.

The arrival of Thomas from Coventry City and the blossoming of Roberts and Miller's partnership had allowed Perryman to move back into midfield, having become something of a valuable nomad in Burkinshaw's team in recent seasons, after making a name for himself in the centre of midfield when breaking through under Nicholson.

Competition for places fierce in midfield, beyond Perryman, Hoddle and Ardiles, Tottenham could also call on the intelligence of Micky Hazard and the dependable Garry Brooke. Gary Stevens and Tony Galvin completed this rich midfield collective of options that Burkinshaw had brought together.

Chief beneficiaries of the opportunities created were the soon-to-be Barcelona-bound Steve Archibald and the deceptive Mark Falco, whose form was impressive enough to leave the experienced Garth Crooks and Alan Brazil in the shadows, to the extent that Crooks was allowed to take in a loan spell with Manchester United, while Brazil would also head to Old Trafford at the end of the season, on a permanent deal.

Merciless against Drogheda United in the first round, Tottenham advanced with a 14-0 aggregate win – the first six obtained at a partisan United Park, a game played on the narrowest pitch the laws of football allows, the remainder of the goals procured back at White Hart Lane, where Burkinshaw offered no respite to the Irish side, when fielding his strongest available 11 and handing them a remit to entertain those who had clicked through the turnstiles, for what was a game that was free of jeopardy.

While Tottenham might have been merciless in how they dealt with Drogheda, there was a different display of class at the end of the second leg, when Perryman led his team-mates in applauding the visitors off the pitch.

Sterner tests lay ahead for Tottenham before the turn of the year in the UEFA Cup. The second round brought a reunion with Feyenoord, fast approaching a decade beyond them facing each other in the explosive 1974 final.

Despite boasting the ageing influence of Johan Cruyff, it was the 21-year-old Ruud Gullit that Burkinshaw was most wary of. The Tottenham manager had observed Feyenoord face PSV, just three days prior to the first leg, a top-of-the-table Eredivisie clash in which Gullit had begun in defence, before moving into midfield, eventually ending the game up front, as his team unsuccessfully sought to turn a draw into a win.

Feyenoord would go on to clinch their domestic double, and while they had dispatched St Mirren in the first round, Tottenham would prove too strong this time around, in a set of games that was billed as Hoddle vs Cruyff.

At White Hart Lane, on an evening when every attempt was made to defuse any potential reprisals for the violence and result of 1974, inclusive of a pre-match skydiving display, Tottenham were ruthless and careless at a ratio of 2:1. Accumulating four goals within a 22-minute span of the first half, the carelessness came in the last 15 minutes, when two away goals were conceded.

After a brace each for Archibald and Galvin, Cruyff clawed Feyenoord's first goal back, before Ivan Nielsen made the second leg look a very different proposition with their second. From 4-0 down in 39 minutes, Feyenoord returned to Rotterdam knowing that a 2-0 victory would be enough to see them through, the very same scoreline that they had beaten Tottenham by in the 1974 final.

Hoddle was the key to each of Tottenham's goals. With great artistry in the build-up, they were all beautifully crafted openings that were enthusiastically converted and massively valuable. Meanwhile, Cruyff's interjection was unsurprisingly majestic. Gullit, however, was lost to an early injury, withdrawn midway through the first half.

At De Kuip a fortnight later, amid scenes of carnage on the terraces, before, during and after the game, Tottenham put in the complete performance. Hoddle outstanding, once again, a goal in each half, the first from Hughton, the second by Galvin, secured Tottenham a 2-0 win to comfortably progress to the third round, on an evening when Clemence pulled off two magnificent saves.

Handed a gargantuan task next, Tottenham headed to the Olympiastadion to face Bayern Munich, the very same venue and team where and against whom they had been beaten 4-1 in the Cup Winners' Cup the previous season.

Without the services of Ardiles, Mabbutt and Galvin, Tottenham showed no signs of psychological scarring from their prior mauling in Munich, where on a frozen night of temperatures of -10, they came to within six minutes of emerging with a hard-earned goalless draw, until falling to a counter-attack, facilitated by Søren Lerby and executed by Michael Rummenigge, a move that began with an off-the-ball incident that left Falco on the turf.

Back at White Hart Lane, Hoddle was again imperious, having been kept on the periphery in Munich, to the extent that Franz Beckenbauer had been amongst his critics. With a point to prove, Hoddle ensured that mocking Germanic words were eaten.

Still counting the cost of injuries, Burkinshaw had been bold in fielding two 18-year-old wingers, in the shapes of Ally Dick and Richard Cooke. The ploy worked perfectly, however, as Bayern were not only unfamiliar with the duo but combined with the determination of Hoddle it made for an uncomfortable night in north London for Udo Lattek's team.

After just 12 minutes, Falco struck the post, a near miss that acted as a clarion call for attack after attack to flow. Perryman was soon seeing a backward header being cleared from the goal line, Hoddle came close with a deflected free kick, an Archibald volley dipped just over Jean-Marie Pfaff's crossbar, a Stevens volley was blocked at close range, while another Hoddle opportunity was pushed over the bar by Pfaff, after a delicate trademark lob.

Incredibly, still goalless at half-time, Tottenham could have been forgiven for thinking it wasn't going to be their night, yet they started the second half in the same frame of attacking mind as they had ended the first.

It took just five further minutes for Tottenham to make their deserved breakthrough, when a floated Hoddle free kick was headed back across goal by Roberts, from where Archibald drilled the ball past Pfaff to level the aggregate scoreline.

Having fought so hard to restore the aggregate parity, Tottenham seemed to freeze for a spell, allowing Bayern the encouragement to strike forward. The Rummenigge brothers both saw chances fall their way, Karl-Heinz forcing Clemence into another fine save, while, when Thomas misjudged a situation, Michael was unable to take advantage, possibly surprised that an opening had presented itself.

In a much more even and nervous game after Archibald's goal, Tottenham's winner was a piece of magic that was created by Hoddle and taken by Falco. With his back to goal around 30 yards out and travelling towards his own half, Hoddle picked out a stunning reverse, looping ball, having caught the run of Falco out of the corner of his eye. The striker latched on to it, sending a diagonal shot across the Bayern penalty area, just out of Pfaff's reach, where it bounced off the inside of the post and spun, seemingly in slow motion, over the line.

A coming together that was always going to leave the winner as one of the favourites to lift the trophy, Tottenham were drawn to face FK Austria Wien in the quarter-finals, followed by Hajduk Split in the semi-finals. These were two challenges that brought different dangers to the ones that had been posed by Feyenoord and Bayern.

Whereas Feyenoord and Bayern represented A-list opponents, against whom Tottenham knew exactly the heights they would have to hit to progress, Wien and Hajduk were much more subtle and mysterious foes.

Within this, Tottenham being cast in the role of favourites seemed to be an uncomfortable fit, at a time when Burkinshaw's side were struggling to shake a run of poor form, in which they had won only four of their next 14 First Division fixtures since overcoming Bayern. They had also toppled out of the FA Cup, to Norwich City, in a fourth-round replay.

Added to this, they had lost the services of the in-form Clemence, while Hoddle was struggling to regain his own fitness after a spell on the sidelines. Miller, Roberts and Archibald were all rated as doubtful, prior to the arrival at White Hart Lane of Wien. It made for a nervous Tottenham performance in the quarter-final, first leg.

All three available, but not fully fit, with all his eggs now in his UEFA Cup basket, Burkinshaw fielded Miller, Roberts and Archibald and it would prove to be an evening of mixed fortunes for the Scottish international.

One goal scored, another disallowed, an open goal missed, also finding himself struck by the ball on the posterior when a Perryman effort came hurtling his way, Archibald didn't even have time to turn the other cheek. When he found the net, it was a goal that took almost an hour in coming and it was soon followed by a determined, but clumsily plundered second goal, this time by Brazil.

A healthy lead to take to Austria, relieved to have Clemence at his disposal once more and with other injured players beginning to drift back into contention, Burkinshaw was able to leave Thomas and the returning Falco on the bench. With the generally misfiring Brazil sneaking the opening goal, it was a gamble that paid off handsomely.

Tottenham's other goal being a wonderful strike into the top corner by Ardiles, Wien's consolation for their free-flowing style of football was to come away from the second leg with a deserved draw, via two equalisers, the first a Herbert Prohaska penalty, after Stevens's abruptness in his own penalty area, the second cleverly taken by the veteran Hungarian international, Tibor Nyilasi.

It left Hajduk as Tottenham's last hurdle in their bid to reach a first major European final in a decade. In Split, Burkinshaw's team walked away with a 2-1 reversal, against opponents that mixed a strong defence with a wider physical approach to the game, laced with a touch of flair.

Until the 67th minute, however, it appeared as if Tottenham were set to return home with a dream victory,thanks to some quick thinking from Falco, who turned the ball in after it was swiftly returned to him in the Hajduk 18-yard box after the striker had had a penalty saved, which had been awarded for the most ridiculous handball imaginable.

Hajduk's late rally was a compelling one, not only scoring two goals, but forcing Tottenham into a desperate rearguard action, on a night of torrential rain. Minus the suspended Stevens, plus Hoddle, after he had been left with no option but to go under the knife for an operation on his troublesome Achilles, just like the games against Wien, the games against Hajduk were heavily booby-trapped ones. Tottenham were subsequently undone by one deflection and a six-yard-box scramble.

In the return game, Tottenham were left to nervously rely upon the 1-0 victory that would be enough to take them through on the away-goals rule. Hazard, their chief source of ingenuity, in the continuing absences of Hoddle and Ardiles, scored the only goal with a smartly taken free kick, beating the outstanding Zoran Simović.

Simović had kept Hadjuk in the game with a string of fine saves, denying Falco, Stevens, Roberts, Hughton and Archibald, in turn inspiring the Yugoslavs to launch themselves forward in search of the goal that would instead take them into the final. Parks, who had returned as cover for the injured Clemence once again, in Split, produced his own brilliant reaction to ensure it was Tottenham who would go on to face Anderlecht.

In the first leg of the final at the Constant Vanden Stock Stadium, Tottenham went toe-to-toe with their hosts, despite being deprived of Hoddle, Ardiles, Clemence and Mabbutt. Clemence was, however, fit enough to take up a place on the bench.

Tragedy marred the game, when the 18-year-old Irishman Brian Flanagan was shot dead by the Brussels bartender, Albert Neuckermans, in a fatal response to further instances of violence and destruction. Sadly, revenge attacks would be launched on the streets of north London a fortnight later.

On the pitch, in a hard-working performance and one which came to within five minutes of being rewarded with an incredible victory, Tottenham took the lead through a Miller header in the 57th minute. Other chances came at both ends, inclusive of Falco passing up an open goal, but, just as Burkinshaw and his players could sense the final whistle was getting closer, Anderlecht levelled the score with five minutes remaining, Olsen in the right place at the right time to force the ball home after a fine reaction save from Parks.

Anderlecht frustrated but relieved, Tottenham pleased but disappointed, it set the second leg up nicely, but, due to the brandishing of a yellow card, it would be a game in which Burkinshaw would have to do without his captain. Perryman was suspended and it meant that Mabbutt was pushed back into action.

The initial 90 minutes of the second leg at White Hart Lane almost read like a complete role reversal of the first game. This time, it was Anderlecht who opened the scoring around the hour mark; this time, it was Tottenham who forced in the late equaliser. Alexandre Czerniatynski took a beautiful goal for the visitors, while Roberts was the hero with a late flourish for the hosts.

There was much to Roberts's equaliser that widely goes forgotten. In a frenzied goalmouth scramble, Falco had a legitimate appeal for a penalty ignored, while Ardiles, thrown on as a substitute, contrived to strike the underside of Munaron's crossbar from around two or three yards.

Yet, as soon as Anderlecht cleared the ball, it was just as quickly delivered once again, thanks to a brilliant looping cross from Hazard, upon which it found Roberts, who stunningly brought it down on his chest, before evading the desperate lunges of Anderlecht's defenders, to steer the ball past the now-exposed Munaron from six yards.

In a dramatic finale, extra time couldn't separate the two sides, and it meant that a penalty shoot-out would decide the 1984 UEFA Cup Final. Burkinshaw's last act as Tottenham manager was to be a duel from 12 yards, with the UEFA Cup as the prize.

While Roberts, as Tottenham's stand-in captain, led by example, confidently dispatching their first penalty, Olsen saw his effort saved by Parks, pushing the ball away to his left. An already electric White Hart Lane was set to go nuclear.

The next six penalties were scored: Falco, Grün, Stevens, Scifo, Archibald and Vercauteren all converted with varying techniques, yet all with at the very least an outer aura of confidence. It was then the turn of Thomas.

Despite his effort being better-placed than some which found the net, the Tottenham full-back's penalty was saved. As the clearly devastated Thomas returned to the centre circle he was consoled by Roberts and Archibald on the pitch and by the Spurs fans all around the stadium, as they sang his name loudly from the terraces.

But, with one last twist in the tale, Parks wrote his name in Tottenham and UEFA Cup folklore, as he pulled off a second spectacular save, this time from the stunned Arnór Guðjohnsen, father of the future Chelsea and Barcelona striker, Eiður. The UEFA Cup was once again in the possession of Tottenham, while Burkinshaw had his wildly celebrated parting gift to the club.

In a season where Tottenham had been bedevilled by a spate of injuries, it was perhaps an act of karma that Vandenbergh was ruled out of the game, picking up an injury 24 hours beforehand. Anderlecht, purveyors of some outstanding football during the 120 minutes, missed his appetite for goals, just as much as they had missed Vercauteren's influence for all but 26 minutes of the first leg, when restricted to only a cameo appearance as a substitute.

With Burkinshaw succeeded by his assistant, Peter Shreeves, Tottenham would go out as holders in the quarter-finals the following season, never to again contest the UEFA Cup within its two-legged final format. Yet, in two defined eras, bridged only by Perryman, White Hart Lane was witness to greatness in the tournament. Pioneers, trendsetters, providers of immense drama and a fair modicum of style, the UEFA Cup seemed a very comfortable fit for the Edmonton area of north London.

Dr Luiz Murgel, the Brazilian delegate, hands over the Jules Rimet trophy prior to the 1966 World Cup to Sir Stanley Rous and Ottorino Barassi, who along with Ernst Thommen were the founders of the Inter-Cities Fairs Cup.

Billy Bremner and Leeds United win the last European Fairs Cup, defeating Juventus in the 1971 final. By the last playing of the tournament, it had finally taken on the shape that the UEFA Cup would carry for the next 26 years.

Ottorino Barassi died in November 1971, just outliving the Inter-Cities Fairs Cup tournament he helped create. He also hid the Jules Rimet trophy under his bed during the Second World War, ensuring it could not be used as a propaganda tool.

Tottenham Hotspur's Martin Chivers outjumps Wolverhampton Wanderers' Frank Munro, to head home the opening goal of the 1972 UEFA Cup Final, at Molineux.

A swamped Tommy Smith holds on to the UEFA Cup, after Liverpool stubbornly repelled Borussia Mönchengladbach's second leg fightback at the Bökelbergstadion, during the 1973 final.

Violence erupted in Rotterdam, between Feyenoord and Tottenham Hotspur supporters, before, during and after the Dutch club's victory in the second leg of the 1974 final.

Allan Simonsen, Jupp Heynckes, Hans-Jürgen Wittkamp and Hans Klinkhammer, on their lap of honour for Borussia Mönchengladbach, at the Diekman Stadion, after they convincingly beat Twente in the 1975 final, for their first UEFA Cup success.

Juventus celebrate winning not only their first UEFA Cup, but their first major European success, and the first of 13 trophies that the club won within Giovanni Trapattoni's first spell as head coach. They narrowly defeated Athletic Club in the 1977 final.

Emlyn Hughes lifts the UEFA Cup, after Liverpool's 1-1 draw against Club Brugge is enough to win the tournament for the second time in three years. In the celebrations that followed, the base of the trophy detached from the top portion.

Bastia supporters during the first leg of the 1978 final, against PSV Eindhoven. A waterlogged pitch at the Stade Armand-Cesari ruined the Corsican club's chances of success.

Berti Vogts leads out the Borussia Mönchengladbach team for the second leg of the 1979 final, at the Rheinstadion, in Düsseldorf. A disputed Allan Simonsen penalty gave them their second UEFA Cup success.

Christian Kulik and his Borussia Mönchengladbach team-mates celebrate his equaliser, against Eintracht Frankfurt, in the first leg of the 1980 final, at the Bökelbergstadion. Frankfurt prevailed in the second leg, however, in what was the last of Mönchengladbach's four finals.

Frans Thijssen and Arnold Mühren take time to pose for the cameras prior to the first leg of the 1981 final, at Portman Road.

IFK Göteborg's pensive, 34-year-old head coach, Sven-Göran Eriksson watches on as his team closes in on winning the 1982 final, at Hamburger SV's Volksparkstadion. Within weeks, he took charge of Benfica, who he would take to the 1983 final.

Chapter Nine

The Appliance of Science

DURING THE first half of the 1980s, a combination of fate and the compelling rise of both old and new, yet dormant, rivals in the Basque Country to the north, and in Catalonia to the east, meant that Real Madrid were made to look impressively human and vulnerable, at a time when the Human League and Duran Duran were all the rage.

When Madrid won the LaLiga title in 1979/80, there would have been incredulous retorts had you suggested to the average, common or garden *Madridista* that they would be waiting six years to see their club crowned Spanish champions again.

In 1980/81, the Vujadin Boškov-led Madrid narrowly lost out on retaining their league title, edged out by Real Sociedad on the head-to-head rule, a league title that would have gone Madrid's way had it been played in the three-points-for-a-win era.

Despite having a month to prepare for it, more pain lay ahead for Boškov's side, when they were beaten in the 1981 European Cup Final by Liverpool in Paris – a poor spectacle played out on long grass at the Parc des Princes that was decided by a late winning goal from an unexpected source: Alan Kennedy.

Domestically, it was the second of three successive seasons where Sociedad played a big role in the LaLiga title race, going on to win it again in 1981/82, having agonisingly missed out in 1979/80, before Athletic Club took the spoils in 1982/83 and

1983/84, succeeded by the Terry Venables-inspired Barcelona in 1984/85.

Concerning times for Madrid, 1982/83 had been particularly painful, as, under the leadership of Alfredo Di Stefano, a promising campaign in which they were fighting on all fronts ended with *Los Blancos* losing out on all prizes.

A title race lost to Athletic by one point, Madrid also fell short against Barcelona in the finals of both the Copa del Rey and the short-lived Copa de la Liga, while in Europe, they were beaten in the 1983 European Cup Winners' Cup Final too, by Alex Ferguson's Aberdeen. To complete the set, they had also been vanquished earlier in the season, by Sociedad, in the Supercopa de España.

Di Stefano relinquished the role of head coach at the end of the 1983/84 season, again having missed out on the major honours, upon where he was succeeded by another former Madrid player, Amancio Amaro.

Amaro had stunningly led the Madrid reserve side, Castilla, to the 1983/84 Segunda División title. Whereas his title-winning side weren't allowed to be promoted, he was, and Amaro inherited a Madrid squad that already contained a selection of his Castilla graduates, after Di Stefano had elevated several throughout his last season in charge.

The pick of this crop was a collective that went by the name of *La Quinta del Buitre*. Led by the stylish goal-getter Emilio Butragueño, whose own nickname was *El Buitre*, he was joined in this group of talent by Manolo Sanchís, Rafael Martín Vázquez, Míchel and Miguel Pardeza.

In the case of Butragueño, his talent was so prodigious that he was called into Spain's squad for the 1984 European Championship finals, despite only having started eight games for Madrid. Míchel, meanwhile, had been kept back with the Castilla side during 1983/84 as he was the dynamo that was propelling them to the Segunda title, yet his Madrid first-team debut had been a goalscoring one, as far back as April 1982, on a day when the Castilla squad stepped up to cover for the first team, who were out on strike.

Only Pardeza wouldn't make a lasting contribution at the Santiago Bernabéu; limited to the periphery of the side, he would eventually become a club legend at Real Zaragoza instead, inclusive of captaining them to victory over Arsenal in the 1995 Cup Winners' Cup Final.

Although all the components for success were in place, Amaro didn't last for the entirety of the 1984/85 season. Beaten convincingly on the opening day, at home to Barcelona, it was a result that saw him chasing control of the situation from the very beginning of the campaign. He was eventually unseated during the two-week gap between the first and second legs of the UEFA Cup semi-finals.

Domestic anxieties had been offset by a UEFA Cup run that had stunningly lurched back and forth from the sublime to the ridiculous. Ineptitude on Madrid's travels was largely matched by dominant home displays.

Embarrassing or simply convincing defeats were absorbed away to Wacker Innsbruck, Rijeka, Anderlecht and Internazionale, to the tune of one goal scored and 11 conceded. Conversely, in the quarter-finals, they met the challenge marvellously, emerging from the first leg at White Hart Lane, with a 1-0 win against the holders, Tottenham Hotspur.

Yet, at the Bernabéu, on their run to the final, they had scored an impressive 17 goals in the competition, conceding only once – a set of games that had included three second-leg fightbacks; in the cases of Anderlecht in the third round and Inter in the semi-finals, from 3-0 and 2-0 deficits respectively.

Amaro played his part in this phenomenon, his finest achievement in charge of Madrid being the club's 6-1 demolition of Anderlecht in December 1984. By the time of the semi-final comeback, against Inter, however, the Madrid hierarchy had turned once again, in a time of need, to the dependable Luis Molowny, who had already led the club for three separate spells.

Previously asked to take the helm, in the wake of the departures of the legendary Miguel Muñoz, the talented Miljan Miljanić and the highly celebrated Boškov, Molowny's varying periods as coach had lasted anything from a short few weeks to a couple of seasons, yet on each occasion he would successfully steady the ship and deliver trophies. Over the course of those four spells, Molowny had placed three LaLiga titles, two Copa del Reys, one Copa de la Liga and two UEFA Cups in the glittering Bernabéu trophy room. As far as Madrid were concerned, Molowny was the perfect man to right the wrongs of others.

Blessed by this influx of young talent and still possessing influential figures such as Santillana, Juanito and Uli Stielike, Madrid had also recruited Jorge Valdano in the summer of 1984. All the components were there in order to strike for success, but the catalyst was missing, until Molowny's reintroduction.

Madrid's back-to-back UEFA Cup successes acted as the springboard for the club's domestic domination of the second half of the decade, a domination that brought with it five successive LaLiga titles, yet, conversely, frustration in the European Cup, where they were beaten in the semi-finals three years in a row, 1987, 88 and 89. This, despite adding the talents of Hugo Sánchez in the summer of 1985 and, later, Bernd Schuster, to their already powerful squad.

Considered by some to be the Bernabéu's greatest European evening, Madrid's comeback against Anderlecht was a game that was arguably an aesthetic prototype of Spain's incredible victory over Denmark at the 1986 World Cup in some respects.

While Anderlecht were by no means shy in creating chances of their own, it just seemed that every time Madrid ventured forward, they were rewarded with a goal, the first of which came as early as the second minute, when Sanchís met a free kick swung in from the right, with his head.

Within half an hour, Madrid had levelled the aggregate score, the second headed home by Butragueño, after some intricate build-up play, while the third was claimed by Valdano, with Anderlecht carved open once again.

A stunning start, a mountain climbed, Madrid then allowed exuberance to get the better of them, as within four minutes of gaining parity, they handed Anderlecht back the advantage, as Per Frimann grabbed what should have been a crucial away goal, a goal that left Madrid needing to score two more.

Before half-time, Valdano had clawed one of those goals back, however, sliding the ball in to end the stunned silence that had enveloped the Bernabéu in the immediacy of Anderlecht's goal.

With 45 minutes in which to get the one goal that would be enough to take them through, Madrid bounced into the second half. Within four minutes of the restart, Butragueño had scored twice, the first a defiant finish, the second laced with an outrageous streak of skill.

A season in which the name Zanussi was emblazoned across Madrid's shirts, in the spirit of sponsorship, this was arguably Amaro's side administering the appliance of footballing science. Unexpectedly surviving into the new year in the UEFA Cup, Madrid then headed to north London, to take on the holders, Tottenham.

Madrid, swimming against the tide, emerged from White Hart Lane with a 1-0 victory, from a game that was far more expansive than the scoreline suggests. A marvellous 90 minutes, in which both teams squandered multiple chances to score, was settled by a Steve Perryman own goal when the ball hit him as it was pushed away by Ray Clemence, leaving the Tottenham captain with no say in the matter.

It was the first time that Tottenham had suffered a European defeat on home soil and the first time that Madrid had procured a win in England.

At the Bernabéu, a goalless draw was enough to see Madrid through to a semi-final clash with Inter, the third of four times the two clubs were drawn to face one another in European club competitions in six seasons, all of which would fall in favour of Madrid.

Beaten at the San Siro, 2-0, by an Inter that boasted the talents of Walter Zenga, Giuseppe Bergomi, Liam Brady, Karl-Heinz Rummenigge and Alessandro Altobelli, Amaro's Madrid were once again fighting a battle that appeared to be lost already when the two teams walked out at the Bernabéu for the second leg.

With Amaro having been relieved of his duties after Madrid's loss at Valencia, Molowny had overseen a numbing 1-0 home defeat at the hands of Hercules before the arrival of Inter. While it wasn't the ideal way to prepare for the visit of one of the Italian super clubs, Inter's recent run of Serie A form had included only one win in their last eight fixtures, a run that saw them drift out of a title race that had at one point been theirs for the taking.

What came next was a game that acted as a microcosm for the following year, under Molowny – a tentative start that spoke of a team lacking in confidence, which was soon swept away in a blizzard of white footballing heat.

Santillana bundled in the first goal, a scrappy affair that wouldn't have looked out of place had it been produced by a group of kids in the park. What the goal lacked in aesthetic beauty, however, it more than made up for in terms of what it then inspired. Within the next five minutes, Madrid had struck the post, had a debateable penalty claim turned down and seen a Míchel effort dip just over Zenga's crossbar.

Three minutes before the interval, Santillana made it 2-0 with a beautifully powered and directed header. It was a goal that served to antagonise Inter, however, as both Rummenigge and Altobelli came close, before half-time arrived.

Second half picking up where the first had ended, it was a game that featured a magnificent battle of brawn and brain between Stielike and Brady. While Santillana was the man whose goals brought Madrid back into the semi-final, it was Stielike's drive and determination that kept them there, at one point pulling off a stunning goal-line clearance from Altobelli.

A story of the old and the new, it was Míchel who snared Madrid's winning goal, just short of the hour, with a beautifully struck, low-flying effort that shot past the outstretched Zenga.

In the 1985 UEFA Cup Final, Madrid's opponents were the season's surprise package, Videoton. Only the second, and to this day last, Hungarian team to reach the final of a major European competition and a team that would have seemed a better fit to a Cup Winners' Cup Final, there was something majestically out of step about Videoton.

The following year, the Hungarian national team would compete in their last major international tournament for 30 years; this was by no means one of the golden eras of Hungarian football.

Videoton's route to the final was one that was littered with evocative eastern European disputes and shock outcomes against western giants. Dukla Praha, FK Partizan and FK Željezničar were navigated at the expense of varying degrees of sweat in the first round, third round and semi-final respectively.

While they had narrowly sneaked past Dukla and comfortably dealt with Partizan, Videoton had come to within three minutes of going out in the last four against Željezničar, until József Csuhay saved the day.

Interspersed between these eastern-flavoured encounters, Videoton saw off the rising force and future giant of French football, Paris Saint-Germain, in the second round, before stunningly defeating Manchester United in the quarter-finals.

It had been with an obscene sense of ease that Videoton unseated PSG, winning both legs of their tie, while Manchester United were shockingly overcome on penalties at the Sóstói Stadion after the two teams traded 1-0 wins.

By the time the first leg of the final came into view, Videoton were struggling to put a team together. Shorn of their most potent threats, not only were they without their prime source of goals, the suspended József Szabó, but they had also lost to injury his regular partner, Lajos Májer. Added to this, Videoton had had to absorb the equally significant blow of losing their best midfielder and talismanic captain, Ferenc Csongrádi.

Armed with only 13 vaguely fit players, even Csongrádi's replacement as captain, Tibor Végh, was an unexpected name on the Videoton team sheet for the first leg, while György Novath was only pushed into action up front due to Szabó and Májer being unavailable, Novath having only recently returned from knee surgery.

Míchel the inspiration, Madrid swept to a 3-0 victory in Székesfehérvár. With Míchel the scorer of the first, with a spectacular volley, and creator of the second and third for Santillana and Valdano respectively, Molowny's side were too strong for the depleted Videoton.

A similar *what if* scenario to Bastia's in 1978, except in reverse, Videoton's 1-0 win at the Bernabéu in the second leg, when they welcomed back Szabó, Májer and Csongrádi, acted as a teaser for what might have been across the breadth of the two games. Májer was the hero for Videoton in the Spanish capital.

Instead, it was to be Madrid winning their first major European honour in 19 years. A success that not only ended an unacceptable drought at the Bernabéu, but also set the foundation of a new wave of glory.

The following season, Videoton again appeared in the UEFA Cup, where this time they fell at the first hurdle, on away goals to Malmo, while Madrid once again went all the way, pairing their retention of the UEFA Cup with their first LaLiga title in six years.

Adding the goals of Hugo Sánchez and the subtle threat of Rafael Gordillo, Madrid didn't just win the 1985/86 LaLiga title, they ran away with it, yet their 1984/85 issues with European football on the road were carried over into the new UEFA Cup campaign.

Imperious at the Bernabéu, but prone to misadventure on their travels, Madrid lost all but once away from home in the 1985/86 UEFA Cup, scoring just twice, while at home they swept all-comers aside, only scoring fewer than three goals in any one game on one occasion, scoring 24 times over the course of their six home games.

A run to the final that included two incredible second-leg fightbacks and one near second-leg capitulation, by the time Madrid faced 1. FC Köln in the 1986 UEFA Cup Final they were back in their rightful place, at the forefront of both domestic and European football.

Brushing off the challenges of AEK of Athens and Chornomorets Odessa in the first two rounds, Madrid's defence of the UEFA Cup appeared to have come unstuck in the third round, when they exited the Rheinstadion with a chastening 5-1, third-round, first-leg loss at the hands of Borussia Mönchengladbach, a defeat that included a José Antonio Salguero own goal.

A resounding second-leg fightback, through a belief made possible by the previous season's overhauling of Anderlecht, saw the perfect display of the new Madrid that was blossoming under Molowny. Two goals each for Valdano and Santillana took *Los Blancos* through, with the clinching goal coming in the 89th minute, one which was almost stumbled over the goal line by the Madrid captain.

Santillana's winning goal wasn't symptomatic of the wider performance, however. While neither Míchel, nor Butragueño made it on to the scoresheet, both were massively influential in Madrid going through.

Míchel was the creator of Valdano's second goal, while Butragueño played a beautifully weighted role in Santillana's first, Madrid's third, a goal which stemmed from a bit of quick thinking from Juanito.

After sneaking past Neuchâtel Xamax in the quarter-finals, where Madrid almost threw away a hard-earned 3-0 first-leg victory, defeated 2-0 in Switzerland by a Neuchâtel side that was inspired by the former Madrid hero, Stielike, Molowny was handed yet another duel with Inter, in the semi-finals.

Almost as if Madrid couldn't function to their full capacity unless given a mountain to scale when it came to mid-1980s European challenges, they limped away from the first leg at the San Siro with a 3-1 defeat.

A marvellous game of football, in which Marco Tardelli opened the scoring before the Italian television director had removed the list of Madrid substitutes from the screen, chances came and went at both ends of the pitch.

Emerging with one away goal, Madrid could feasibly have headed home with four or five, while the three goals that Inter did claim could easily have been doubled, with Altobelli guilty of two stunning misses.

When Valdano forced the ball over the Inter goal line in the 87th minute, Madrid were in possession of a hugely valuable scoreline, which was then diluted within 60 seconds when, with his second own goal of the campaign, Salguero majestically lobbed his own goalkeeper, to make it 3-1 to the hosts.

Without the services of Valdano for the return game, Santillana was back, having sat out the first leg. It was at a vibrant Bernabéu that the *Madridistas* witnessed yet another startling UEFA Cup comeback, this time from a position where frustration seemed set to be the theme of the evening.

Made to wait until the 43rd minute to make the breakthrough, at 90 minutes Madrid had matched Inter's San Siro score of 3-1, to take the semi-final into extra time, with three of the four goals coming from the penalty spot, two to Sánchez and one to Brady.

Santillana was to prove the extra-time hero, with the two goals that took his team into the final once again, the first with his head, the second guided home after his almost 34-year-old legs carried him the type of distance that 108 minutes of football against Inter should have rendered impossible.

After the drama of Inter, and before that Neuchâtel and Mönchengladbach, the final was unsettlingly sedate. A 5-1 first-leg victory at the Bernabéu over a Köln side that had struggled domestically all season, despite possessing the quality of Harald Schumacher, Pierre Littbarski and Klaus Allofs, had seen the opening goal fall to the visitors. Madrid then streaked away into the distance with goals from Sánchez, Gordillo and two for Valdano, before the last of the night came from Santillana, who had made a late cameo appearance as a substitute. A 2-0 defeat followed a fortnight later in a Köln gesture that was too little, too late.

Back-to-back UEFA Cup winners, Madrid's lingering reunion with the LaLiga title and then the dawning of the Champions League meant that the Bernabéu would play host to just three more UEFA Cup campaigns, the best of those being a run to the semi-finals in 1991/92, while they have never graced the Europa League with their presence.

Arguably a footnote within a litany of bigger successes for Madrid, the UEFA Cup wins of 1985 and 1986 should never be downplayed. They acted as an oasis to an arid club, both in terms of it being almost two decades without gaining European honours, plus it being three years since they had won a trophy of any major description.

As stepping stones go, this UEFA Cup one was the foundation for the last great era of true domestic hegemony at the Bernabéu. A Madrid era that even their most ardent detractors tend to respect, if not for the flood of silverware, then certainly for the style with which they played.

Chapter Ten

The Great Pretenders

THE 1988 UEFA Cup Final was contested by two of football's great outliers.

Approaching the final, neither Bayer Leverkusen nor Español could boast the most glittering of trophy rooms. Still to this day, that remains the case.

Bayer Leverkusen are a unique oddity. A team formed in 1904, by the employees of the pharmaceutical company, Bayer AG, Leverkusen are a team that goes by the nickname of *Die Werkself,* which roughly translates itself into 'factory football club'.

A near recluse of an entity, until a late 1970s rise that took them from the outer reaches of the complicated, regionalised third tier, Verbandsliga, to the Bundesliga in just four years, Leverkusen have been an ever-present in the top flight of German football since the summer of 1979.

When Leverkusen walked out for the first leg of the 1988 UEFA Cup Final, there is a good chance that they were as surprised as everybody else. A team that had not only never won a major honour, they had not even reached a major cup final before, while their highest Bundesliga finish had been sixth, and this was just their second European campaign.

The LaLiga side were arguably just as bemused to find themselves in the final as Leverkusen were. While Español could point to previous domestic cup successes in Spain, the last of those two Copa del Reys had been won in 1940. Added to this, their European adventures, prior to this one, had been sporadic and generally short-lived, with a run to the quarter-finals of the 1961/62 Inter-Cities Fairs Cup being their best effort, during a season when they were relegated to the Segunda División.

While individual finalists had risen in surprising circumstances before, two underdogs at once was a rarity. Yet, the two protagonists were led by coaches of substance, both of whom would eventually take charge of their respective national teams: Erich Ribbeck with Germany, Javier Clemente with Spain. Español could count themselves as blessed to have acquired the services of Clemente, who had led Athletic Club to their LaLiga title successes of 1982/83 and 1983/84.

Still operating under the name of Español (it wouldn't be until February 1995 that the club reverted to the Catalan spelling of Espanyol), 1987/88 was a wild season at the Estadi de Sarrià. Labouring domestically, to the point that relegation loomed a little too alarmingly, Español's split personality helped them to some truly eye-catching exploits in the UEFA Cup.

Giants slain, a resounding semi-final comeback achieved and a spectacular capitulation unfolding in the final, Español's run had it all.

Led on the pitch by the Español legend, Diego Orejuela, Clemente's team also leant upon the experience of one of his former Athletic Club cornerstones, the former Spanish international Santiago Urquiaga, bringing together a team of mavericks, blossoming talent and a sprinkling of players who had something to prove.

Alongside Orejuela and Urquiaga, Clemente had at his disposal the Denmark international John Lauridsen, the dangerous but unpredictable Michel Pineda, the future Barcelona coach Ernest Valverde, Sebastián Losada on loan from Real Madrid, the former Real Zaragoza legend Pichi Alonso, who had failed to live up to his Zaragoza days during his time at Barcelona, inclusive of being one of the players to miss in the

1986 European Cup Final penalty shoot-out, plus the steadily rising star Miquel Soler, who would soon be bound for both Barcelona and the 1988 European Championship. This was a promising eye-of-the-storm coming together that was backed up by the Cameroon international goalkeeper Thomas N'Kono.

Español had qualified for the 1987/88 UEFA Cup on the back of an impressive third-placed LaLiga finish the previous season. Before Christmas, they had dispensed with Borussia Mönchengladbach but, far more stunningly, Arrigo Sacchi's AC Milan and Giovanni Trapattoni's Internazionale.

This being the Milan of Franco Baresi, Paolo Maldini, Carlo Ancelotti, Ruud Gullit and Marco van Basten, it was quite incredulous that Español could think they were allowed to travel to Italy and return with a 2-0 victory against the team that would sweep to the Serie A title by the season's end. Domestically, Español would rise no higher than 11th position all season.

With Milan banished from the San Siro, the game was played in Lecce, where a goal a few minutes before half-time from Javier Zubillaga was added to by Alonso shortly after the restart, to leave Sacchi and his expensively assembled stars dazed and confused. On the brink of an all-encompassing greatness, it is a result that has fallen beneath the radar of football history. By the end of the following season, while Milan were winning the European Cup, Español would be relegated to the Segunda División.

Second leg navigated with a goalless draw, Clemente could have been forgiven for thinking he and his team were cursed, when handed more Milanese opponents in the third round. This time inclusive of a trip to the San Siro, it was with an intelligently guided header that the substitute, Lauridsen, obtained Español their equaliser, with only eight minutes remaining, cancelling out Inter's one and only goal, scored in the first half by Aldo Serena.

It was an evening where Inter had played with a nervous disposition, having been embarrassed on home soil in the previous round by the Finnish part-timers, Turun Palloseura, who beat them 1-0 at the San Siro. Back at the Sarrià, it was Español's captain, Orejuela, who took aerial advantage of Trapattoni's team, to send them into the quarter-finals.

Leverkusen, meanwhile, had swept aside FK Austria Wien in the first round, before they were made to work for their passage beyond Toulouse and Feyenoord.

In Toulouse, during the first leg, Ribbeck's side gained a valuable lead, through Christian Schreier's opening goal, which was eventually levelled from the penalty spot by Alberto Tarantini, the Argentinian World Cup-winning full-back, who inexplicably ended up in the employment of Birmingham City just a short few weeks after helping his nation defeat the Netherlands for football's biggest prize. Schreier was again the hero a fortnight later, with the only goal of the return game.

A wildly open first half at Feyenoord came next, as the hosts clawed their way back from 2-0 down to level the game on the brink of half-time. In as impressive an example of a game of two halves as you could hope to find, no further goals were added in the second half. Falko Götz edged Leverkusen through, with the only goal of the second leg.

Into the quarter-finals, Leverkusen were drawn to face a Barcelona side that was within a bitter internal civil war between players and president over the culpability of escalating tax bills, a discord that would eventually lead to the arrival, as coach, of Johan Cruyff, followed by a mass culling of the squad he inherited.

In the first leg, Barcelona managed to put their problems to one side, returning to the Catalan capital with a precious goalless draw, but at a sparsely populated Camp Nou they were hit by the sucker punch of a ruthless counter-attack, the ball eventually slammed home by the Brazilian international, Tita, close to the hour mark, just as Luis Aragonés's men were increasing the pressure. It was to be the only goal of the game.

In another close call in the all-Bundesliga semi-final against Werder Bremen, a goal on the hour in the first leg proved to be the difference. Alois Reinhardt took advantage of a poor clearance from an in-swinging corner, bouncing the ball in off the inside of Oliver Reck's left-hand post from the edge of the Bremen penalty area.

Another goalless second leg ensured that it was Leverkusen, rather than Bremen, that would reach the 1988 UEFA Cup Final, despite Bremen being armed with the goalscoring threat of the excellent Karl-Heinz Riedle. A stunning achievement, this was a Bremen side that would eventually finish 20 points ahead of Leverkusen, in clinching the Bundesliga title during what was still the two points for a win era.

If Leverkusen's run to the final had been a magnificent example of determination, focus and belligerence, Español's had been incredulous and hypnotic. Having seen off the powerhouses of Gladbach, Milan, and Inter in the quarter-finals, they eased past FC Vítkovice 2-0 on aggregate, both goals scored in the first leg at the Sarrià, Lauridsen with a spectacular free kick in the first half, Pineda with a marvellously opportunistic near-post finish in the second half.

It set Español up with a semi-final clash against Club Brugge, whose own run to the last four had been one layered in drama. Beaten finalists in 1976, 12 years on the Belgians had been forced to complete a series of second-leg comebacks in the first three rounds, impressively overturning 2-0, 3-1 and 3-0 deficits against Zenit Saint Petersburg, Red Star Belgrade and Borussia Dortmund respectively. It meant that the 2-2 draw they escaped Athens with, after their quarter-final encounter with Panathinaikos, was something of a bonus.

Mesmerising on the front foot and questionable defensively, Brugge were powered by the vision of the legendary Jan Ceulemans and the goals of the former Anderlecht UEFA Cup winner, Kenneth Brylle. Unfortunately for them, however, having been drawn at home in the second leg all the way through, they were now faced with hosting the first leg of the semi-final.

Managing to frustrate Brugge for long periods at the Olympiastadion, it wasn't until three minutes before the interval that Ceulemans finally made the breakthrough, before Español contrived to give them another goal midway through the second half, via a Josep María Gallart own goal.

Two weeks later, it was at a vibrant Sarrià that Español pulled off the great comeback. A 3-0 victory clinched in the 119th minute, with a penalty shoot-out looming, it had taken only eight minutes for Clemente's side to give themselves a foothold in the game, simultaneously setting off Brugge's alarm bells that yet another away-day nightmare was about to befall them.

Orejuela, leading by supreme example, guided in a fine, yet unorthodox diving header to open the scoring, while it was another headed goal, this time from Losada, that levelled the aggregate score, in the 61st minute, rising at the back post.

All-square at 90 minutes, it was now a test of extra-time nerve and it was one that was passed by Español. Pichi Alonso pounced on a near-post spill by the Brugge goalkeeper, Philippe Vande Walle, to send the Sarrià into unbridled rapture.

A first leg that wasn't as one-sided as the scoreline suggests, Leverkusen paid the price of profligacy, while Español scored three times within a 12-minute span that stretched each side of the interval.

Losada struck first, on the stroke of half-time, with a powerful header, getting on the end of the most perfect of crosses from Soler. It was a goal that came just two minutes after Orejuela had seen a goal of his own disallowed.

Within three minutes of the restart, Español had their second of the evening, Soler driving the ball into Vollborn's bottom left-hand corner after a build-up that mixed magical skill with a goalmouth scramble that wouldn't have looked out of place had it unfolded on a muddy and sloping pitch in an FA Cup fourth qualifying round game somewhere in Northumberland.

Not to be outdone, Losada, who had been one of a string of Español players that could have laid claim to their second goal, had he connected with the ball cleanly, scored the third with less than an hour played. He produced a marvellous diving header low to Vollborn's left-hand post, Valverde supplying the cross, having taken advantage of some loose play by Leverkusen.

Easing off after their third goal, no more were added, and Español would count a heavy cost a fortnight later as they fell to the most spectacular second-leg UEFA Cup Final unravelling in the entire history of the tournament.

Español benefited from a controversial early decision from the referee, Jan Keizer, who contentiously disallowed a goal from Tita, who had swooped in when N'Kono released the ball from his hand to kick downfield, dispossessing the Español goalkeeper to roll it into an empty net. The visitors were widely in control of their destiny until the 57th minute.

From here, Clemente's side hit the self-destruct button and it was a mistake between N'Kono and his defenders that opened the door to Leverkusen, as Tita prodded in a scrappy effort that sneaked over the line at the near post.

The goal having increased the volume of the atmosphere perceptibly, Español suddenly froze, while an inspired Leverkusen grabbed their second goal just six minutes later.

Tita having broken the second-leg deadlock, Ribbeck then made the bold decision to withdraw the Brazilian, replacing him with Klaus Täuber, whose introduction was an explosive one. Within 60 seconds of his arrival on the pitch he had supplied the cross for Götz to stoop home a header for 2-0.

Regaining a modicum of composure, Español managed to repel Leverkusen until the 81st minute, eventually succumbing to a goal from the South Korean legend, Cha Bum-kun, who had won the UEFA Cup with Eintracht Frankfurt eight years earlier. More commonly referred to as Tscha Bum, he met a wonderfully directed free kick with a towering header, leaving N'Kono with little hope of stopping it.

Leverkusen shocking themselves almost as much as stunning their opponents, as the game drifted into extra time it was Español that held the greater control of the game, without carving the winning opportunity, and it meant that the game would lapse into a penalty shoot-out.

Apart from that amazing 24-minute span of the second leg, in which Leverkusen scored the three goals that levelled the aggregate score, it was Español who mostly dictated the pattern of play over the course of the 210 minutes of the 1988 UEFA Cup Final. It was a pattern that was carried into the penalty shoot-out as with Clemente's team stepping up first, when Ralf Falkenmayer's kick was saved by N'Kono – a miss that was bookended by successfully converted spot kicks from Alonso and Job – it handed the Catalan side the early advantage, despite Vollborn's attempts at imitating Bruce Grobbelaar's wobbly legs routine from the 1984 European Cup Final.

In a complete about-turn of fate, however, while Leverkusen were on target with their next three kicks, Español missed their next three, to gift wrap the UEFA Cup for Ribbeck and his players. Evocatively, it was the heroic Losada who missed the kick that ended the contest.

With one of those outcomes that has the power to change entire landscapes, Español went into their spiral towards the following year's relegation, while Leverkusen were now taken that little bit more seriously as a power in the Bundesliga, going on to win their very first domestic honour five years later and cultivating an environment that would take them all the way to the 2002 Champions League Final.

By 1995, Español were Espanyol, their name change coinciding with a rise in on-pitch fortunes. By 2000, they had ended what was by then a 60-year wait for a major honour, winning the Copa del Rey, a success they repeated in 2006, using that as a springboard in returning to the UEFA Cup Final in 2007, where they again lost out in a penalty shoot-out, this time on a one-off occasion at Hampden Park against Sevilla.

A stadium forever linked to Leverkusen whose 2002 Champions League Final loss was also inflicted at Hampden Park, while Español and Leverkusen's UEFA Cup Final is one that is a little too easy to skim past when running your finger down the list of tournament winners; in terms of their standing in the game, as opposed to the result they produced, they actually combined to provide one of its greatest-ever stories.

Chapter Eleven

As Stylish as it Gets

THERE IS a classic, BBC Sport ident of the late 1980s and early 90s where two balls orbit the earth multiple times and are accompanied by a simple, yet unmistakable and uplifting eight-second tune that is initiated by what sounds, at least to my untrained ear, to be a deep bass drum. In later years, there were updated and now retrospectively dated versions of it, which never quite hit the spot in the same way as the original one did.

That 1988–92 version of the BBC Sport ident had a certain gravitas to it. It suggested that something important was about to happen. In June 1990, when Luciano Pavarotti's take on 'Nessun Dorma' was tagged on the end of this classic BBC Sport ident, broadcasting alchemy occurred. Hairs would involuntarily rise on the back of the neck at the very sound of it, which was utterly confusing to an increasingly moody 16-year-old, who was besotted with Primal Scream, The Farm, the Stone Roses, The Charlatans, The Soup Dragons and the 1960s psychedelia movement.

At least in visual and sensory terms, Italia 90 was the most unremittingly stylish World Cup ever. In association with the host broadcaster, Rai, it was the first to be transmitted and recorded in High Definition, thus the images that were beamed back from Rome, Milan, Turin, Naples, Bari, Florence, Udine, Verona, Cagliari, Bologna, Palermo and Genoa were crystal-clear ones.

181

Unlike in previous World Cups, they were accompanied by commentaries that didn't sound as if sent down a yoghurt pot and a length of taut string, or maybe the surface of the moon. And then there was those dots, down the side of the screen, the line struck towards the bottom, when a player was being identified by surname and age. To the naked eye, Italia 90 looked beautiful.

Everything to do with the 1990 World Cup finals felt futuristic. The stadiums, some of which looked like spaceships and were light years ahead of their British counterparts, cast the most wonderful shadows across their pitches as the hot sun struck the roofs of the stands. The kits were largely iconic, many of which have been rehashed at later tournaments and it was blessed by an African nation going as far as the quarter-finals for the very first time.

Added to this, 'World in Motion' was hard to dislike and as far removed from 'World Cup Willie', 'Back Home' and 'Ron's 22', in terms of World Cup songs, as it was possible to travel.

Sleight of hand and act of illusion, however, the football at the 1990 World Cup wasn't all that pretty to watch. On the morning of Boxing Day 1990, Des Lynam confessed as much, in a review of the tournament. For everything the 1990 World Cup offered in respect of style and sophistication, it lacked in footballing substance.

West Germany, the eventual winners, were taken for granted. Expected to win it, they did so in a metronomic manner. Deserved world champions, they had the focus, drive and stubbornness that they had displayed in previous major tournaments, but without a bewitching maverick of the likes of a Günter Netzer or a Bernd Schuster. Nor did they have the hypnotic goal-getting of a Gerd Müller, the free spirit of a Karl-Heinz Rummenigge, the dastardliness of a Harald Schumacher, or even the vaguely underhand aura of a Paul Breitner.

The 1990 West Germany was one of immense strength and balance. While they could boast the presence of stars, such as the Internazionale trio of Andreas Brehme, Lothar Matthäus and Jürgen Klinsmann, there was something strikingly textbook about Franz Beckenbauer's team. If compared to a portrait, they were the finest painting-by-numbers project ever, as opposed to a masterpiece. There was certainly talent throughout the team, but the sometimes questionable character of previous squads was sadly missing.

Essentially, West Germany were a bit too, well, cuddly, I suppose. The World Cup was used to *Die Mannschaft* taking up the role of the Bond villain of the piece, be that by defeating the Netherlands in the 1974 final, their shameless result of convenience with Austria in Gijón, Schumacher's mowing down of Patrick Battiston, or how they even denied France a helping of karma in Mexico four years later by beating them in the semi-finals once again.

And this is what the 1990 World Cup sold to you. It gave with one hand yet took away with the other. Even when watching from afar, the sights and sounds were food for the eyes and ears, which in turn distracted the brain from being too critical about the football being served up.

Brehme, Matthäus and Klinsmann were not the only members of the West Germany squad that played their club football in Serie A during the 1989/90 season. Beckenbauer also called up the services of AS Roma's Thomas Berthold and Rudi Völler.

Within weeks of the final whistle being blown on the 1990 World Cup, Karl-Heinz Riedle was a Lazio player, while over the course of the next two years, Serie A would absorb another four members of West Germany's victorious squad. Thomas Häßler headed to Roma in the summer of 1991, while Stefan Reuter and Jürgen Kohler both signed for Juventus, where a year later Andreas Möller joined them.

Italy, its glamourous league, its beautiful stadia, plus its iconic and high-paying football teams couldn't have had a more attractive advert for its already alluring wares than it did in the summer of 1990.

A magnet to the great and the good of football, despite a much maligned Argentina being branded a one-man team, Carlos Bilardo's squad had contained seven Serie A players, while beaten semi-finalists, England, would see their two fastest-rising stars, Paul Gascoigne and David Platt, fall under the jurisdiction of Lazio and Bari respectively by the summer of 1991. Although a cruciate ligament injury would eventually delay Gascoigne's debut in Rome for so long that Platt had moved on to Juventus by the time he did.

These were not the only instances either. Czechoslovakia, the Soviet Union, Brazil, Sweden, Yugoslavia, Uruguay and the Netherlands all had ingredients within their squads that played their club football in Italy. Serie A was the centre of the footballing universe and it had been for some time.

When the 1990 World Cup ended, many viewers couldn't let go and they dived headlong into an adoration of Serie A, which was eventually made easier by Channel Four cleverly acquiring the rights in 1992, just as live top-flight English football fell into the hands of Sky.

James Richardson, Peter Brackley, Kenneth Wolstenholme and an array of guests and summarisers who had played in Serie A during the 1980s became essential viewing on a Saturday morning and Sunday afternoon, upon which a generation of football hipsters fell in love with Zdeněk Zeman's Foggia.

For the few people who had lived in a house with a BSB 'Squarial', they had been watching live Serie A games since the beginning of the 1990/91 season, straight off the back of the World Cup, a broadcasting entity that was soon swallowed up by Sky.

Prior to this, viewers in Wales had been blessed by Serie A highlights from the beginning of the 1988/89 season on S4C's weekly football show *Sgorio*. With Ian Rush having departed Liverpool for Juventus in the summer of 1987, and Mark Hughes still being a Barcelona player as the 1987/88 season ended, the duo of Serie A and LaLiga highlights, with a projected added Welsh interest, was a forward-thinking one.

What the S4C programming executives didn't see coming, however, was that both Rush and Hughes would be back in the First Division by the time *Sgorio* made its debut transmission. Yet, to lovers of great football, this mattered little.

In Serie A, 1988/89 meant Napoli's Diego Maradona attempting to wrestle the title back from the AC Milan of Ruud Gullit, Marco van Basten and Frank Rijkaard, only to see the Inter of Brehme and Matthäus run away with it instead, while Michael Laudrup failed to spark a slumbering Juventus. The Serie A of the 1980s and 1990s was a beautiful yet merciless beast, a ruthless 18-team league, from which four were relegated; an environment where only the strongest survived and superstars were to be found at every turn.

Title handed over to Inter, Milan compensated themselves by winning the European Cup for the first time in 20 years, while the rapidly rising Sampdoria reached and lost the European Cup Winners' Cup Final, to Johan Cruyff's Barcelona.

Up until this point, scepticism and frustration had been the order of the day from Serie A's teams when it came to the UEFA Cup. In the first 17 seasons of the tournament, there had only been one Italian finalist, this being Juventus's run to glory in 1977.

Conversely, over the course of the last nine campaigns of the two-legged final era of the UEFA Cup, only once was there a final that did not contain a Serie A club, while three of those nine finals were all-Italian encounters. Added to this, the first two one-off UEFA Cup finals, of 1998 and 1999, were won by Inter and Parma; 1989 to 1999 almost represented a monopolisation of the UEFA Cup by Serie A.

It was a run of success that was started by Napoli. Edging nervously past PAOK, Lokomotive Leipzig and Bordeaux before Christmas, the quarter-final draw paired *I Partenopei* with one of their great northern nemeses, Juventus.

All appeared to be lost when Napoli returned south from the first leg having suffered a 2-0 defeat, thanks to an unexpectedly spectacular opener from the future Cowdenbeath defender, Pasquale Bruno, followed by an unfortunate own goal on the stroke of half-time from Giancarlo Corradini, on a blustery Turin evening when Juventus's overconfidence in not over-extending themselves for further second-half goals would prove crucial.

A fortnight later, the San Paolo arguably witnessed its finest night, when Maradona led his team to a stunning comeback that included a 120th-minute winning goal, just as a penalty shoot-out loomed large.

It was Maradona himself who got the ball rolling, with a coolly dispatched penalty within ten minutes and, when Andrea Carnevale arrowed a beautifully struck shot into virtually the same spot Maradona had picked out with his penalty, from just outside the 18-yard line only seconds before half-time, it was a goal that was greeted in such an enthusiastic manner that the recently installed roof on the cavernous San Paolo was rigorously stress-checked.

Deliriousness at the equalising goal was offset by a loss of momentum for Napoli as the second half began. Their second goal had come at the perfect moment, but the half-time interval was an unwelcome one. After such a high-tempo and productive first 45 minutes, the next 75 were much more in keeping with a traditional Serie A tactical stalemate.

Just as the game was being drawn towards an inevitable looking duel from 12 yards, Napoli dealt the fatal blow to Juventus. Alessandro Renica would prove to be the unlikely hero, when he powered home the winner, via what could easily have been his left shoulder as his head, even barging Maradona out of the way to get there, to light the pyro fuse to one of the biggest parties that San Paolo and Naples had ever seen.

One European giant overcome in the last eight, in the semi-final Napoli were handed the challenge of subduing the mighty Bayern Munich. It was a challenge that they were more than capable of meeting.

A 2-0 win in the first leg at the San Paolo, thanks to an emphatic finish from Careca and a towering header by Carnevale, was complemented by a second-leg 2-2 draw at the Olympiastadion in which Napoli were always one step ahead of their opponents.

Goalless until just beyond the hour, all four goals were condensed to a 20-minute span in which Careca twice put Napoli ahead, only to see Bayern promptly, yet forlornly equalise on each occasion within a short few minutes, firstly through Roland Wohlfarth and then by Reuter.

Napoli's goals, meanwhile, were beautifully gifted, the first via Maradona capitalising upon comical Bayern defending, to set Careca up, the second taken on the break, as Bayern pushed on in a bid to find the three goals they now needed to reach the final.

Awaiting Napoli in the 1989 UEFA Cup Final were another Bundesliga opponent, this time in the shape of VfB Stuttgart, who had reached their first major European final, predominantly on the back of a succession of closely contested ties against Tatabányai Bányász, Dinamo Zagreb, Groningen, Real Sociedad on penalties and then an evocative west vs east semi-final, against Dynamo Dresden.

Shorn of the suspended Klinsmann for the first leg of the final, Stuttgart were not expected to give Napoli so tough a game at the San Paolo. Maybe it was the weight of being the favourites, having always been the indefatigable underdogs, but it was a nervous and disjointed Napoli that went in for half-time at 1-0 down.

Maurizio Gaudino, a West German born to Italian immigrants and a lifelong Napoli supporter, struck Stuttgart's goal at the San Paolo. Hit from distance after a free kick was rolled his way, it was a powerful effort, but one that Giuliano Giuliani should have dealt with.

Saved by a disputed Maradona penalty and a close-range Careca strike that came just three minutes from the end, the full-time whistle was met with relief at the San Paolo. While Napoli had been totally dominant during the second half, much of it had been laced with desperation and an ever-increasing sense of aggression from the home side.

All set up for a dramatic second leg when Alemão struck first in the 18th minute, it meant that for the remainder of the evening, Stuttgart were never closer than needing two goals to win the UEFA Cup, despite once again having the services of Klinsmann to call upon.

One in, one out; while Stuttgart welcomed Klinsmann back, they had lost the defensive qualities of their injured captain, Guido Buchwald. Emboldened by their first-leg performance, Arie Haan, the Stuttgart coach, opted for a change of formation, dispensing with a sweeper and pushing two up front, after Fritz Walter had mostly toiled alone in Naples where he was only occasionally supported by Gaudino pressing on from midfield.

Napoli's untidily procured, but crucial lead, lasted for less than ten minutes, before Klinsmann timed a back-post run to perfection, getting on the end of a beautifully swung corner to head past Giuliani.

Having found their way back into the final, Stuttgart's hopes were again dashed nine minutes later. When a Maradona corner was sent straight back to him with a defensive header, instead of bringing the ball down and assessing his options, the Napoli number 10 instinctively went with head tennis, directing it back towards the Stuttgart six-yard box, where it was cleverly finished by Ciro Ferrara, who guided it past the surprised Eike Immel.

Leading 4-2 on aggregate, with two away goals now wiping out the one Stuttgart had scored at the San Paolo, it was a strike which meant the game had to finish within 90 minutes. Extra time and penalties were out of the equation and when the two teams returned for the second half, Haan's side needed three goals, without reply, to lift the UEFA Cup.

In a position to pick and choose when to attack during the second half, Napoli absorbed Stuttgart's early pressure, before striking forth again shortly after the hour. Careca once more the marksman, he was on the end of a swift counter-attack in which Maradona showed immense unselfishness to ignore the temptation to go for goal himself.

Less than half an hour to play and, with Stuttgart needing four goals, Napoli took their foot off the accelerator. When Gaudino found the net, with 20 minutes left, via a huge deflection off Fernando de Napoli, which was so pronounced that it was credited as an own goal, it was a strike that Stuttgart greeted with no more than a rueful celebration.

Di Napoli, experiencing a mixed night at the Neckarstadion, was then the key to Stuttgart levelling the second-leg score at 3-3, in the 89th minute, when his looped, under-hit back pass was nodded past Giuliani by the substitute Olaf Schmäler.

Ending 5-4 on aggregate, the generosity of the result to Stuttgart did nothing to dampen Napoli's joy. In the five years Maradona had been with the club, he had led them on the pitch from habitual bottlers and underachievers, to their first Serie A title as part of a domestic double and now onward to European honours.

As holders, Napoli would only go as far as the third round in 1989/90, crashing out spectacularly, 8-3 on aggregate to Werder Bremen. Redoubling their focus domestically instead, a second Serie A title would be celebrated at the San Paolo at the season's end.

Napoli winning the 1989 UEFA Cup Final didn't just break Serie A's 12-year drought in the tournament, it also opened the floodgates for other Italian teams to prosper throughout the next decade.

A year later, with Rai's iconic World Cup graphics now in operation, the 1990 UEFA Cup Final marked the first all-Italian collision at the prize-giving end of a major European tournament. It was also a coming together that was shrouded in controversy and rancour.

Mighty Juventus, up against the perpetually tormented Fiorentina, it was a set of games that played its part in what was quite possibly the very zenith of Italian club football's position, as being the high plateau of quality, above cloud level, compared to all other leagues and eras.

In those rambling weeks of pre-World Cup anticipation, all three major European trophies ended up in the possession of Serie A clubs. While Juventus and Fiorentina battled it out for the UEFA Cup, Milan retained the European Cup and Sampdoria went one better than 12 months earlier, in their pursuit of the Cup Winners' Cup. With Maradona and Napoli taking the Serie A title, Italy was the undisputed centre of the footballing universe.

Intrigue and sleight of hand hovered over the 1990 UEFA Cup Final – a Juventus side led by the World Cup-winning captain, Dino Zoff, up against fellow *Azzurri* world champion, Francesco Graziani and his Fiorentina.

Going into the final, there was already a bone of contention in existence between the two clubs, stemming from the culmination of the 1981/82 Serie A title race, when Fiorentina were denied the spoils on the final day under circumstances that saw both sides locked on the same number of points with just 15 minutes left to play.

On that fateful day, shortly before Italy's successful 1982 World Cup campaign, Liam Brady's winning penalty for Juventus, away to Catanzaro, was unimpeachable. Yet, Fiorentina cried foul, over what had appeared to be a perfectly valid first-half shout for a Catazaro penalty. Coupled to their own goalless draw away to Cagliari, during which Graziani had a goal cruelly disallowed, it made for the perfect series of events for conspiracies to flourish and open wounds to fester.

Added to this, as the two teams walked out for the first leg at the Stadio Comunale, rumours had begun to circulate that Fiorentina's most precious asset, Roberto Baggio, was set to be sold during the summer. As it would take a world-record fee to attain his services, an unthinkable sale to Juventus was no longer an impossibility.

Polarising routes taken to reach the 1990 UEFA Cup Final, while both teams had lost just one of the ten games it took to reach this point that is where the similarities ended. Juventus, winning eight times, scoring 17 goals along the way, were freewheeling bohemians when compared to Fiorentina's austerity football. In the case of *La Viola*, they had scored four goals fewer than the number of games they had played in reaching the final.

Zoff's *I Bianconeri* comfortably overcame Górnik Zabrze, Paris Saint-Germain and Karl-Marx-Stadt, before being made to sweat that little more profusely during the quarter-finals and semi-finals, by Hamburger SV and 1. FC Köln respectively.

Meanwhile, Fiorentina had kept seven clean sheets, but failed to score more than a single goal in any one individual game in ushering Atlético Madrid, Sochaux, Dynamo Kyiv, Auxerre and Werder Bremen out of the tournament, from their temporary base at Perugia's Stadio Renato Curi.

With the Stadio Artemio Franchi out of commission, due to upgrades being made ahead of the World Cup, Fiorentina had decamped to Umbria, more than 90 miles away from home, where they suffered a season of domestic struggle, remaining on the periphery of a wide-open relegation battle that was being contested by the entire bottom half of Serie A, in some cases right up until the last minutes of the campaign.

This domestic sufferance was compensated by their tentative European adventures. Fiorentina's run to the final included one penalty shoot-out, two away-goals advancements and no bigger winning aggregate margin than two goals. None of this was pedestrian enough to discourage the passion of Fiorentina's support, however, so much so, that crowd disturbances marred the second leg of the semi-final against Werder Bremen and brought the sanction that their home leg for the final would instead take place on a neutral ground.

At the Stadio Comunale, the first leg took less than three minutes to spring to life. A bursting run down the right from Salvatore Schillaci drew the attention of three Fiorentina players and left a huge expanse in the penalty area for Roberto Galia to exploit, from where he rolled the ball beneath the exposed Landucci.

Rather than wilt under the early pressure, Fiorentina responded positively to the setback and it was Renato Buso who levelled the scores, within seven minutes, with a wonderful near-post diving header that cut across a startled Stefano Tacconi, after some determined work from Alberto Di Chiara. Marco Nappi had already forced the Juventus goalkeeper into a smart save, before Buso equalised.

It was a goal that prompted Fiorentina's best period of the entire span of the two legs of the final. Dictating the pace and flow of play, Graziani's players hit swiftly on the counter-attack and were precision personified when it came to their passing. Chances came Fiorentina's way, but they went untaken, with Baggio missing a golden opportunity on the half hour when he attempted to chip the ball over the advancing Tacconi instead of taking it around him, having been sent through on goal by the uncontrollable Nappi.

When Juventus lost their captain, Sergio Brio, at half-time, it appeared that everything apart from more goals was going Fiorentina's way, despite their own loss of Luboš Kubík at the interval. It all changed, however, in one controversial moment just short of the hour, when a ball into the Fiorentina penalty area fell the way of Angelo Alessio, whose spectacular effort was deflected into the sightlines of Pierluigi Casiraghi, who prodded it home for a 2-1 Juventus lead.

Rightly furious, Fiorentina's players complained vehemently about the goal, as Casiraghi had blatantly shoved Celeste Pin before the ball dropped to Alessio. It was an obvious infringement and one that should have been picked up easily by the officials, but it would instead go down as another dose of Florentine 'proof' of habitual Juventus chicanery.

To add insult to injury, Luigi De Agostini snared Juventus a third goal with 17 minutes remaining. Struck from distance, it

The Danish international, Kenneth Brylle, scores the only goal of the first leg of the 1983 final, for Anderlecht against Benfica. A 1-1 draw at the Estádio da Luz, a fortnight later, meant Belgium had its first and only UEFA Cup success.

Keith Burkinshaw, the departing Tottenham Hotspur manager, with the trophy he left the club as his farewell gift, in 1984.

Camacho and Santi Uana get to grips with the UEFA Cup, after defeating 1. FC Köln in the 1986 final. It was a second successive glory for Real Madrid, after they had defeated Videoton of Hungary 12 months earlier.

Billy Kirkwood tries to find Dundee United a way back into the second leg of the 1987 final, at Tannadice Park, against a dangerous, determined, and talented IFK Göteborg. It was the second cup final defeat in just four days for the Scottish side.

Cha Bum-kun holds the trophy aloft after Bayer Leverkusen's remarkable second leg comeback in the 1988 final. The man known as 'Cha Boom' was also a winner eight years earlier, with Eintracht Frankfurt.

Diego Maradona celebrates as Napoli overcome a powerful Bayern Munich side to reach the 1989 final, in which they defeated another Bundesliga opponent, VfB Stuttgart.

The Juventus coach Dino Zoff and his goalkeeper Stefano Tacconi, after winning the 1990 final against Fiorentina. Despite this success being added to the Coppa Italia, which they won the previous month, Zoff was ruthlessly sacked a few weeks later.

Roberto Baggio in action
for Juventus during the
1993 final, against Borussia
Dortmund. Baggio had been
in the Fiorentina side that was
defeated by Juventus in the final
three years earlier.

Juventus and Parma line up prior to the second leg of the 1995 final, a game that took place at the San Siro, in Milan, due to a combination of a rental dispute and poor attendances, at the Stadio delle Alpi.

Bixente Lizarazu, of Bordeaux, breaks free of the attention of Bayern Munich's Jürgen Klinsmann, during the second leg of the 1996 final. The German team comfortably won the UEFA Cup for the first time, with Franz Beckenbauer on the touchline.

Schalke's Olaf Thon takes the acclaim at the San Siro, as the Bundesliga outfit shock an expensively assembled and Roy Hodgson led Internazionale, in a penalty shoot-out to win the last two-legged final.

The first single legged final, played at the Parc des Princes, was won by Internazionale, who via a Ronaldo masterclass, destroyed Sven-Göran Eriksson's ambitious Lazio side. The hooped shirts Inter were wearing seemed as jarring as the loss of the two legged final.

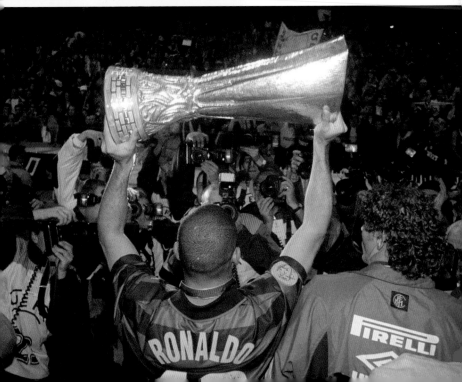

5-4! Gary McAllister's free kick skims off the head of the Deportivo Alavés defender, Delfí Geli, past the despairing punch of his own goalkeeper and into the net, for Liverpool's golden goal winner, in the 2001 final at the Westfalenstadion.

Rebranded and repackaged. The UEFA Europa League is a tournament that barely resembles the UEFA Cup, as was, yet is its linear continuation, while the Inter-Cities Fairs Cup goes unrecognised by UEFA as its official predecessor.

was a goal which was entirely stoppable, yet deceived Landucci, dipping in front of him, then bouncing up and over the Fiorentina goalkeeper. Any hopes that Graziani had of turning the final around were lost there and then.

A goalless draw between two Serie A teams, as occurred in the second leg of the 1990 UEFA Cup Final, would suggest a stereotypical *Calcio* stalemate, if simply judging a football match by its scoreline.

There was, however, more than meets the eye. Sent over 300 miles to Avellino, Fiorentina's 'home advantage' was enveloped in pyro smoke and swept away in a sea of black and white flags and scarves.

Juventus, a team whose domestic powerbase of support doesn't lay solely in Turin, but instead across the length and breadth of Italy, were well backed at the Stadio Partenio, an unexpected, yet electrically atmospheric venue for the second leg. When the first game took place, the identity of where the return game would be played was still undetermined.

It was through a strategic masterclass that Juventus completed the job of claiming their second UEFA Cup. Subduing Nappi and Dunga simply cut the supply line to Baggio. Fiorentina were progressively left to resort to frustrated and wayward efforts at goal, from distance.

Even Juventus being down to ten men for the last half hour made little difference to an increasingly resigned Fiorentina, after the dismissal of Bruno. The trophy headed to Turin, the psychological wounds and conspiracy theories to Florence.

Regardless that there had been a defined winner and loser, both clubs went on to shoot themselves in the foot over the course of the immediate weeks and months ahead. Zoff, one of the greatest goalkeepers of all time, tends to go criminally undervalued as a coach. Despite winning the UEFA Cup in 1990, just weeks after having won the Coppa Italia, beating Arrigo Sacchi's Milan, no less, he was sacked in the summer by an impatient Agnelli family, whose insatiable desire was the Serie A title. It was an incredibly rash move, even by Italian football standards and the following season would be a forgettable one for *I Bianconeri*, completing it without a trophy, or even European qualification.

Fiorentina, meanwhile, not only lost out on the UEFA Cup, but on Baggio too, albeit for a world-record transfer fee. Amid the violent uprising in response to his sale to Juventus, *I Viola* president, Flavio Pontello, was forced to lock himself away in his own stadium, while the riots outside caused at least 50 injuries and led to nine arrests.

As a collective, however, Serie A had never been in such rude health. Despite winning the UEFA Cup, it was into the Cup Winners' Cup that Juventus went for the 1990/91 season, where they were joined by the holders, Sampdoria. Milan, having again won the European Cup, were joined by the Serie A champions, Napoli, making it two Italian representatives in both competitions, to go along with their four UEFA Cup qualifiers. This meant that in 1989/90, only six clubs neither gained European qualification nor wound up relegated.

A year beyond Juventus and Fiorentina, the UEFA Cup Final was again contested by two Serie A teams, yet it came with a heavy German influence. At a time when Italian teams were only allowed to field three non-domestic players, a rule that UEFA would soon implement for their own club competitions, of the six combined permitted foreign players involved in the 1991 UEFA Cup Final, between Inter and AS Roma, five of them were German.

At the San Siro, Matthäus and Brehme had been joined by Klinsmann in the summer of 1989, while at Rome's Stadio Olimpico, Völler and Berthold offered goals and defensive solidity respectively. Only the Brazilian, Aldair, was the exception to this blanket German hegemony.

In the league, Roma struggled for consistency, despite hiring the man who had put Napoli on top of Italian football and delivered them the 1989 UEFA Cup, Ottavio Bianchi.

This is where a wonderful family tree effect came into play. Bianchi's return to the UEFA Cup Final, just two years after winning it with Napoli, also saw him reunited in opposition of Klinsmann, who had been part of the defeated Stuttgart team in 1989.

Added to this, one of Bianchi's first recruits at Roma was Carnevale, from his former club, yet he would soon lose the services of his new signing, after the striker, alongside the future Italian international goalkeeper, Angelo Peruzzi, was found guilty of using the banned substance, Phentermine, which had been present in a weight-gain suppressant that both players had used.

This marvellous interlinking of UEFA Cup stories was further amplified in the shape of Sergio Battistini, who had been in the Fiorentina team that had lost out to Juventus in the 1990 final. He returned for the 1991 final, as an Inter player.

Despite Roma's Serie A inconsistencies, they were imperious in the UEFA Cup, throwing in a run all the way to the Coppa Italia Final for good measure. On a considerably sounder European footing than Inter were, Roma reached the UEFA Cup Final without losing a single game.

A testimony to how strong the UEFA Cup's field of teams could be, Roma's path to the final took them past Benfica, Valencia, Bordeaux, Anderlecht and Brøndby, the last of which gave Bianchi's side its biggest scare, when the Danes incredibly came to within two minutes of reaching the final instead, despite not even managing to score a goal of their own.

Goalless in the first leg at the Brøndby Stadium, when the game switched to Rome for the second leg, *I Giallorossi* were in control, but also in possession of only a narrow one-goal lead. Just beyond the hour, Sebastiano Nela contrived to score the own goal that levelled the second-leg scoreline and inadvertently handed Brøndby the away-goals advantage. It wasn't until the 88th minute that Völler played Roma's 'get out of jail free' card, when obtaining an untidy, but wildly celebrated winner. It was also a goal that denied the UEFA Cup its most outlandish finalist since Videoton, six years earlier.

Yet, Roma's flirtation with the unthinkable against Brøndby wasn't symptomatic of the rest of a run which had started with them being reunited with their former coach, Sven-Göran Eriksson, who was now at the helm of a Benfica side he had led to the European Cup Final only four months earlier.

Fast out of the blocks, Carnevale scored in the very first minute of the campaign, much to the anger of a Benfica defence that was vehement in its protestations of handball. With no further goals added to the first leg, there was still all to play for at the Estádio da Luz in the return game.

Giuseppe Giannini killed off any hopes Benfica had of launching a comeback in under 30 minutes, however, when he was in the right place at the right time to be the beneficiary of a rebound off the home goalkeeper, Silvino, after he had blocked an effort that came at the end of a surging run by Völler.

Next, a resurgent Valencia were navigated, with Ruggiero Rizzitelli scoring a crucial away goal, for a 1-1 draw at the Mestalla, before the job was nervously completed back at the Stadio Olimpico a fortnight later.

Again, Giannini was one of the heroes, with a cool finish, when the ball bobbled toward him, in the 37th minute, setting him free to run through on goal, where he placed it into Silvino's bottom left-hand corner.

Midway through the second half, Völler then planted a penalty into the top right-hand corner, at the end of an excessively long run-up, for 2-0. All thoughts of a sedate meander to the full-time whistle were then spoilt when Roma gifted Valencia a way back into the game, via a penalty of their own, with just under 20 minutes still to be played. It was a relieved Bianchi that welcomed his players off the pitch at the end.

Conversely, Roma's third-round opponents were dealt with easily, as Bordeaux were dispatched 7-0 on aggregate,

Völler starting the rout when capitalising upon an error by the visiting goalkeeper, the Cameroon international Joseph-Antoine Bell.

In a performance of substance by Roma, the Bordeaux side that was swept aside, 5-0, at the Stadio Olimpico contained an ageing, but still effective Patrick Battiston, the prolific Netherlands international, Wim Kieft, the French international midfielder, Jean-Philippe Durand, plus the blossoming Didier Deschamps and a fast developing Bixente Lizarazu.

With only seconds remaining of the first half of the first leg, Völler struck again, with yet another penalty that included a marathon run-up, sending his kick straight down the middle. The German international then completed one of the most gift-wrapped hat-tricks imaginable, when confusion between goalkeeper and defender opened the door to an open shot at goal for Völler, just five minutes beyond the restart.

A brace from Manuel Gerolin then dissipated any lingering notions Bordeaux might have harboured of producing a second-leg fightback. Bell, once again culpable for Roma's fourth, could do very little to stop the final goal of the evening.

Despite the presence of an 18-year-old Christophe Dugarry for the second leg, it was a steadily imploding Bordeaux that was defeated 2-0 at the Stade du Parc Lescure, by virtue of another Völler penalty, this time of a Panenka style, plus a late strike from Stefano Desideri.

By the end of the season, Bordeaux had been demoted to the second tier of French football, for financial irregularities, having finished in mid-table.

Having already dispensed with the previous season's beaten European Cup finalists in the quarter-finals, it was the turn of the team that lost the 1990 Cup Winners' Cup Final, Anderlecht. Apart from drawing Inter themselves, Roma were arguably handed the toughest draw, in the last eight.

For all but the last minute or so of the first half of the first leg, this seemed to be proved correct, until Desideri opened the scoring for Roma. A free kick sent in low from the left-hand side, aimed towards the near post, was deflected past the blind-sided Filip De Wilde.

If the opening goal constituted a foothold in the game for Roma, then a stranglehold was taken during the second half. The insatiable Völler arched in a beautiful free kick in the 74th minute, which was then followed, just three minutes later, by Rizzitelli finishing off a magnificent team goal, to give Bianchi's side a commanding lead to take to Brussels.

At the Constant Vanden Stock Stadium two weeks later, Roma were in no mood to throw their advantage away. Völler, again, showed himself to be the man for the big occasion, collecting another hat-trick, but one that wasn't as generously allowed, compared to the one he scored in Bordeaux. This time it took a beautifully weighted lob, a wonderful glancing header and a powerfully struck half-volley, with his back partially to goal, after a determined chase down of the ball, to earn his trio of goals from Anderlecht. Even a couple of belated goals for the home side couldn't tarnish what had been an impressive individual and collective performance.

While Roma had been hypnotic upon their way to the final, Inter had shown both sides of their classic split personality. A club that had so many gifts at their disposal during the 1980s, a ten-year span in which their two biggest rivals had spent half the decade each in a state of, at best, flux, at worst, chaos, Inter had failed over and over again to take advantage of the opportunities that fell their way, even during the first two seasons after the arrival, as head coach, of Giovanni Trapattoni.

Serie A title finally won in 1988/89, a patchy autumn meant that the defence of their crown was always a few steps out of reach as the 1989/90 season unfolded. Inter also conspired against themselves in the European Cup, where they shockingly fell at the first hurdle, to Malmo.

It left Trapattoni and Inter with a point to prove in 1990/91. Domestic honours would prove elusive once more, but the UEFA

Cup would be theirs and it was to be Trapattoni's parting gift to the club, before returning to Juventus.

Marvellously gifted, this was an Inter side that shouldn't have made life as hard for itself as it did. Strengthened in the summer of 1990, not only by the arrival of Battistini from Fiorentina, but also by that of Antonio Paganin from Udinese, the evolution of Trapattoni's side had hinged as much on the recruitment of the likes of Aldo Serena, Nicola Berti and Alessandro Bianchi, as it had upon the much celebrated Germanic triumvirate of Brehme, Matthäus and Klinsmann.

In the case of Klinsmann, he had arrived to enhance Inter's post-title-winning team, only to, arguably, upset the balance of the line-up, at least compared to how Ramón Díaz had operated during Trapattoni's *Scudetto*-winning campaign.

Going into the 1990/91 campaign, it wasn't only Inter who were stunned by the sweeping tide that took Sampdoria to the Serie A title. Added to this, a quarter-final exit from the Coppa Italia meant all Trapattoni's eggs were placed in his UEFA Cup basket.

A run that couldn't be more symptomatic of an era of excess and underachievement, Inter's path to the 1991 UEFA Cup Final was a marriage of them being utterly ruthless at the San Siro, yet startlingly vulnerable on the road.

Just as in the previous season, Inter's European hopes were almost upset at the first hurdle. This time, it was Rapid Wien who were the threat and, having been beaten 2-1 in the first leg at the Gerhard-Hanappi-Stadion, Trapattoni's men needed extra time back at the San Siro to secure a route into the second round.

While Rapid were subtly dangerous opponents, Inter should have had no problem in progressing, given that Matthäus's away goal had been procured so early in the first encounter. Yet, it was with only 12 minutes remaining at the San Siro that Berti finally made the breakthrough, powering in an effort from the edge of the area to breach the stubborn visitors.

In the right place at the right time, within five minutes, Berti had struck once again. A goal that was expected to be the hammer blow to Rapid, Inter were rocked back on their heels, when Franz Weber plundered the goal that took the tie into extra time, with only two minutes remaining. Klinsmann would settle the issue, however, in the 101st minute, with a deftly taken finish.

Through to the second round, they were drawn to face Jozef Venglos's Aston Villa, with First Division clubs having been freshly readmitted to European competition after the Heysel ban. At Villa Park, there were no signs of continental rustiness from the Midlands club, who had seen off the challenge of Baník Ostrava in the first round.

A thunderous first-half strike from Kent Nielsen was coupled with a well-worked goal by David Platt in the second period, in a performance that gained a result that set Venglos's team up with a golden opportunity to take an iconic scalp.

Back in Milan, however, an early goal from Klinsmann left Villa on thin ice, where they were undone in a stereotypically Anglo-Saxon footballing manner, as opposed to a more forensically typical Italian style. It was via a long ball that Klinsmann seemed to tip the ball past Nigel Spink, for the opening goal of the game.

Opportunism rather than artistry could be suggested to have been the path to Inter's second goal, the goal that levelled the aggregate scoreline, shortly beyond the hour. Villa's inability to clear a free kick led to Berti driving the ball across the six-yard-box and into Spink's bottom left-hand corner.

Disorientated and vulnerable, Villa's defence simply could not cope from that point onward. A winning goal seemed inevitable and it came in the 74th minute, courtesy of Bianchi, who forced the ball through Spink's legs, when catching it on the volley, beyond the back post.

Difficult to think that any team other than Inter would be going through from here, it still didn't mean there weren't some ambiguities to the goal that did it for them – a hint of offside and a possibility that the ball crossed the byline, before it was crossed for Bianchi to score, circulated Inter's winner.

Bianchi had been the key element for Trapattoni. Suspended for the first leg, he dominated the midfield during the second leg. While enthusiasm and the sense of occasion had sustained Villa a fortnight earlier, at the San Siro there was a clear chasm between the two teams in terms of technical ability.

It was with another 3-0 San Siro masterclass that Inter cruised past Partizan in the third round. The only occasion, other than in the final itself, that Trapattoni's side was drawn to play at home first, they prospered thanks to a beautifully crafted opener by Matthäus, a thumping header from Andrea Mandorlini and a third that was generously gifted by the Partizan goalkeeper, Goran Pandurović, when he opted to meet a free kick with a badly misjudged double-fisted punch, which was eventually put away by Bianchi, after an untidy exchange of passes, deflections and blocks.

In Belgrade, Matthäus was the man with the equaliser on the night, for a 1-1 draw, easing Inter onward, to the quarter-finals, where they were handed an all-Italian clash with Atalanta.

Whereas most of Roma's opponents on the way to the 1991 UEFA Cup Final were blatantly talented and dangerous ones, Inter's were arguably masked with uncertainty over just how good they were. In both the quarter-final and semi-final, Trapattoni would err towards caution when plotting a way past Atalanta and Sporting.

Identical aggregate scorelines of 2-0 were garnered, via conservative goalless draws attained away, followed by 2-0 wins back at the San Siro. Against Atalanta, set pieces were again Inter's friend, Serena meeting a free kick on the hour, unmarked, from six yards, with an unstoppable header, while Matthäus struck from distance, when a free kick was rolled across his sightlines, just three minutes later.

Sporting's resistance, in the last four, was broken earlier in the second leg. Matthäus was merciless from the penalty spot within 15 minutes, while 20 minutes later it was Klinsmann who was the hero, taking advantage of slack marking and an open goal, to end the threat of the Lisbon club.

So, it was the split personality of Inter and the sure-footed Roma who went head-to-head in the 1991 UEFA Cup Final. Perhaps unsettled by their opponents being domestic ones, Roma were wounded in a 15-minute second-half span, where Matthäus was again brutal from 12 yards after a penalty was won, before a turn of skill and burst of speed from Klinsmann down the left resulted in Berti putting the ball into an unguarded Roma net, with 18 minutes left to play. Beset by crowd disturbances, missiles and flares were thrown to and from the away section, on an evening when fire raged on the terraces.

At the Stadio Olimpico two weeks later, Trapattoni opted for as tight a defensive shield as possible, punctuated with sporadic counter-attacks. It was an approach that frustrated Roma, until Rizzitelli managed to force one past an inspired Walter Zenga, with just seven minutes remaining.

It was beyond a combination of Roman profligacy, wonderful goalkeeping and disciplined, yet, at times, desperate Milanese defending that Trapattoni finally delivered Inter what was the perfect parting gift, before heading back to Juventus. The 1991 UEFA Cup was the club's first major European honour in 26 years.

For Roma, having had to stand and watch an opposing team lift European silverware in their own bearpit for the second time in seven years, there would be the consolation of Coppa Italia success a few weeks later, against the title-winning Sampdoria.

Without Trapattoni, Inter's defence of their UEFA Cup ended with a first-round defeat at the hands of Boavista, a result that proved to be the scene-setter to a hugely forgettable season for *I Nerazzurri*.

With other contemporary Serie A giants waylaid elsewhere, it was left to a couple of evocative names of yesteryear to carry the flag for Italy in the 1991/92 UEFA Cup. While Genoa would fall one round short of the final, Torino did make it to the showpiece event.

Under the guidance of Emiliano Mondonico, the early-1990s Torino tends to be a widely under-celebrated entity, given that it fell short in its objectives and finds itself historically hemmed in by the Milan of Sacchi and Fabio Capello, an evocative Sampdoria, the Napoli of Maradona and Careca, the Germanic-inspired Inter and even the attempts of Baggio to lead a Juventus resurgence.

Blessed by the presence of the future Italian international goalkeeper, Luca Marchegiani, captained by Roberto Cravero, Torino also boasted the stubborn defending of Pasquale Bruno, who won the UEFA Cup with Juventus in 1990, the Italian international Luca Fusi and the late blooming Roberto Mussi, whose own international career began at the age of 30 and took him to the World Cup Final in 1994.

Added to this solid defensive foundation, Mondonico's midfield was a beautifully balanced unit. Rafael Martín Vázquez, Enzo Scifo, Giorgio Venturin, Roberto Policano and Gianluigi Lentini all brought something different, yet strikingly intelligent to the team. Before long, Lentini would be the most expensive footballer in the world.

At the top of the tree came Walter Casagrande, the Brazilian international. Looming on the periphery of the team was an 18-year-old Christian Vieri.

Progression to the semi-finals was a journey in which Torino had to avoid a series of potential banana skins, with opponents that shouldn't be tipping Serie A clubs of substance out of Europe, yet most of which were capable of doing so if underestimated, inclusive of the very same Boavista side that had accounted for Inter, who Mondonico's team were thrown into the path of in the second round.

A run that began with a splurge of goals against KR Reykjavík, in which Scifo was enjoying the shooting practice,

Boavista were circumnavigated thanks to two goals that combined great fortune and determined perseverance. The first, from Lentini, came when chasing in a rebound off the Boavista goalkeeper, Ivan Pudar, when he couldn't hold on to a free kick with only two minutes on the clock. The second came from Enrico Annoni, being from even closer, when the ball dropped to him after it agonisingly span past Pudar in a similar way to how Wim Kieft's goal for the Netherlands eluded a despairing Pat Bonner during the 1988 European Championship, except this time the ball having struck the post and landed at the feet of Annoni, with the goal at his mercy.

Paired with AEK Athens in the third round, a 2-2 draw in the Greek capital was obtained thanks to two headed goals, the first from Casagrande, the second from Giorgio Bresciani. Casagrande was a striker of whom so much was expected as he went into the 1986 World Cup with Telê Santana's Brazil, only to see his potential go unfulfilled on football's most elevated stage.

Bustling, in the image of a traditional English centre-forward, Casagrande was required to work alone up front, for most of his time, by Mondonico. Physical and difficult to knock out of his stride, he wasn't a stereotypical Brazilian goalscorer, more a player with a European styling, or that of one of the more forthright or bludgeoning South American nations. Arguably a Brazilian Mark Hateley, what he lacked in terms of naked Copacabana Beach skill, he more than made up for in being ruthlessly blunt in front of goal. A sledgehammer of a striker; a prototype of Diego Costa, in some respects.

Casagrande scored the only goal of the return game, at the Stadio delle Alpi. Another header powered home that suggested he must have had the neck muscles of a lion.

In the quarter-finals, Torino avoided a cluster of European royalty. With Real Madrid, Liverpool and Ajax among the field of teams remaining, Mondonico was instead handed Boldklubben 1903 and a relatively sedate trip to Denmark.

A goal procured in each half, matched to a clean sheet kept, meant that Torino had effectively booked their semi-final spot by the end of the first leg. Casagrande, again on target with the first, through a gloriously untidy effort bundled in at the back post, was complemented by Policano, powering the ball into the roof of the net, from just outside the penalty area, when a free kick was rolled into his path.

Back in Turin, Casagrande provoked the only goal of the second leg, when a marvellous run of his was enough to panic Ivan Nielsen into turning the ball past his own goalkeeper.

If Torino's run to the semi-final was one in which they mostly had to cope with the subtly unsettling concept of being favourites to progress through each round, in the last four they were undoubtedly back in the more comfortable position of being the underdog.

Real Madrid were aiming for a third UEFA Cup success and it was they who stood in the way of Torino and a first major European final. It was a coming together that also represented a reunion between Vazquez and his former club.

At the Santiago Bernabéu, Casagrande blew the semi-final wide open when he broke the first-leg deadlock, capitalising on Francisco Buyo being taken by surprise and by the lack of height, plus the unusual trajectory of Policano's cross, shortly before the hour. When the Madrid goalkeeper spilled the ball, it was the Torino number 9 that took full advantage.

Within seven minutes, Madrid hadn't just levelled the scores, but snatched the lead. Firstly, Gheorghe Hagi finished smartly, after some wonderful build-up play by the fabulously gifted Míchel, before Fernando Hierro powered home a forceful header, meeting another Míchel contribution beyond the back post.

Damage done by Casagrande's away goal, however, as swift, stylish and devilishly handsome as Madrid's riposte had been, they walked into the Stadio delle Alpi bearing gifts. With only seven minutes gone, Ricardo Rocha scored a spectacular own goal, to give Torino both the lead on the night and put them on the road to the final with their away-goal advantage.

While it didn't alter Madrid's need for a goal to save themselves, Luca Fusi made it 2-0 with less than 20 minutes left, making the most of some dazzling play from Lentini. It was a bittersweet night for Fusi, as the yellow card he picked up ruled him out of the first leg of the final.

Faced with the unenviable challenge of overcoming a resurgent Ajax in the 1992 UEFA Cup Final, the chance of a third successive all-Italian crescendo fell narrowly short, when the Genoa of Carlos Aguilera, Stefano Eranio, Branco and Tomáš Skuhravý lost out in Amsterdam, having already overcome Oviedo, two trips to Bucharest and a Liverpool side that was making its first foray back into European competition after the Heysel ban.

A work in motion, Louis van Gaal's Ajax would evolve dramatically during the next three years, to the point that of the 16 players to collect a UEFA Cup winners' medal in 1992, only three of them would be present in 1995 to be handed a Champions League winners' medal, one of those being Edwin van der Sar, who in 1992 acted as the back-up goalkeeper to Stanley Menzo. This was also an Ajax that possessed the bright stars of Dennis Bergkamp and Wim Jonk, who would soon be spirited away to Serie A.

Without the suspended Fusi and the injured Policano, for the first leg of the final Torino were coaxed into an open game of football at the Stadio delle Alpi, by Van Gaal and his Ajax side. A 2-2 draw ensued, in which Casagrande, twice, heroically equalised, after *de Godenzonen* had twice taken the lead, with a goal each side of the interval, firstly from a Jonk effort from distance and then by a Stefan Pettersson penalty.

Not only a target man, Casagrande proved in the first leg of the final that he could play with the ball at his feet too, when either the need arose, or the will overcame him. Sharp and sensory in claiming his first strike, the second required some fleeting footwork and quick thinking. Dragging the ball along with him, as if it were a small, unruly, uncontrollable and yapping lapdog that was always one wrong move or bobble away from escaping his possession, Casagrande advanced, then dinked it over Menzo, as he dropped to the turf.

With a goalless draw at Amsterdam's Olympic Stadium in the second leg, the 1992 UEFA Cup Final went the way of Ajax – a major stpping stone on the way to them becoming European champions, for a fourth time.

For Torino, however, it was something that represented a missed opportunity and perhaps the point of detachment in Italian football, where their great Turin rival, Juventus, and the two Milan giants began to fully monopolise Serie A.

Apart from the brief renaissance of the Roman figures of Lazio and Roma, which marked the end of the last Millennium and the beginning of the new, since Sampdoria's 1990/91 title win, the Serie A trophy has only avoided the possession of Juventus, Milan or Inter on three occasions, the last of those being the 2004/05 version, which Juventus were stripped of, as part of the *Calciopoli* scandal.

By the start of the 1992/93 season, Lentini was wearing the red and black stripes of Milan, while within a year, Casagrande was back in Brazil. Mondonico would lead his team to Coppa Italia success in 1993, yet this wonderful Torino era was dissipating and he himself returned to Atalanta in 1994. By 1996, Torino were back in Serie B, with the highs of a UEFA Cup Final and a third-place finish in Serie A seemingly as if they were a lifetime ago, rather than just four years past.

In time, Mondonico would return to Torino, guiding the club back to Serie A in 2000, while Lentini, the most expensive player in the world in the summer of 1992, would never hit the peaks that his potential suggested he would. Surviving a high-speed car crash in August 1993, Lentini escaped with his life, but also with a vastly altered footballing horizon, which included his own return to Torino, where he played a role in Mondonico's promotion-winning team.

Turin again featured heavily in the 1992/93 UEFA Cup. Torino fell at the second hurdle, to Dynamo Moscow, while Trapattoni's Juventus went all the way to glory 16 years after he had led the club to their 1977 success.

Roberto Baggio finally had a major honour of substance to show for a career that had, up until this point, shined due to his redoubtable individual talents, rather than the accumulation of trophies and medals.

Falling short in the 1990 final with Fiorentina, against Juventus, Baggio's first three years with *I Bianconeri* had coincided with Juventus continuing to chase its tail, in their attempts to put themselves back among the winners' circle. Try as Trapattoni might domestically, Capello's Milan were simply on another planet, however.

Juventus had failed to acclimatise to a world without Trapattoni, when he departed in the summer of 1986, to such a pronounced level that the Trapattoni who returned in 1991 was not only handed his own legacy to live up to, but, also, the damage his absence had done to the club was there for him to unpick.

A distant runner-up to an undefeated Milan, in the 1991/92 Serie A title race, Juventus had also lost out in the Coppa Italia Final, to the fast maturing Parma. Rather than using that as a launchpad for an even greater challenge to Milan's supremacy, 1992/93 proved to be a domestic step backwards. Trapattoni's team went out of the Coppa Italia at the semi-final stage, while the gap between them and *I Rossoneri* in the league was extended, not shrunken.

Solace was taken in the UEFA Cup, though; the tournament that Trapattoni had used as his parting gift to Inter. Arguably, success in the very same tournament is what proved to be the bedrock upon which a new era of Juventus vitality was constructed.

Anorthosis Famagusta were ruthlessly dealt with, 10-1 on aggregate, the Cypriots' only goal being procured by the future Newcastle United curiosity, Temuri Ketsbaia. This was target practice for Juventus that included goals for Baggio, Möller, Gianluca Vialli, Antonio Conte, Moreno Torricelli, Fabrizio Ravanelli, Jürgen Kohler and Pierluigi Casiraghi.

A jewel-encrusted Juventus, could also call upon the skill and unpredictable nature of Paolo Di Canio, plus the £8m percentage playing of David Platt, a man who would suffer throughout the campaign as Juventus's odd man out, during an era where four would not condense into three when it came to the club trying to field their permitted foreign trio.

Platt would often be sat in the stands, watching on, as the German duo of Möller and Kohler would be regularly joined by the Brazilian international, Júlio César. Given that César and Kohler formed Trapattoni's central defensive partnership, Platt would be left to fight it out with Möller for the last berth, often losing out. The England international did, however, make a huge contribution, with the only goal of the second-round encounter with Panathinaikos. It was a beautifully taken effort, which hints of what Platt might have been able to do in the black and white stripes, had he not had to contend with Möller.

Another glut of goals was plundered in the third round, against Sigma Olomouc, one of which was a deliciously impudent lob from Dino Baggio, during the first leg, before the return game provided Juventus with another chance to find their goalscoring range.

Panathinaikos's stubbornness aside, Juventus had cruised into the quarter-final, where the strength of the challenges was suddenly heightened. Trapattoni's one and only reversal of the run was delivered by Benfica, at the Estádio da Luz, in the first leg of their last-eight clash. Vialli's away goal was a precious prize, however, and the second leg was an untidy, but one-sided encounter, as the visitors' vulnerability in central defence was exposed within two minutes of the start, via a set piece, by

Kohler, with Dino Baggio and Ravanelli adding second-half strikes.

In the semi-final, the Paris Saint-Germain of George Weah and David Ginola were ready and waiting to ambush. At the Stadio delle Alpi, in the first leg, the two linked midway through the first half, to give Artur Jorge's side the lead. It took a second-half Roberto Baggio masterclass to turn the evening around for Juventus. A stunning first-time drive into Bernard Lama's bottom right-hand corner was followed by a trademark free kick, which was *Il Divin Codino* at his very best.

At the Parc des Princes, just over a fortnight later, Baggio scored the only goal, deep into the second half, when all the while at the back, Trapattoni's team repelled PSG's attempts to work their way into a game in which they had needed only one goal to take the away-goal advantage.

Borussia Dortmund stood between Juventus and a first major trophy in three years. Four years prior to them facing one another in the Champions League Final, there was something of an unofficial twinning of the two clubs, between 1993 and 1997. It was also a coming together that acted as a reunion of sorts, as in Dortmund, Möller found himself up against one of his former clubs, while Reuter's stay at Juventus had amounted to one season, before heading back to the Bundesliga, at the Westfalenstadion.

By the time of the 1997 Champions League Final, Möller had returned to Dortmund, where both he and Reuter were joined by Kohler, who was of course in the Juventus side for both legs of the 1993 UEFA Cup Final.

An utterly commanding set of performances, Trapattoni won what would prove to be his only piece of silverware, during his second spell in charge of Juventus. Within a year, he himself was off to the Bundesliga, for the first of two explosive spells in charge of Bayern Munich, having laid what would at last be Serie A-winning foundations for Marcello Lippi.

It was through a marvellously worked free-kick routine that Dino Baggio converted, in the 26th minute, to cancel out

Michael Rummenigge's early opener, during the first leg, in Dortmund. From that moment on, there was only going to be one winner. Four minutes later, Roberto Baggio had made it 2-0, with a finish that any predatory penalty-box poacher would be proud to call their own.

A third goal snared, with 16 minutes to go, Roberto Baggio again on target, with another that could have been plucked from the Vialli textbook on goalscoring, and it left Dortmund with an insurmountable mountain to climb when they travelled to Turin for the return game.

Even the absence of the influential Antonio Conte, who was suspended for the second leg, did nothing to disrupt the flow and energy of Juventus's performance at the Stadio delle Alpi, which effectively picked up where it had left off at the Westfalenstadion.

Within five minutes, Juventus had carved Dortmund open and Dino Baggio had added to his impressive contribution of UEFA Cup goals for the campaign. A defensive midfielder of great discipline, while he would move on to Parma in 1994, departing Juventus with only one Serie A goal for the club, conversely, he struck five times in the 1992/93 UEFA Cup, three of those coming across the breadth of the two legs of the final.

Operating as the late interloper into the Dortmund penalty area, it was Dino Baggio again who scored Juventus's second of the night, meeting a free kick with a fine glancing header shortly before half-time. A hopeless position to be in, the visitors conceded one more goal in the second half, with Möller benefiting from a lucky ricochet after some beautiful build-up play.

Perhaps the most telling thing about Juventus's 1993 UEFA Cup Final victory is just how unequivocal the gulf between the two teams was. Trapattoni's side finished fourth in Serie A in 1992/93, eclipsed not only by Capello's seemingly bulletproof Milan, but by Osvaldo Bagnoli's Inter and Nevio Scala's hypnotic Parma too. In the Bundesliga, Dortmund also finished fourth, yet despite the domestic leagues of Italy and Germany both being of elite standing, Serie A was off and away on such an untouchable plateau that Juventus's counterparts in the 1993 UEFA Cup Final were made to look distinctly amateur.

Herein worked a magnificent symbiosis that helped Germany, and West Germany before reunification, dominate on the international scene. The best German players would head to Serie A, where they would be refined in terms of technical ability. Added to their inherent collective work ethic, this made for the perfect environment in which to win the World Cup and the European Championship.

Italian players, meanwhile, would often wilt under the pressure of representing their national team. There has always been an all or nothing element to *Gli Azzurri*, which has left them as likely to trip over their own feet at major international tournaments, in the group stages, as they are to reach the business end.

German and Italian players are generally as studious as each other, but consistency seems to come easier to the Germanic personality. In this respect, it shouldn't be classed as a surprise that while the Milan of Sacchi and Capello swept up league titles and European Cups, and their Serie A rivals enjoyed a growing monopoly of success in the UEFA Cup, these glories came during an era in which the national team failed to win their own World Cup in 1990, following this by failing to qualify for the 1992 European Championship. Yet, in comparison, West Germany won in 1990 and, as a unified Germany, they reached the final in 1992, while their club teams struggled to make an impact in European competitions.

Even in reaching the 1994 World Cup Final, the accusation was that Roberto Baggio had dragged Italy there, single-handedly. Both before and after this, there were shadows cast over their 1982 and 2006 squads that won the respective World Cups they took part in. In both instances, those squads were backed into corners, from where they didn't just come out fighting, but claimed the prizes on offer. Perhaps the Italian national team can only fulfil its generation upon generation potential when the mood lighting is dipped to a specific degree. Yet, none of this could ever dent Serie A's well-deserved sense of superiority.

A third UEFA Cup success for Juventus, a third for Trapattoni, this one was much more domineering than his success with Inter had been in 1991. Whereas Trapattoni's 1990/91 Inter had been emphatic on home soil and conservative in their approach to travel, his 1992/93 Juventus felt like a team that was on an aesthetically pleasing mission, as much as they were one for the trophy itself.

This was a success for Juventus that played its part in setting the scene for the remainder of the decade; this was a success that would be followed by three Serie A titles, one Coppa Italia win and glory in the 1996 Champions League Final, going on to lose the next two finals – a spree of success and near misses that came Juventus's way before the end of the century, in which they reclaimed the baton as Italian football's most pre-eminent club from Milan.

In defence of their UEFA Cup, Juventus went out in the quarter-final, yet Serie A's grip on the tournament was showing no signs of loosening. Inter came back for more glory, in 1993/94, while Cagliari set off on a wonderful run to the semi-final.

For Inter, 1993/94 was a white-knuckle ride, one in which they flirted with relegation to Serie B and won only two of their last 14 league games, to eventually limp home, in 13th, just one point ahead of the relegated Piacenza.

Against all recognised laws of footballing gravity, this was an Inter that was blessed by the presence of Bergkamp and Jonk, signed from Ajax, playing in the same team that still contained many of Trapattoni's UEFA Cup winners from 1991.

Led by Osvaldo Bagnoli, the man who had taken Verona to the Serie A title almost a decade earlier, the man who was behind Genoa's early 1990s rise to prominence, Inter had finished as runner-up to Milan the previous season and much was expected of them this time around. However, the wheels stunningly fell off domestically.

Pairing Bergkamp with the Uruguayan international, Rubén Sosa, should have been a match made in heaven, yet his arrival, alongside that of Jonk, unsettled a squad that had thrived last time around, as much through the endeavours of Igor Shalimov as they had any other player.

Shalimov, a Russian, suffered the same fate with Inter in 1993/94 that befell Platt at Juventus the previous season. Four foreign players contesting three permitted berths will undoubtedly have brought an awkwardness to the squad, where newcomers needed to prove their worth immediately. This can be increased to five contesting three berths, when considering the expensive, yet underperforming Darko Pančev, who Bagnoli had little appetite for.

Added to this, while Inter's fresh intake of talent from Ajax struggled to get to grips with their new environment, Bagnoli's domestic recruits were workmanlike rather than spectacular additions. Gianluca Festa, Francesco Dell'Anno and Massimo Paganin arrived from Cagliari, Udinese and Brescia respectively, Massimo being the brother of the existing Inter player, Antonio Paganin.

Losing Matthäus, Brehme and Klinsmann in one fell swoop during the summer of 1992 was ultimately too much too soon when it came to the revamping of the post-Trapattoni Inter. Seemingly assimilated without trauma during 1992/93, it was in 1993/94 that the reverberations began to rock the club.

Domestic unease, however, was offset by Inter embracing the UEFA Cup like a long-lost friend, a place where they appeared to be able to relax, away from the weekly ordeal of league games. Bergkamp, for example, scored as many goals in the UEFA Cup as he did all season in Serie A, despite playing 20 more games in the league, compared to in Europe.

A success obtained while hovering just above the Serie A trap door, the San Siro would not only welcome the UEFA Cup in 1994, but Milan would spectacularly dismantle Johan Cruyff's Barcelona in the Champions League Final too. It was a performance from Capello's team that consigned Inter's achievement to the shadows.

When tripping off the names involved in the 1989 to 1999 run of Italian UEFA Cup winners and beaten finalists, from Napoli in 1989 to Parma in 1999, the 1994 version of Inter is arguably the one to fall under the radar the easiest. This is not only due to the exploits of Capello and Milan, but by the feeling that Inter's bigger story in 1993/94 was their unexpected battle with relegation. You can also add to this that the 1993/94 Inter wasn't the best UEFA Cup-winning Inter side of the 1990s.

Trapattoni's 1990/91 vintage draws the attention a lot more readily than the 1993/94 one. It can also be levelled that this time around, with Austria Salzburg being their opponents in the final, there is a nonchalance that Inter should be prevailing in such circumstances. When a big team attains an expected glory, it is by no means a tarnished glory, yet neither is it one which wins itself wider respect and admiration. It is limp handshakes all round, rather than broad smiles and backs being slapped.

Very little could be taken for granted about this new, vulnerable Inter, though. Even less so after Bagnoli was relieved of his duties in February after a San Siro defeat at the hands of Lazio. Domestic inconsistencies aside, he had delivered Inter into the quarter-final of the UEFA Cup before his departure. Gianpiero Marini was the man to nervously guide them over the finish line.

Marini, a defensive midfielder for Inter during the 1970s and 80s, with an eye for the occasional spectacular effort from distance, had been a player of great standing. He was an unused substitute for Italy in the 1982 World Cup Final, having played a part in all but one game in the tournament up until then, quite likely denied involvement against West Germany due to

Enzo Bearzot being forced to replace Francesco Graziani, with Alessandro Altobelli, in the early minutes of the game.

As coach of Inter, his spell in charge would stretch to just three months, losing eight of his 12 Serie A games, yet plotting a way through the latter stages of the UEFA Cup, overseeing a success that was totally out of proportion to what was a campaign of stunning misadventure.

Under Bagnoli, for the first three rounds, on UEFA Cup performances alone, you would never have guessed that Inter were heading toward such dangerous domestic territory. Rapid Bucureşti were clinically dispatched, the standout moments over the two games being a wonderful Bergkamp hat-trick in the first leg, inclusive of a stunning twisting volley and a delicate lob, while in the second leg, Jonk hit a devastatingly punishing goal, in reply to a lazy and poorly selected ball being played out by the Rapid goalkeeper, Leontin Toader.

Apollon Limassol were navigated in the second round, although not without a second-leg encounter that didn't know when to give up. Another piece of Bergkamp intelligence had secured Inter a 1-0 victory at the San Siro, but at the Tsirion Stadium, Apollon brushed off the early blow of being 2-0 down in under ten minutes, to eventually push Bagnoli's side to a 3-3 draw.

A goal for Shalimov, on a rare outing in place of Jonk, Bergkamp also claimed another, only to see Milenko Špoljarić and Slađan Šćepović drag Apollon back on to level terms, all within the first half hour of the game.

When Fontolan scored for Inter seven minutes before the interval, a game of delightful skill and ineptitude appeared to be settled. Apollon had one last roll of the dice, however, when they gave their visitors some time to sweat out the final few minutes, thanks to a third goal of their own, from Giorgos Iosifidis.

Bagnoli's last UEFA Cup duties for Inter were carried out against a Norwich City side that had remarkably knocked Bayern Munich out in the previous round, even winning at the

Olympiastadion, where they became the only British side to beat Bayern in the iconic stadium that had hosted both the 1972 Summer Olympics and the 1974 World Cup Final.

Two 1-0 victories were procured by Bergkamp, firstly from the penalty spot at Carrow Road and then via a burst of speed and a nerveless one-on-one, with Bryan Gunn, back at the San Siro. Drawn to face Borussia Dortmund in the quarter-finals, Bagnoli was jettisoned by Inter three weeks prior to the first leg. Inter, while underachieving yet again, were not a club in any mortal danger at that point. Inter were sat in sixth position in the Serie A table. It was change for the sake of change and seemingly the reactionary whim of a club president that had grown tired of his demands for perfection not being met, while Milan and Silvio Berlusconi continued to rule, both in Serie A and across the continent.

Ernesto Pellegrini's unwillingness to wait until the end of the season to make a change almost met with calamitous repercussions. Under Marini, Inter plummeted. Obtaining the job when Bagnoli's reign ended after a Coppa Italia exit to Sampdoria and that Serie A defeat, at home to Lazio, Marini's start was far from being a dream one.

Beginning with a defeat at Piacenza, Marini picked up just one point from his first three games. From here, his next task was to take his dispirited Inter to the Westfalenstadion to face Dortmund in the first leg of the quarter-final.

Escaping the pressures of Serie A's unforgiving pitches, Inter were excellent in Dortmund – sharp interchanging of passes, intelligent movement off the ball, strong yet inventive across the midfield, disciplined in defence. For Dortmund, meanwhile, it was like a rerun of the first leg of the 1993 final against Juventus. Despite Inter's week-to-week woes, there was still a clear chasm between the great and the good of Italian and German club football.

Two outstandingly converted goals from Jonk, within a three-minute span of the first half, were consolidated by the temporarily reprieved Shalimov in injury time. It would prove to be a crucial extra goal, given that Dortmund had snatched one back five minutes from the end through Michael Schulz.

When play resumed, 16 days later, in Milan, Inter were in for a rude awakening with Michael Zorc and Lars Ricken scoring just before the break and shortly after the restart, respectively. It was a relieved Antonio Manicone who struck on the counter-attack, with nine minutes remaining, just as Dortmund were pushing forward in their bid for a winning goal.

From being empirical at the Westfalenstadion, to largely insipid at the San Siro, this was a definitive example of the extreme sweet and sour sides that the 1993/94 Inter possessed. A fantasy first leg, away, followed by a serious attempt to self-destruct at home, it couldn't get any more Inter than that.

Nervously through to the semi-finals, Inter were paired in an all Serie A clash with an overachieving Cagliari. Caught within such an uncertain season and maybe feeling that attack would be the best form of defence after their Dortmund experiences, Marini's team simply went for broke in the first leg at Cagliari's Stadio Sant'Elia.

Twice taking the lead, Inter eventually had to make do with a 3-2 defeat that came equipped with two vital away goals, the first a beautifully guided header from Fontolan, just six minutes in, the second coming from a marginally deflected Sosa strike, shortly beyond the hour. Cagliari's responses came from the Belgian international, Luís Oliveira, the habitual journeyman Antonio Criniti and the future Italian international full-back, Giuseppe Pancaro.

With a sense of the intrepid, Inter supporters could have been forgiven for expecting the worst when they arrived at the San Siro for the second leg. However, what they witnessed was the version of Inter that had dismantled Dortmund during the first leg of the quarter-final.

A 3-0 victory fell the way of Inter, not by luck, but through an inspired performance from Bergkamp, who scored the opening goal with a hotly disputed first-half penalty, before setting up the next two, in the second half, for Berti and Jonk. If there were any internal resentments at Inter towards Bergkamp and Jonk, then they were not on display that evening.

Austria Salzburg were the surprise opponents awaiting Inter in the 1994 UEFA Cup Final, the club that now goes by the contemporary and controversial name of Red Bull Salzburg. Just the third time an Austrian side had reached a major European final, Salzburg's route to their showdown with Inter took in duels with DAC Dunajská Streda, the beaten 1993 Cup Winners' Cup finalists, Royal Antwerp, a stunning second-leg fightback in the third round against Sporting CP, Eintracht Frankfurt on penalties, a tie that offered up the peculiar sight of a German team being vanquished in a shoot-out from 12 yards, then Karlsruher SC, on away goals in the semi-final.

A hard-earned place in the final that nobody could suggest was unmerited, Salzburg were packed with Austrian internationals and had just claimed their first Austrian Bundesliga title, yet they were a team without a talismanic star. They were instead a collective that pulled together as one, led by a captain who was fast approaching his 39th birthday and a richly deserved retirement.

Heribert Weber had made his first appearance for the Austrian national team as far back as 1976, playing a part in both the 1978 and 1982 World Cups, inclusive of the game that would become known as the 'Disgrace of Gijón', against West Germany, when a result of convenience put Algeria out of the tournament and altered the way group stages of major tournaments of the future would be ended. He had also been in the Rapid Wien side that played Everton in the 1985 Cup Winners' Cup Final.

Salzburg didn't solely rely upon domestic players, however, as they did boast a Brazilian playmaker in the shape of the journeyman, Marquinho, and the goals of the Croatian international, Nikola Jurčević, who damagingly missed the first leg. Jurčević also had his compatriot Damir Mužek for company in the squad.

Tight and compact, Salzburg had kept an impressive seven clean sheets on the way to the final, yet had scored just 11 goals in their ten games. Their defensive solidity was what made the manner of the goal they conceded in the first leg all the more shocking, as Salzburg uncharacteristically switched off when a free kick set Berti loose in the penalty area, from where he controlled the ball masterfully and finished beautifully, ten minutes before half-time.

Back at the San Siro, the second leg ended in the same scoreline, although Inter were made to wait over an hour for their breakthrough. Sosa's measured pass gave Jonk the opportunity, which he impudently took with the outside of his left foot, chipping the advancing Otto Konrad with what was almost a stabbing technique.

To end a fraught campaign by lifting the UEFA Cup was an incredible achievement for Inter. Talented, yet disjointed, it is very telling of the club's trials and tribulations that, despite the positive final flourish to the season, they supplied only one player towards Sacchi's Italy squad for the World Cup finals that summer. Berti.

Meanwhile, Inter's success in 1994 also represented a subtle line being drawn in the sand by UEFA. Almost imperceptible in retrospective terms and something I'd forgotten all about entirely until the research took me there, by the beginning of the 1994/95 season, the UEFA Cup had taken its first defined step in a new and unsettling direction.

Chapter Twelve

The Disappointing Homogenisation of the UEFA Cup

WHEN GROUP stages were introduced to the 1991/92 European Cup, swiftly followed by the 1992/93 rebranding of the tournament to the UEFA Champions League, the pistol was fired on radical change, in not only European football's governing body's elite tournament, but in a domino effect upon the UEFA Cup and the European Cup Winners' Cup too.

By 1999, the Cup Winners' Cup had been consigned to the history books and footballing museums. While it had been quite rightly classed as the second-most important of the trio of major European tournaments, with one round fewer and, more often than not, a weaker field of teams than the UEFA Cup, in an era where commercialism and modernisation was now the watchword of football's dealmakers, the Cup Winners' Cup was soon earmarked for demolition.

A tournament that represented the old currency of football, it had jarred to an extent when Juventus, as the 1991 UEFA Cup winners, didn't defend their prize as holders, instead as Coppa Italia winners, going into the 1991/92 Cup Winners' Cup.

Next on the agenda was the thorny issue of just why UEFA's third-grade tournament largely boasted the strongest line-up of teams. To be fair, that was a peculiarity, but it was a peculiarity that made the tournament what it was. Once you begin to compromise that quirk, then you alter the personality of the tournament entirely.

The season 1994/95 saw a format change implemented in the UEFA Cup, partly due to the proliferation of the former eastern European collectives, but also due to UEFA wanting to sharpen the field of teams for the evolving Champions League.

No longer was being in possession of a domestic league title a guarantee of participation in Europe's biggest competition. If your national coefficient wasn't up to scratch, then the bouncers wouldn't let you through the door of the Champions League.

It meant the 1994/95 UEFA Cup had a preliminary round tagged on to it and the tournament became a refuge for 22 displaced league champions, inclusive of evocative names such as Dinamo Tbilisi, Slovan Bratislava and Ararat Yerevan, while clubs like Linfield and Shamrock Rovers lost their chance to host the biggest teams on the continent. European football's haves were now being cocooned away from the have-nots.

The UEFA Cup, as was, had three more seasons left to run, before the Champions League began to absorb teams that hadn't even won their domestic league title, from the 1997/98 season onward. The very same season the UEFA Cup Final became a one-off game.

For those final three seasons of the two-legged final era, however, much beauty could still be found and for Serie A's clubs, initially at least, it was a case of business as usual.

While Inter's 1994 UEFA Cup-winning team supplied only one player to Italy's World Cup squad, conversely, Nevio Scala's Parma supplied five players to Arrigo Sacchi's cause. A club enjoying a hypnotic rise to power, they had won the Cup Winners' Cup in 1993, and now they had the UEFA Cup in their sights too.

As holders, Inter went out at the first hurdle, bundled out, on penalties, when renewing acquaintances with Aston Villa. The familiar image of Juventus would return for the 1995 UEFA

Cup Final though, where they were joined by the hipster's 1990s Italian team of choice, Parma.

Parma were a wonderful entity. The 1995 UEFA Cup Final was their third major European final in succession, having defeated Royal Antwerp in the Cup Winners' Cup Final at a sparsely populated Wembley in 1993, before losing as holders to Arsenal in Copenhagen a year later. They would go on to reach another UEFA Cup Final, in 1999.

Dripping with talent, Scala had constructed a team that shook the established order in Serie A. Luca Bucci, his goalkeeper, had gone to the World Cup as back-up to Gianluca Pagliuca and Luca Marchegiani, while in the USA he had been joined by team-mates Luigi Apolloni, Antonio Benarrivo, Lorenzo Minotti and Gianfranco Zola. Two other members of Sacchi's World Cup squad, Roberto Mussi and Dino Baggio, would also be recruited by Parma for the new campaign, the latter swooped for when Juventus signed both Didier Deschamps and Paulo Sousa. The Dino of the Baggios, no relation of Roberto, would come back to haunt Juventus in the most emphatic of manners.

Strong throughout the squad, Scala could also call upon the fantastic Massimo Crippa, the former Italian international Alberto Di Chiara, who was the first Parma player to represent Italy, plus the massively underrated Gabriele Pin, the skilled yet inconsistent Marco Branca and the experienced former Italian international goalkeeper, Giovanni Galli, who acted as Bucci's back-up until a prodigiously talented 17-year-old, going by the name of Gianluigi Buffon, made his presence felt. They also had an emerging Stefano Fiore within their ranks.

All this domestic talent was then accentuated by Parma's shrewd eye for foreign influences. The commanding Portuguese international, Fernando Couto, was joined by the intelligent and versatile Argentine, Roberto Sensini, with awe and wonderment supplied by the unpredictable, yet hypnotic Colombian, Faustino Asprilla. Tomas Brolin was also still a Parma player.

Never possessing the consistency to take the Serie A title, the closest Parma came was in 1996/97, when they finished runner-up to Juventus, beyond the departure of Scala, under the guidance of Carlo Ancelotti.

Very much a cup team, between 1992 and 2002 Parma won the Cup Winners' Cup, two UEFA Cups, one European Super Cup, three Coppa Italia and one Supercoppa Italiana. There were also other near misses. Parma were universally admired and feared. They certainly caught the imagination.

A 1-0 first-round, first-leg defeat, at Vitesse Arnhem, was overcome by a brace of goals from Zola, back at the Stadio Ennio Tardini. The first of those goals was a trademark free kick from a ridiculous distance, the second a case of being in the right place at the right time to take advantage of an unguarded net, with less than 20 minutes to play.

Juventus progressed to the second round, in part due to CSKA Sofia fielding the ineligible Petar Mihtarski, scorer of two goals in the Bulgarians' 3-2, first-leg victory, against the Turin giants. Marcello Lippi's side were later awarded a 3-0 win, clocking up an 8-1 aggregate success, with their 5-1, second-leg win being allowed to stand, despite Mihtarski scoring for CSKA once again.

Crippa was the man with the decisive goal in the first leg of the second round against AIK, in Stockholm, for Parma. Taken adroitly on the volley, it was a massively characteristic goal from a player who was often overshadowed by Asprilla and, prior to this season, Brolin. In the return game, Minotti struck twice, in a scrappy game where the goals suited the ambience.

For Juventus, the second round brought them two very stubborn games against Maritimo, in which the growing importance of Fabrizio Ravanelli was evident. Lippi's Juventus would go on to break their nine-year Serie A title drought this season, and while Roberto Baggio played a vital role, he sat over three months out after picking up a serious knee injury against Padova in November.

It was in the absence of Baggio that Alessandro Del Piero truly blossomed, with the team displaying a new steely resolve, balance and more direct style of play. Baggio would depart Turin for AC Milan in the summer of 1995, as Lippi sought to eliminate the concept of his team ever having to place over-reliance on any one given player, especially one who held as much power as Baggio did. Del Piero would become a talismanic figure for Juventus, yet he always seemed to be part of a wider framework, compared to Baggio, who would be given the ball and be expected to create magic for both himself and others.

Just a short few days before damaging his knee against Padova, Baggio was in inspired form in the first leg of Juventus's third-round encounter with Admira Wacker, in the Austrian capital. With skill to burn and composure that wouldn't have looked out of place if leading the Vienna Philharmonic Orchestra, it is quite eerie to watch the footage of this performance, armed with the knowledge that the injury, which would start the clock ticking down on his removal from the club, was only three days away, an injury sustained on a Serie A occasion, when he scored the first goal of a 2-1 victory. Without Baggio, his team-mates laboured to a 2-1 win in the second leg.

While political subterfuge and manoeuvrings occurred in the Juventus camp, during the third round Parma were involved in a marvellously entertaining 180 minutes of football, against Athletic Club. The first leg was settled by just the one goal, a fantastic glancing near-post header from the future Athletic head coach, Cuco Ziganda, when getting on the end of a beautifully tempting swinging cross from the right, at a stunningly atmospheric old San Mamés.

In reply, Parma were widely superior a fortnight later, when David Elleray was the man keeping a watchful referee's eye over the game. A Zola dip of the shoulder and fine finish was added to before the break when the liberated Dino Baggio prodded in the second.

Within three minutes of the restart, Baggio powered home the second, after a delightfully outrageous ball was played for him to run on to, direct from the outside of Zola's left foot. With the game seemingly over, this is where it got a little trickier, as despite Couto drilling in a fourth goal when the ball fell invitingly at his feet following a scramble for a free kick that was angled in towards the Athletic penalty spot in the 64th minute, it was a gift that fell between two goals scored by the visitors, both of which dragged the Basque side to within one goal of the away-goal advantage.

It meant that the final 15 minutes were played out on a knife-edge.

Nerve held, Parma advanced to a quarter-final that was a closer call than they might have imagined, when the draw paired them with Odense BK. A Zola penalty, early in the second half of the first leg, was all that separated the two teams.

For Juventus in the last eight, Eintracht Frankfurt were dispatched via a 4-1 aggregate scoreline that was far closer than meets the eye. A 1-1 draw at the Waldstadion, in which Giancarlo Marocchi bobbled one in from distance to open the scoring only to see Jan Furtok level the game was followed by a 3-0 victory for Lippi, back in Turin, who now had Roberto Baggio back at his disposal.

Not as conclusive as it may sound, Juventus's goals in the second leg all came in the last 13 minutes, the last two from the 87th minute onward, while Frankfurt desperately pushed on in their search for a way back into the game. It was Conte that broke the deadlock, before Ravanelli swept in the second on the counter. Del Piero then completed the scoring when springing the Frankfurt offside trap.

With Dortmund and Bayer Leverkusen progressing to the semi-finals, the steadily maturing Dortmund defeating Lazio in the quarter-finals, it resulted in two Serie A vs Bundesliga clashes in the last four. Juventus tangled with Dortmund yet again, while Parma were handed Leverkusen.

Contrasting fortunes, Juventus were fortunate to walk away with a 2-2 draw from the first leg in Milan's San Siro, a game switched from Turin's Stadio delle Alpi due to a rental dispute and unsatisfactory attendances. Twice Dortmund took the lead and Lippi was reliant on a Roberto Baggio penalty and late Kohler strike to avoid defeat. For Dortmund, their goals came from the ex-Juventus duo Stefan Reuter and Andreas Möller, the latter being a glorious strike from distance. This was a very different Dortmund compared to the one that had been unable to give Juventus a game of substance in the 1993 UEFA Cup Final.

Parma, meanwhile, headed to Leverkusen for the first leg of their semi-final, where they returned to Emilia-Romagna with a valuable 2-1 victory. Dino Baggio, a fine player in a Juventus shirt, was proving an absolute revelation in the colours of Parma and it was he who equalised, after the gifted Paulo Sérgio had drawn first blood, with the Italians undone at a corner.

Baggio's leveller, when it came, was one which was bestowed with luck. A wild diagonal pass fell into his possession on the right-hand side of the Leverkusen penalty area and he struck his shot too centrally, albeit rising. Rüdiger Vollborn, the Leverkusen goalkeeper, got a hand to it, yet as the ball looped upward, it didn't have the legs to clear the crossbar. Baggio was wheeling away to celebrate before the ball had dropped over the goal line.

Again, Baggio was key to Parma's winning goal; latching on to a long ball out of defence, it was his determination that gave Asprilla the opportunity to thread the ball into the Leverkusen net, amid a sea of legs and flailing arms. Just five minutes separated the goals of Baggio and Asprilla during the early exchanges of the first half.

At the Stadio Ennio Tardini, Parma were simply too strong for Leverkusen. Despite a determined start by the visitors, Asprilla was in the right place at the right time to profit when Vollborn parried an effort from distance, which had taken an awkward bounce on its way towards goal. Only four minutes had elapsed.

Careless in possession of the ball, it was ten minutes into the second half that Leverkusen's generosity gave Asprilla his second goal of the game, a goal that was ruthless, yet one he was almost sheepish in taking, celebrating it with a more lethargic version of his trademark cartwheel and stomach punch to the air.

For Parma's third goal, Asprilla turned provider, driving the ball into the Leverkusen half, before playing through the perfect ball for Zola to run on to and coolly place beyond the exposed Vollborn, with his defence having been holding far too high of a line.

This game was a platform in which Asprilla displayed his full repertoire of skills and talents. A player, no matter what team you support, who could only provoke admiration and joy from the spectator when in such irresistible form. Throw Zola alongside him for good measure and it made Parma compulsive viewing. They were simply mesmerising at times.

Juventus, with much to do in the other semi-final, were quick out of the blocks at the Westfalenstadion. Dortmund were left to rue a lack of defensive concentration when Sergio Porrini wonderfully headed home a Roberto Baggio corner in the sixth minute.

In an explosive start to the game, four minutes later the former Juventus man, Júlio César, drove in the equaliser, as Dortmund pulled off an excellent free-kick routine. César's shot arrowed just above the turf, through a fragmented Juventus wall, after it was cheekily rolled into his path. Less than two years on from being roundly outclassed by Juventus in the 1993 UEFA Cup Final, two years on from this latest meeting in the 1995 semi-final, it would be Dortmund's time, in Munich, in the Champions League Final.

On this occasion, however, unlike in 1997, this was a Juventus that still possessed the talents of Baggio. Just beyond the half hour, he was the man to decide the outcome of the game, with yet another act of footballing genius, angling a beautiful and precise free kick into the top left-hand corner, marginally clipping the underside of Stefan Klos's crossbar. Baggio's celebration took him into a spontaneous embrace with Lippi that belied the tensions that were thought to be escalating between the two.

No further goals added, Dortmund having been without the services of Möller, it set up an incredible 40-day span, where Parma and Juventus faced one another in a series of games of gigantic standing. First up were the two legs of the UEFA Cup Final, a pair of games that would be followed by a crucial Serie A clash and the two legs of the 1995 Coppa Italia Final.

Two closely contested games, the first leg was settled within five minutes of the start when Dino Baggio got on the end of a cutting diagonal pass from Zola, to hook the ball past the advancing Michelangelo Rampulla. From there, the game became a physical one, with six yellow cards being brandished, four of them to Parma, three of which resulted in the second-leg suspensions of Apolloni, Pin and Sensini.

Parma's Baggio would complete his revenge in the second leg, where Scala's heavily restructured side didn't only have suspension issues to navigate, but fitness concerns over Benarrivo, who had lasted only seven minutes of the first game. In a game that once again took place at the San Siro, he would be withdrawn at half-time.

Welcoming back Crippa and calling on the emerging Stefano Fiore, Massimo Susic also stepped up to cover in defence, for Apolloni. Still, the odds were stacked against Parma as soon as Vialli scored a stunning goal to level the aggregate scoreline, ten minutes before half-time. Collecting a long and arcing ball out from left-back, Vialli was swift and devastating in converting it, striking the ball at the first time of asking with such power that it ripped past Bucci and into the top right-hand corner.

Depleted and on the ropes, Vialli's goal could have easily been the beginning of the end of Parma's hopes, yet they adapted, and in another bruising encounter, this time seven yellow cards being shared, Dino Baggio struck the hammer blow to Juventus in the 53rd minute when he headed in the goal that left their hosts needing two to lift the trophy. Against his former team, it was a sweet moment for a man who was too readily discarded. Baggio's exuberant celebration said it all. And with that, Parma became the last Italian winner of a two-legged UEFA Cup Final.

In the days and weeks that followed, Juventus were more than compensated, when clinching their first Serie A title in nine years, with a 4-0 victory against their UEFA Cup Final conquerors. They followed this up with a convincing two-legged victory over Scala's side in the Coppa Italia Final. It made for the peculiar conundrum that Italy's representatives in the 1995/96 Cup Winners' Cup would be the UEFA Cup holders, Parma, having lost the Coppa Italia Final to the Serie A champions, who would instead contest the Champions League.

In the wake of this seven-season stretch of Serie A domination, 1995/96 had provided something of a UEFA Cup culture shock, where, for the first time since 1988, no Italian team reached the final.

When AC Milan and AS Roma were bundled out at the quarter-final stage, they had been the last Serie A teams standing in the tournament. Within this sudden power vacuum, the Bundesliga took its chance and grabbed the glory. In the absence of the rising Dortmund, who were called away on Champions League duties, it was left to Bayern Munich to take advantage of the situation.

For Bayern, the 1990s had been a harsh decade, up until this point. While they had won the Bundesliga in 1993/94, it was a standalone success and one that came in a season in which Franz Beckenbauer stepped into the role of head coach midway through, after the Christmas sacking of Erich Ribbeck, when a limping Bayern were sat in fourth position and looking anything but potential champions.

Despite making two European Cup Final appearances and reaching a further seven major European semi-finals, since Beckenbauer had kicked his last competitive ball as a player for the club, it was fast approaching 20 years since Bayern had tasted success on the continent.

Even domestically, Bayern were no longer the monopolising force of old. When they clinched the Bundesliga title in 1989/90, it was a fifth success in six seasons. In comparison, in the following six campaigns, they lifted the iconic *Salatschüssel* only once, while even the domestic cup, the DFB-Pokal, had remained elusive since 1986.

Bayern had not only had to contend with the rise of one challenger, but a cluster of them. Success for Kaiserslautern was emulated by VfB Stuttgart and Werder Bremen, while Eintracht Frankfurt came close too. Then came Ottmar Hitzfeld's Dortmund.

Desperate measures called for desperate transfer dealings, and in the summer of 1995, Bayern went on a trolley dash. In came Thomas Strunz, Andreas Herzog and Ciriaco Sforza, scalped from Bundesliga rivals, Stuttgart, Bremen and Kaiserslautern respectively, while from the Premier League they lured Jürgen Klinsmann from Tottenham Hotspur, then tempted Emil Kostadinov to depart Deportivo La Coruña and LaLiga. A second busy summer in succession; 12 months earlier, Bayern had recruited Oliver Kahn, Markus Babbel and Jean-Pierre Papin.

In the Bundesliga, Hitzfeld and his Dortmund team were far too coherent a force for the Fantasy Football version of Bayern to regain domestic top billing, instead taking the runner-up spot, finishing six points adrift of the champions. With yet another early exit from the Pokal, it meant that Bayern's best hopes of honours lay in the UEFA Cup.

During their bid to regain their place at the forefront of German football, Bayern's ambitious plans had brought Trapattoni to the club, in succession to Beckenbauer, who stepped down after delivering the Bundesliga title in 1993/94. A volatile union that lasted only one season, it didn't stop the Italian from returning to the club within a year of his departure, yet it was in his 12-month absence that Bayern lifted the UEFA Cup.

Casting around for a successor at the end of Trapattoni's first spell in charge, Bayern had turned to the Bremen legend, Otto Rehhagel. It was an ill-judged relationship and one in which the coach fell out with almost everybody he crossed paths with. Rancour abounded, public slanging matches erupted, player mutiny became a very real possibility and, when Rehhagel's request to move Papin on came to nothing, then all control was lost.

Amid all of this, Bayern's results were not particularly poor. Always a step or two behind Dortmund, there was a feeling that Bayern were playing instinctively, performing in spite of Rehhagel's presence, rather than because of it.

Lost in translation perhaps, rumblings of discontent had included a theory that Rehhagel was supplying his Bayern side with no tactics to speak of. One person's lack of tactics is, however, another's idea of expressive freedom.

Personality clashes are one thing, but to suggest that Rehhagel wasn't a coach of immense talent would be nonsense. This was a man who arrived at the Olympiastadion having won two Bundesliga titles at Bremen, along with the 1992 Cup Winners' Cup and three Pokals, the first of those at Fortuna Düsseldorf. For good measure, beyond his fractious spell at Bayern, he would guide Kaiserslautern back out of the 2. Bundesliga and onward to the *Salatschüssel* the very next season, eventually pulling off international football's most seismic shock, when he led Greece to glory in the 2004 European Championship.

Sometimes, what seems like the perfect union can be too explosive. The struggle for power becomes too much and something must give. See Brian Clough's 44 days in charge of Leeds United for reference of this phenomenon. A collection of big personalities and egos, all of which react against one another.

Bayern's run to the 1996 UEFA Cup Final was an eclectic one. Beaten at home in the first round, first leg by Lokomotiv Moscow, in front of just 16,000 at the Olympiastadion, Rehhagel's team corrected themselves in the Russian capital with a 5-0 victory. With four goals run in before half-time, Bayern simply overpowered their hosts, largely via goals that exploited Lokomotiv weaknesses in the full-back areas. The profiteers were Klinsmann twice, Herzog, Scholl and Strunz.

In the second round, Bayern were handed a dying breed of a tie, when paired with Raith Rovers. Instances of European royalty going up against provincial labourers was on borrowed time and this was an occasion that fleetingly offered up the iconic image of the Olympiastadion scoreboard glowing a second-leg scoreline of FC Bayern 0 Raith Rovers FC 1.

It mattered not that Bayern had comfortably won the first leg, 2-0, in a game that took place over the other side of the River Forth from where Raith were based. Their Stark's Park home, in Kirkcaldy, was scheduled for comprehensive renovation in the summer of 1996, so the decision was made to switch the game to Edinburgh, to Hibernian's Easter Road. A commercially more rewarding experience for the club, it came at the price of relinquishing the projected advantage of inflicting a more rustic environment of Rehhagel's Bayern superstars. When Klinsmann ran in the second of his two goals, there was a laid-back, pre-season air to it all.

It was Halloween when Raith walked on to the Olympia-stadion pitch for the second leg. Danny Lennon's opener came from a free kick that flew past Kahn with the help of a deliciously deft deflection. A goal that came two minutes before half-time, it meant that those who had travelled from Kirkcaldy had the entirety of the interval to stare lovingly at the scoreboard, while Sam Leitch's magnificently under-researched 1970s line of 'They'll be dancing in the streets of Raith tonight' won itself a tongue-in-cheek comeback that was eventually rehashed on a famous night for Total Network Solutions a short few seasons later.

Too strong in the second half, it still took Bayern and Babbel a goal that some players in the Highland Football League would be sheepish to call their own to win the evening, 2-1.

From a careless start in the first round against Lokomotiv, to a touch of arrogance in the second round against Raith, Bayern then went stratospheric when faced with a trio of past champions of Europe.

Utterly ruthless in their dealings with Benfica and Nottingham Forest, in the third round and quarter-final respectively, Bayern scored 14 goals over the course of those four games, with eight of them on their travels. Five of them came beside the River Trent, at the City Ground, against Frank Clark's Forest.

Klinsmann was particularly brutal in his treatment of Benfica in the first leg of the third round. Plunderer of a first-half hat-trick, within a minute of the restart, at the Olympiastadion, he had a fourth goal to his name for the evening. The former Stuttgart and Inter man would score two more during a 3-1, second-leg victory in Lisbon.

In the quarter-finals, Bayern were left in a winning yet vulnerable position at the end of the first leg. Forest returned to the East Midlands with a precious away goal, scored by the unlikely source of Steve Chettle, with a header that might well have been intended as a centre to his onrushing team-mates.

Any aspirations Forest harboured of rolling back the years to their European Cup-winning era evaporated in a blizzard of mistakes, deflections and shortcomings in the second leg. Klinsmann walked away from these two games with another three goals, while Bayern's fourth goal, on a cold Nottinghamshire night, was even scored by the misfiring Papin.

Given the demanding task of facing Johan Cruyff's Barcelona in the semi-finals, it made for two games that were defiantly for the purists, the type of games that would not be allowed to escape the greedy clutch of the Champions League for much longer.

In the first leg at the Olympiastadion, Barcelona carved Bayern open in the 15th minute, with Óscar scoring a goal that was entirely in the image of Cruyff's mind's eye. Despite this, Cruyff was just a short few weeks away from departing the Camp Nou, in a decision that was taken out of his hands, the endgame of a power struggle, between coach and president, with José Luis Núñez casting the decisive vote of no confidence.

Patiently biding their time, Bayern eventually procured a well-worked equaliser seven minutes into the second half, when Marcel Witeczek drilled the ball beneath the Barcelona goalkeeper, Carles Busquets, the father of the future Barcelona legend and World Cup winner, Sergio Busquets.

Five minutes later, Scholl edged Bayern in front, capitalising on some disjointed Barcelona defending. On a rain-lashed Munich night, on a deteriorating pitch, the visitors now seemed to be there for the taking, after they had been so domineering throughout the first half.

What came next was a gift of a goal, which enabled Barcelona to head home with a crucial second away goal and a 2-2 draw. In unseasonable weather for the first week in April, where rain had now turned into sleet, Babbel's careless and misjudged back pass fell straight into the possession of Gheorghe Hagi, who coolly dispatched it past the exposed Kahn.

Advantage very much belonging to Cruyff and Barcelona, Núñez would have been left in a difficult position had his club reached the 1996 UEFA Cup Final, which in turn would have consolidated the loosening grip of the coach.

At the Camp Nou, however, in a game where both coaches were under increasing pressure from escalating boardroom and dressing-room divisions, Barcelona struck an image of nervousness that betrayed the hard work they put in during the first leg, in Munich, to gain such a compelling foundation from which to strike for the final.

Bayern, meanwhile, were relaxed and fluid in the opening exchanges, without creating too many opportunities in the final third. Combative in winning the ball and determined in his drive forward, Christian Nerlinger came close with a long-range effort in the 22nd minute that had Busquets beaten, yet curled away from his left-hand upright.

Three minutes later, there was an incredible 16-second span, where both teams could have opened the scoring. A low and powerful free kick from Gheorghe Popescu thudded into the clutches of Kahn, who swiftly set in motion a counter-attack, in which Christian Ziege's lobbed effort looped agonisingly over Busquets's crossbar at the end of a stunning burst of speed.

These were shots across the bows from the visitors, warnings that went unheeded by Barcelona. A pensive-looking and clock-watching Cruyff seemed to be reading the signs, however. Eight minutes before half-time, Dietmar Hamann powered into the Barcelona penalty area, his effort at goal going just wide of the base of Busquets's left-hand post.

Any hopes of reaching the interval without conceding were swept away five minutes before Cruyff had the chance to regroup in the dressing room. It was left to Babbel to capitalise on the trajectory of a parried save by Busquets.

Rehhagel's finest hour as Bayern coach, Barcelona's second-half pressure was absorbed with a consummate sense of ease, their second goal springing from yet another desperate run towards Kahn, by Luis Figo. From here, Bayern broke away, at the end of which a deflected shot from Witeczek eluded the grasp of Busquets for 2-0. Despite Iván de la Peña grabbing one back for Barcelona, with just two minutes remaining, it was Bayern that came closer to adding more goals, as the final whistle drew ever closer.

From jubilation to incredulousness, when Bayern proceeded to take just one point from their next two Bundesliga outings, during which any realistic chance of winning the title was relinquished, Rehhagel was shown the door. The first leg of the 1996 UEFA Cup Final was only days away.

Just as he did in 1993/94, in stepped Beckenbauer, in a bid to steady the volatile ship. In a near-mirror image, Bayern's opponents in the final, Girondins de Bordeaux, had also sacked their coach for domestic issues. Slavoljub Muslin had been replaced by the former Bayern defender, Gernot Rohr, in early February, with the club locked in a very real relegation battle.

Against the laws of footballing physics, Bordeaux had been flirting with relegation, with a squad that contained the future World Cup winners, Bixente Lizarazu, Christophe Dugarry and, even more impressively, Zinedine Zidane.

These domestic struggles were offset by their incredible run to the UEFA Cup Final, however. Vardar and Rotor Volgograd were overcome with only moderate effort, before Real Betis were dealt with in the third round.

This was a Betis side that had no discernible problems in European travel, having won away to both Fenerbahçe and Kaiserslautern, prior to rolling into Bordeaux. Still under the guidance of Muslin, the first leg was all a little too easy for the home side, while in the return game at a rainswept Estadio Benito Villamarín, Zidane scored within three minutes with an outrageously taken left-foot strike from over 40 yards.

A goal that was pure Zidane, it left Betis needing four to progress and, while they did claw two back before half-time, it was a challenge that proved to be beyond *Los Verdiblancos*.

What came next was simply stunning. In the quarter-finals, Bordeaux were drawn to play an AC Milan side that was edging towards the last acts of Fabio Capello's first spell in charge of the club. This was a Milan side that was less than two years beyond categorically dismantling Cruyff's Barcelona, in the 1994 Champions League Final.

Now led by Rohr, when Bordeaux departed the San Siro with a 2-0 first-leg defeat, the outcome seemed obvious, for this was a Milan that could still boast talents such as, not only Franco Baresi and Paolo Maldini, but also Alessandro Costacurta, Christian Panucci, Marcel Desailly, Stefano Eranio, Dejan

Savićević and Roberto Baggio. They also fielded the 19-year-old Patrick Vieira.

Back in Bordeaux the unexpected unfolded, however, as, on an atmospheric night at the Stade du Parc Lescure, Rohr's side overpowered Capello's Milan. It was a result that broke the spell which *I Rossoneri* had held over the rest of Europe, ever since Arrigo Sacchi had brought Ruud Gullit, Frank Rijkaard and Marco van Basten to the club.

With the sometimes maligned Dugarry in a mood for devastation, it was Didier Tholot who opened the scoring, with only 15 minutes played, a goal that Milan's reserve goalkeeper, Mario Ielpo, could have done more to stop, a goal in which Lizarazu made an outstanding contribution.

No further first-half goals, Dugarry then made himself the hero, with two goals in a seven-minute spell from the 63rd minute – clinical finishing, in situations that were generated by Zidane. While Bordeaux's comeback was one of shock and awe, Milan's inability to rise to meet the threat of Bordeaux head on was just as surprising, when one goal would have been enough for Capello's side to take a place in the semi-final, on the away-goal rule. Milan's failure in Bordeaux marked the shifting of European football's tectonic plates.

A couple of 1-0 victories over Slavia Prague saw Bordeaux into the final. The first leg, at the Stadion Evžena Rošického, was decided by another fine piece of interplay between Zidane and Dugarry, while in the return game it was Tholot who put away his own rebound, after a wonderful solo run.

Again, Bordeaux had cast off their domestic problems to excel in the UEFA Cup. This was a Slavia side that would supply five members of the Czech Republic squad, which just a couple of months later would reach the 1996 European Championship Final, inclusive of the future Liverpool and Manchester United players, Vladimír Šmicer and Karel Poborský. They also had the presence of the former Queens Park Rangers goalkeeper, Jan Stejskal. Of course, in the semi-finals of that summer's international tournament, the roles would be reversed, and it was Zidane, Dugarry and Lizarazu who were on the losing side.

In the first leg of the final at the Olympiastadion, with Beckenbauer at the helm of Bayern, out went Witeczek and back came Papin. For Bordeaux, both Zidane and Dugarry were suspended. Helmer opened the scoring with a thumping header ten minutes before the break, while on the hour, Scholl scored a beautiful goal, weaving his way through the Bordeaux defence, before planting the ball into Gaëtan Huard's bottom left-hand corner.

Welcoming back Zidane and Dugarry, any hopes Rohr had of overturning Bordeaux's first-leg deficit were still circulating at half-time, with the second-leg score deadlocked at 0-0. Eight minutes beyond the restart, however, Bayern landed the killer blow and it was Scholl who once again delivered it, after a clever piece of ball movement and a subtle deflection. Twelve minutes later, Kostadinov added another, with a glancing header from an in-swinging corner, muscling his way into the Bordeaux six-yard box.

It was with a heavy element of frustration that the substitute, Daniel Dutuel, scored with a low and powerfully struck free kick, to give Bordeaux their only goal of the 1996 UEFA Cup Final. Even this didn't prove to be the last say, as Klinsmann helped a Strunz effort from distance, past Huard, for his 15th UEFA Cup goal of the campaign.

For Bayern, never having won the UEFA Cup before, it completed the set, having won the Cup Winners' Cup in 1967 and having collected a hat-trick of European Cups in the mid-1970s. With this, they emulated Ajax and Juventus, who had both achieved the same feat, prior to Bayern.

Despite this Bundesliga hiatus, Bayern taking the UEFA Cup to Germany for the first time in eight years was seemingly a case of Serie A business as usual, as the Roy Hodgson-led Inter reached the 1997 UEFA Cup Final, the tournament's very last two-legged showpiece event.

It was a game that represented the wind of change. No longer were clubs bound by the three-foreigner rule and, while such freedom was a great thing for players, for the clubs it introduced the concept of careless error when it came to recruitment. They could now be less measured in their approach to transfers, they could be more speculative, scattergun in some instances.

After initially relaxing the limit to four foreign players, UEFA removed all restrictions with the dawning of the Bosman ruling. Hodgson's Inter, for instance, had fielded Jocelyn Angloma, Javier Zanetti, Ciriaco Sforza, Paul Ince, Youri Djorkaeff, Aron Winter and Iván Zamorano in 1996/97, while the following season, when Luigi Simoni took the very same club to the first one-off UEFA Cup Final in 1998, Angloma, Sforza and Ince had been moved on, the former two after only a year. Zanetti, Winter, Djorkaeff and Zamorano had been added to by the arrivals of Taribo West, Zé Elias, Diego Simeone, Benoît Cauet, Nwankwo Kanu, Álvaro Recoba and, of course, the world's best player, Ronaldo. This was a massive difference to Trapattoni fielding Matthäus, Brehme and Klinsmann.

Inter lost out to Schalke in the 1997 UEFA Cup Final, on penalties. The stubbornness of the Bundesliga outfit had brought them to within six minutes of prevailing in the 180. Coached by Huub Stevens, the former Netherlands international, Schalke were a compelling mixture of promising components and hard-working players that fell beneath the radar.

Current German international, Olaf Thon, was complemented by future *Die Mannschaft* graduates, Jens Lehmann and Thomas Linke. Stevens's side was also boosted by the influence of his compatriot, Johan de Kock, the Czech midfield duo, Jiří Němec and Radoslav Látal, with the Belgian international, Marc Wilmots at the tip of the formation.

UEFA Cup aside, the 1996/97 season was one of general disarray for Schalke. Early season inconsistencies saw Stevens's predecessor, Jörg Berger, out of a job, less than a week beyond guiding the club past Roda JC Kerkrade, in the first round.

There would be something quite apt about Inter being Schalke's opponents in the last two-legged UEFA Cup Final. Their run to glory mirrored Inter's 1994 success in some respects. Domestic misadventure offset by claiming a piece of European silverware. Bordeaux's run to the 1996 final had been achieved within this spirit too, of course.

Inter were on a far more even keel in 1996/97 compared to the previous three seasons. Not everybody's manager of choice, the pragmatic stylings of Hodgson made it a harder job to alleviate points from Inter. Not always the prettiest of football, it was certainly effective, and their notoriously soft centre began to toughen up, something which acted as a bedrock from which the club could eventually flourish the following decade, under Roberto Mancini.

Inspired by the form and the goals of Maurizio Ganz, apart from labouring their way through a penalty shoot-out in the second round against Grazer AK, it was relatively plain sailing for Hodgson and Inter in reaching the 1997 UEFA Cup Final.

Despite this, Inter's supporters largely stayed away from the San Siro until the semi-final, in which they faced the Monaco of Fabien Barthez, Enzo Scifo, John Collins, Emmanuel Petit, Victor Ikpeba, Sonny Anderson and the rapidly rising Thierry Henry. Led by Jean Tigana, this was a side that also had at its disposal an emerging David Trezeguet and the future Manchester City cult hero, Ali Benarbia.

Three goals to the good inside 40 minutes of the first leg in Milan, Ganz on target with two more, Inter conceded a late away goal to Ikpeba. When the same man scored in the return game, with over 20 minutes remaining, it made for a nervous end to what should have been a sedate path into the final at 3-0 up.

Having eliminated Anderlecht in the quarter-finals, Inter had great momentum as they approached the final. Heading toward a respectable third-place finish, they were the clear favourites.

Schalke's route to the final, beyond Roda, took them past Trabzonspor in a bludgeoning and physical encounter, then Club Brugge, inclusive of a wonderful goal from Michael Büskens, with an orange ball, in the Belgian snow.

Results garnered via an almost traditionally British approach to football, leaning heavily on aerial tactics, neither Valencia nor Tenerife had an answer to Schalke in the quarter-final and semi-final respectively.

In a first leg of two penalties against Tenerife, one conceded, one missed, Schalke overcame the disappointment of an opportunity untaken by edging the second leg, in extra time, with two more headed goals, this time from Linke and Wilmots.

It proved to be a final of great symmetry. Schalke took the first leg, 1-0, while Inter won the second leg by the same scoreline – Wilmots with a wonderful strike from distance in Gelsenkirchen, Zamorano forcing home the only goal with just six minutes remaining at the San Siro.

Yet, any deflation Schalke might have experienced at conceding such a late aggregate equaliser was soon offset by Salvatore Fresi's sending off. Down to ten men, Inter played the percentages during extra time and the most explosive moment was reserved for the 119th minute, when, with a penalty shoot-out looming, Hodgson was almost accosted by Zanetti, when the Inter coach withdrew him, in favour of Berti, for the impending duel from 12 yards.

Regardless of Hodgson's alterations, Zamorano and Winter missed their spot kicks, so when Wilmots stepped up to take Schalke's fourth, it proved to be the one that won the UEFA Cup. Ince, for the second time in under 12 months, had lost on penalties at the hands of German opponents, while Berti didn't even get to take the spot kick he had been brought on for.

Within 48 hours, the Blackburn Rovers-bound Hodgson and Inter had parted company and the deal to bring Ronaldo to the San Siro had escalated. A campaign that acted as a handover towards the dawning of a new era, 117 teams had taken part in the 1996/97 UEFA Cup, the all new second preliminary round kicking off just nine weeks after Bayern had won the 1995/96 edition.

This collection of 117 teams had been drawn from 47 different federations; it included 32 national champions, who had been excluded from the Champions League, three teams who had gained entry via the Intertoto Cup and another three by virtue of prospering through the UEFA Fair Play system.

It was all a far cry from the first playing of the UEFA Cup in 1971/72, a campaign in which 64 teams set out for glory, or at least for a sense of European adventure. In the case of Vllaznia, of Albania, their adventure ended before it began, when they were denied visas by Austrian immigration, having been drawn to face Rapid Wien, while there was tragedy in Eindhoven, when PSV's opponents, the East Germans, Hallescher FC, were caught up in a fire that broke out at the hotel they were staying at, the Hotel 't Silveren Seepaerd.

Amongst the nine fatalities in Eindhoven was the 21-year-old Hallescher midfielder, Wolfgang Hoffmann. His surviving team-mates understandably withdrew from the game they had arrived to play.

A smaller Europe in the late summer months of 1971 compared to its expanded nature by 1997, change took a long time to come, but when it arrived, it was swift and far-reaching. As late as 1993/94, the UEFA Cup remained a 64-team tournament, yet the fragmenting former Eastern Bloc nations saw that number grow to 87 the following season.

Not only were the geographical boundaries altering, but the aesthetics of football were too. By 1996/97, added to the breaking of the restrictions on foreign players per team, came the wider implementation of squad numbers, names on the back of shirts and increasingly choreographed goal celebrations. It was very much a case of out with the old and in with the new and it seemed that the two-legged final was a product of the old.

So, for better or worse, change after change came and eventually the UEFA Cup became the UEFA Europa League. A set of events that is akin to a band you love still touring today, except that of the five musicians involved, only one of them is from the original line-up. Either that, or it hints of *Only Fools and Horses*, where Trigger's civically celebrated, trusty and long-serving broom, has only had its pole and head replaced a small number of times each.

While not all change requires frowning at, in my humble opinion, the Europa League is a pale shadow of the tournament it sprang from. While the winner of the competition is handed the same trophy that the Tottenham Hotspur captain Alan Mullery was awarded on 17 May 1972 after his team had seen off the challenge of Wolverhampton Wanderers in the very first UEFA Cup Final, the current-day version of the tournament is completely unrecognisable in not just format, but also aura, from what it was when it was born.

Essentially, the Europa League is the MK Dons of European club football tournaments. There is a sad sense of franchise about it. A beautiful trophy and a piece of footballing history misappropriated as the prize to a tournament that doesn't deserve it. The presenting of it provokes a similar sensation to the one engendered when the classic Football League Championship trophy is awarded to the winners of the English second tier – a trophy far more beautiful and historically evocative than the unsatisfactory silverware that the Premier League hands to its victors.

A claim could be made that the relationship between the UEFA Cup and the Europa League is so tenuous that they don't even feel like the continuation of the same tournament. Can it really be said that when Manchester United prevailed in the 2017 final against Ajax, it felt like success in the same tournament as the one Ipswich Town prospered in when overcoming another team from the Netherlands in the final 36 years earlier? In this respect, the UEFA Cup unarguably harbours a closer relationship with the Inter-Cities Fairs Cup than it does with the Europa League. Despite this, UEFA still refuse to recognise the Fairs Cup as the lineage precursor to the UEFA Cup.

It was from the 1997/98 season onward that the UEFA Cup began to give away the ingredients that made it unique. The switch from the two-legged final to a one-off game was the first step on the road to today's unrecognisable offering, via a general homogenisation that included the tournament swallowing up the Cup Winners' Cup, in 1999.

When Luigi Simoni's Inter defeated Sven-Göran Eriksson's Lazio, at the Parc des Princes in Paris, in the first one-legged UEFA Cup Final in May 1998, it delivered a very clever piece of sleight of hand.

It was the third all-Italian UEFA Cup Final of the 1990s. Given that Parma would go on to win the 1999 final, there was only one UEFA Cup Final throughout the entire decade to not have at least one Italian competitor. In the era of Channel 4's *Football Italia*, it meant an extra bonus event for all lovers of James Richardson, Peter Brackley and Kenneth Wolstenholme, albeit with Des Lynam, Barry Davies and Alan Hansen over on the BBC instead.

With Ronaldo inspiring a star-studded Inter to glory in 1998 against an expensively assembled Lazio, the switch from a two-legged final to one wasn't mourned in the way it should have been.

It wasn't immediately obvious, but a slow puncture was in evidence. The 1997/98 season had also been the first one in which the Champions League permitted more than one team per nation to take part. Teams that would have gone into the UEFA Cup instead of the Champions League, had the previous season's format been in operation, based upon where they finished domestically in 1996/97, included Barcelona, Parma, Bayer Leverkusen, Newcastle United, Feyenoord, Paris Saint-Germain and Sporting CP. That is a significant siphoning of talent.

Worse was to come. When the 1999/2000 UEFA Cup campaign began, new blows had been sustained by the tournament. Absorbing the Cup Winners' Cup was billed as a strengthening exercise for the UEFA Cup. A streamlining process that killed one tournament and forever altered and eventually weakened another. This 'new' UEFA Cup set sail, with an extra round added to it, yet it was also handed 24 teams that had been knocked out of the Champions League. This amounted to the 16 teams that were eliminated at the third and final Champions League qualifying round, plus the eight third-placed teams that were knocked out at the elite tournament's group stage. This gave us the concept that the UEFA Cup was no more than a consolation prize.

Rather than the UEFA Cup absorbing the Cup Winners' Cup, as was the projected concept, the UEFA Cup was digested by the Champions League, with the remnants becoming a refuge for football's c-list overachievers and sleeping giants.

For LaLiga, Serie A and Bundesliga clubs, by the 1999/2000 season they were being awarded four Champions League berths. The Premier League was allowed three, eventually upping to four from 2002/03. The UEFA Cup wasn't being diluted: it was being drowned.

In 2004/05, unwieldly five-team group stages were introduced, further chipping away at the remaining plus points the UEFA Cup still possessed. Then, in 2009/10, the tournament was renamed the Europa League. The trophy aside, the cosmetic surgery was complete. As most of Europe's iconic teams are annually shepherded into the Champions League, each time an AC Milan or a Manchester United ends up within the clutches of the Europa League, you can hear the once clandestine whispers of European Super Leagues increase in volume.

The UEFA Cup became a figure of fun to some. Chants of 'Thursday night, Channel 5' were directed at the supporters of big clubs that had found themselves in the tournament, scorned by fans whose clubs were dining at the top table in the Champions League.

Mid-ranging teams whose supporters had only previously dreamt of European adventures pulled their hair out as they travelled the continent, only to see weakened line-ups take to the field, as their better players were rested for Premier League games that weekend. Bolton Wanderers, for instance, rested players in the last 16 in 2008 for upcoming Premier League games, when the quarter-finals and a potential shot at their greatest contemporary glory was suddenly within touching distance.

Almost seen as a curse to be involved in, Burnley's sluggish 2018/19 domestic campaign was widely blamed upon the early start they had to make for Europa League qualifiers. It was all a long way from the intoxicating heights of Inter facing AS Roma in the 1991 final.

Yet, it would be churlish of me to suggest that the post-1997 UEFA Cup – and indeed the Europa League era – hasn't shown some signs of soul. It's just that they came in a rapidly differing tournament.

Ronaldo was hypnotic against Lazio in that first one-legged UEFA Cup Final in 1998, while Parma were the vision of perfection a year later.

Liverpool and Deportivo Alavés shared one of the greatest major European finals of all time, in Dortmund, in 2001, when Gérard Houllier's side prevailed 5-4 thanks to an extra-time, golden goal, own goal winner. The next two finals offered more drama as Feyenoord defeated Borussia Dortmund 3-2, before José Mourinho's FC Porto beat Celtic by the same score 12 months later. Mourinho would lift the trophy again 14 years on, as manager of Manchester United. Glasgow's other giant, Rangers, reached the final in 2008, their first major European final since 1972.

Middlesbrough's run to the 2006 final was one of wonder and amazement, with a cluster of comebacks that send a shiver down the spine. It was an achievement that Fulham matched in 2010, Hodgson again reaching the final, 14 years after taking Inter there, while Chelsea were twice successful. Russia and Ukraine had their glories and FC Porto prevailed again in 2011, in an all-Portuguese final against Braga in Dublin.

Through it all, however, a Spanish domination came to the fore, beginning with Rafael Benítez and Valencia and continuing with Sevilla and Atlético Madrid.

Yet, the 2019 final in Baku felt like we had reached the high-water mark of Europa League excess – two London teams being sent across the expanse of Europe to play in a sparsely populated stadium, in a city where not everyone was made to feel they would be welcome or, in some instances, safe.

As of the lockdown summer months of 2020, eight clubs have now won the tournament after first being knocked out of the Champions League. Galatasaray were the first, in 2000, against Arsenal, who themselves had also exited the group stages of that season's Champions League. Arsène Wenger's side became the first of 11 teams to exit Europe's premier club tournament, only to go on and reach, yet lose, the final of its secondary tournament.

When Chelsea won the Europa League, under Benítez in 2013, for ten days they held the unique status of being both the holders of the Europa League and the Champions League. Knocked out at the 2012/13 group stages during their defence of the Champions League, it was a week and a half beyond Chelsea beating Benfica, in Amsterdam, at the 2013 Europa League Final, before Jupp Heynckes's Bayern Munich succeeded the west London club as Champions League winners, at Wembley, against Jürgen Klopp's Borussia Dortmund.

Despite these quirks, the Champions League safety net aspect remains an unsatisfactory one for the Europa League, as does the prize of a place in the following season's Champions League for the tournament winner. The advent of this means that you can feasibly exit the Champions League before the group stages and finish outside the top four of your domestic leagues, but still reach the following season's Champions League, via winning the Europa League Final.

Now we live with the spectre of the reintroduction of a third UEFA club competition. Initially given a working title of Europa League 2, eventually bestowed with the moniker of the UEFA Europa Conference League, we are entering a world where extra football is being served up during an era when more is less. It just makes me feel that having one version of the Europa League is bad enough, let alone us suffering two. It just serves to convince me that the past is where the beauty of UEFA's major tournaments predominantly rests.

Afterword

IN WRITING this book, it was originally dreamt up to be a natural sequel to *A Tournament Frozen in Time*, yet it gave me more than that, it summoned up the sensation of how the true UEFA (Yoofa) Cup felt, it reheated that distinct personality of the UEFA Cup, a tournament which perfectly complemented the European Cup and the European Cup Winners' Cup. Three siblings with distinct personalities, which were easy to detect, if you were paying enough attention.

While yes, the European Cup was the senior member of this marvellous triumvirate of tournaments, neither the UEFA Cup nor the Cup Winners' Cup were bedraggled bystanders, there only to doff their moth-eaten cloth caps in subservience to their older and debonair sibling, the one with the all-year-round tan, the bleached white smile and the twinkle in the eye. The UEFA Cup, just like the Cup Winners' Cup, was the most compelling of supporting actors, in a wonderful three-part act to the European club competition season.

Comparatively and in contemporary terms, there is a distinct 'uptown' and 'downtown' division between the Champions League and the Europa League. If upon the classic Monopoly board the Champions League is represented by Mayfair, while the Europa League isn't exactly Old Kent Road, it isn't much more than Vine Street. Under these terms and conditions, the UEFA Cup and the Cup Winners' Cup were the much more sought-after Oxford Street and Piccadilly.

As part of this book, I spoke to many people, drawn into in-depth conversations that once again ended up veering toward pub chat territory, eventually walking away from each one having not shifted from my standpoint by even a millimetre. Not out of stubbornness, but out of idealism, or basically due to the timing of my birth and the chronological positioning of where my most impressionable football-watching years sat. Roughly the age span of 7–18, which in my case translates to 1981–92, a perfectly timed span in which to render a person forever unsettled by the dawning of both the Champions League and the Premier League. After which, football began to provoke pockets of disappointment.

I'm sure I'm not alone in that phenomenon. I am a great believer that when you ask people which their favourite World Cup is, then a sizeable majority will identify the first one they were fully conscious of. The first World Cup where your parents allowed you to stay up late to see the end of the Brazil vs Soviet Union game; the first World Cup where you had the Panini sticker album and the associated wall chart.

Every World Cup from that point on is measured in terms of how the first one made you feel. My version of this is 1982 and, for every World Cup since, I've always had a vague sense of disappointment when a nation that took part in Spain then fails to qualify for the latest one. Hence, I was delighted when Peru qualified for the 2018 World Cup, while I sit impatiently, waiting for El Salvador to return to football's biggest stage one day.

You can never repeat those most impressionable years. You only have one crack at it. It is why, for me, *Sportsnight* and *Midweek Sports Special* are sacrosanct and one of my greatest moments in writing and authorship was being granted a telephone audience with the marvellous Nick Owen, a year or so ago, a man who is as lovely as his television appearances suggest.

There is a warm glow to your most impressionable years. The rough edges are forgotten, while the sensory experiences linger. I can remember how football used to 'feel' back then. That wonderful sense of the occasion it had, which no longer seems possible, given the amount of football you can now obtain access to, even within a global pandemic.

I myself have been condescending about an era of football that took place throughout my 20s, 30s and into my mid-40s. I'm guilty as charged. That 1981–92 era that is essentially my 'sweet spot' will be looked down on by football watchers who were around to fully appreciate the 1960s and 70s, while there will still be children of the 1940s and 50s that lament the post-minimum wage era. Nature will insist upon being nature and nobody wants to acknowledge that their most impressionable era might not be the greatest of all eras.

Talking to people who aren't old enough to remember the two-legged final era of the UEFA Cup, I pitied them for what they had missed out on, while contending that their impressionable eras just weren't as comparable to mine.

Then it dawned on me that this type of thinking is absolute nonsense. Every football era has great beauty and unbearable ugliness. There are always rough edges to go with the smooth. We just forget the rough edges the further time elapses from those personally impressionable eras.

Just as last time, when writing this book I encountered my shortcomings as an interrogator. A habitual conversationalist, the topic would always revert to how the UEFA Cup made people feel, rather than any search for technical and tactical data, or the inside line on anecdotes of punch-ups between team-mates, journalists or supporters. I can't weave the accounts of others, to take you to the internal workings of the subject matter. I do, though, greatly admire those that can.

I am simply not one of those writers that can take you to a topic. What I can do, though, is bring you to my esoteric and nonconformist spec on the terrace, from where I can point out recurring patterns, underappreciated oddities and generally gaze at my own navel.

I did indulge in the aesthetics, however. It always comes down to the aura.

The journalist and musician Philippe Auclair spoke of how French people of his generation get teary-eyed when it comes to Claude Papi, who reached the 1978 UEFA Cup Final with Bastia, yet how Bordeaux's run to the 1996 final made little impact on him, again something that speaks of the power of those impressionable years we all live through.

Conversely, when talking to Jamie Carragher, a man with hands-on experience of winning the tournament, he felt passionately that Liverpool's achievement in 2001 is massively underappreciated, as they had largely been a club in disarray two years earlier.

As ever, when it comes to football watchers, there always tends to be a recall image that immediately springs to mind for people, whether that is a goal or a piece of skill that is conjured up by the mind's eye when the name of a player or a certain game is mentioned or, in this case, a specific tournament.

Aidan Williams, the author and Newcastle United supporter, automatically confessed that he would never forget Faustino Asprilla's magnificent celebration, after scoring against Metz on their way to the quarter-finals in 1996/97.

Rangers supporter Ross Kilvington recounted the feeling that Nacho Novo's clinching penalty engendered, in their 2008 semi-final against Fiorentina, something that has never been diluted, despite going on to lose the final, while Dylan O'Connell talked about the time when Bayern Munich took on Cork City in 1991, where the midfielder Dave Barry, who worked as a plumber and played part-time, was told by Stefan Effenberg he looked like his granddad, only for Barry to go on and score, having turned up for the game fresh from having fitted a sink.

Alain Meskens spoke of his pride in his team, RWD Molenbeek, reaching the 1976/77 semi-finals, where they went out to Athletic Club, without losing a game. Meanwhile, Rod

Helsby proudly showed off his Barcelona cushion, the very same type of cushion that Joey Jones bounced off the heads of supporters at the 1976 semi-final, first leg. He also talked of getting into Anfield for 10p, for the replaying of the rained-off first leg of the 1973 UEFA Cup Final.

Damian Atkins was one of many to drift off to his 'happy place', that is Tony Parks's decisive save in the 1984 UEFA Cup Final penalty shoot-out, an event that meant Mark Budd missed the last train back to Bristol, only getting home on the milk train.

Matthew Leslie cited Heart of Midlothian's run to the quarter-finals in 1989, where they went out to Bayern Munich, having beaten them at Tynecastle, which was a similar experience to Scott Derry, who is still blown away by what he considers to be the loudest night he's ever known on the Holte End, when Aston Villa beat Internazionale in 1990/91, before going out at the San Siro a fortnight later.

Ian Kelly regaled me with St Mirren's tales of pleasure and pain, when self-destructing against Hammarby, and seeing Johan Cruyff and Ruud Gullit rock up at Love Street with Feyenoord, while the theme of glorious failure was picked up by the Queens Park Rangers supporter, Martin Kelly, who mused about the time his team was ordered to take on FK Partizan, at Highbury, due to UEFA's insistence that Loftus Road's plastic pitch was unsuitable for football consumption. A 6-2 victory was subsequently thrown away in Belgrade and out went QPR.

A myriad of Ipswich Town supporters simply stated, '1981'. In most instances, these were conversations that drifted to those impressionable eras.

Before picking up this book, you might, or might not, have read its predecessor, *A Tournament Frozen in Time*. As debut books go, it travelled a wholly unexpected distance, eventually being shortlisted for the 2020 Football Book of the Year by the Football Writers' Association. I was humbled, not only by that, but simply by the kind words that flowed across social media. I never once grew tired of seeing an image of a book I wrote, in all manner of backdrops, both near and far, tipping up in outposts such as Russia, Australia and the USA. One of my son's teachers even asked him if I was a relation, after he had read the book. Being what I would only ever class as an accidental author, I thank you for taking the time to read this one.

Michael Calvin, the prolific author of some of the most majestic football literature ever, once shared his opinion that the key to writing books is to nail the start and then sprint for the finish line.

A significant percentage of this book was written during the lockdown of a global pandemic, juggling the, at times, psychedelic experience of home schooling seven- and 12-year-old children. Entire days passed, where it felt like I could no longer blink.

If writing a book in normal circumstances is akin to sprinting your way through a marathon, then doing it while home schooling is like completing a marathon in a novelty outfit. The 'difficult second album' being written in exceptional times. It was a challenge and I hope you have enjoyed reading it.

The UEFA Cup really was where the cool kids hung out.

Also available at all good book stores

9781785315534

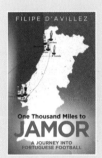

9781785316258

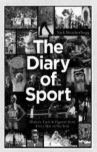

9781785316289

9781785316654

9781785316791

9781785317194

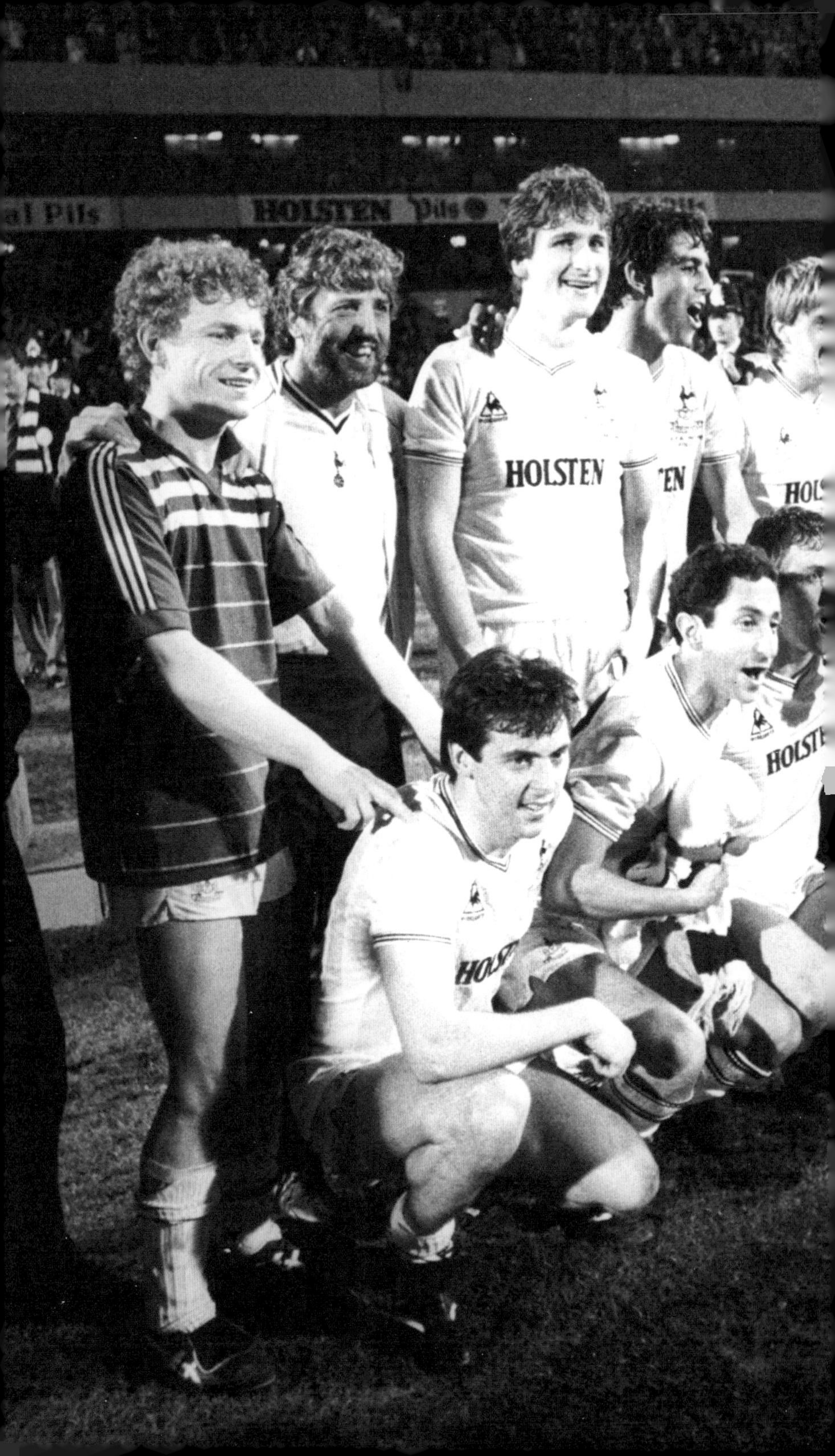
HOLSTEN Pils
HOLSTEN
HOLSTEN